The incomparable master has
returned from London,
resettled in New York,
and gathered together
this absolutely splendid collection of
twenty-two delicious morsels created by
the man who is to humor what caviar
is to mere food.

What more need be said than that
Vinegar Puss includes such unforget-
table delights as...

VINEGAR

801

PUSS,

by S. J. Perelman

SIMON AND SCHUSTER : NEW YORK

For Irene

Copyright © 1942, 1970, 1971, 1972, 1973, 1974, 1975 by S. J. Perelman
All rights reserved
including the right of reproduction
in whole or in part in any form
Published by Simon and Schuster
Rockefeller Center, 630 Fifth Avenue
New York, New York 10020

All these pieces appeared originally in The New Yorker, *with the exception of* *"Nostasia in Asia" from* Travel & Leisure, *"The Machismo Mystique" from* McCalls, *"Mad About the Girl" from* Holiday, *and "The Art Is Long, the Crisis Fleeting" from* Escapade.

Designed by Irving Perkins
Manufactured in the United States of America
By American Book–Stratford Press, Inc.

1   2   3   4   5   6   7   8   9   10

Library of Congress Cataloging in Publication Data

Perelman, Sidney Joseph, 1904–
   Vinegar puss.
   Short stories and essays.
   1. Title.
PS3531.E6544V5   813'.5'2   74–26719
ISBN 0–671–21964–2

Contents

Missing: Two Lollapaloozas—
No Reward

INDIAN ACTRESS LEAVES 13 PRODUCERS IN LURCH

Film producer Gunwantrai N. Naik has filed a case in the court of the Presidency Magistrate against actress Rajshree for having put him to serious loss by leaving India in the midst of shooting his Hindi color film "Deedar." . . . Some 13 producers are said to be left in the lurch with unfinished films on hand, in which Rajshree has the leading part.

—Variety.

Like Noel Coward said, only mad dogs and Englishmen go out in the midday sun, and, brother, was he right. When I ran out of the Taj Mahal Hotel in Bombay that noon, I was mad clean through—I was boiling. I knew if I stayed in that room one minute longer, listening to Donna Crumbshaw chew me out, she'd wind up with a fat lip and me with an assault-and-battery charge. There's only so much you can take from a woman, and she'd been dishing it out ever since we left Hong Kong. Anyway, by the time I put a couple of drinks under my belt, I worked the whole thing out of my system. I was going to apologize, eat crow, offer to kiss and make up just to keep peace in the family, but that envelope on the bed told me that the picnic was over. The message inside was wrapped around a dozen century notes, and it read, "Sorry, I guess it was all a mistake. Goodbye and no hard feelings, except you owe it to yourself to drop dead and free the world of a roach. The enclosed should see you through to New York. Yours, Donna."

So that was the end of the golden dream that had started in Altman's luggage department, of all places, less than two months before. Sitting there in Bombay, I remembered how gorgeous she looked the first afternoon I saw her, during our midwinter clearance sale. Fishmouth, the section manager, had called me over to wait on her, saying she needed a matched ensemble for an around-the-world tour. With some lucky stiff, I thought, sizing up the bedroom eyes and the chassis inside the tailored suit. Everything about this broad spelled class, *crème de la crème, Social Register;* she was the greatest. On the off chance that there might be a spot of action for yours truly, I asked my standard question—what kind of luggage did her husband prefer—and got a lovely surprise.

"I couldn't care less," she said. "I just divorced him. That's why I'm going around the world—to forget."

"And I'm the kid that can help you," I murmured to myself, giving her the little smile I copped from Laurence Harvey, worldly-wise but terribly sympathetic to her problems. Well, she made her choice without much salesmanship, so I had lots left over to sell myself. Once I had her name and address from the charge plate, the rest was easy—the phony anxiety about whether our warehouse had this exact pattern, could I call her after I checked, etc., etc. She went right along with the gag; what a comfort it was in this day and age to meet someone obliging, someone who really cared. . . .

Listening to us, you could have predicted what would happen, and it did—pronto. The first bar we met in was nowhere near her apartment, but the others got closer and closer, and finally the animal in us won out. It was a good, torrid romance, a contest between two civilized people to see which could be more savage when the shades were down. But all of a sudden the complications began. One morning, Fishmouth comes into the stockroom where I'm grabbing a little shut-eye for my hangover. He had one, too, it seems, and there wasn't room for both in the section, so I better nurse mine at home hereafter. When Donna heard the news, she clapped her hands. "Marvy—now we can go on the trip together! Think of it, honey. By next week you'll be on the beach at Waikiki."

"I'm on the beach right here," I said. "I don't even have next week's room rent."

"You won't need it," she said. "I'll advance you the money and you can pay it back out of your first million. Now, you get your outfit at Brooks tomorrow while I call the travel people. Yippee!"

Well, I wasn't too keen about the arrangement, but I figured it'd only spoil Donna's pleasure if I kept on squawking, so I gave in. Everything was peaches and cream, as I said, up to Hong Kong. We billed and cooed like lovebirds in Honolulu and Manila, and then, at the Peninsula Hotel in Kowloon, the fun turned sour. Donna started bitching about the heat, the traffic noise, and the outrageous prices. Her real hangup, though, was jealousy. If I even looked at another dame, she raised the roof, carried on about how fickle and heartless I was. Some of those Chinese heads are pretty zoftick, and when they wink at a person you can't help but smile back. Our second day there, I was just slipping the babe at the cigar stand a fatherly feel when in walks Donna. Man, what a tantrum. She practically foamed at the mouth. And the language! Well, I wasn't going to stoop to her level, so I cut out, had a few beers, and wound up with a couple of chicks at a taxi-dance hall. From that moment on, she never let up on me. Morning, noon, and night in Singapore, Bangkok, and Calcutta, she used any excuse to needle and chip away at me, but Bombay was the clincher. She mislaid a diamond clip in a drawer or suitcase, God knows where, and, instead of asking in a nice way had I seen it, she accused me of hocking it.

I was furious, but I controlled myself. I gave her a cold little smile like Barton MacLane on "The Late Show." "Are you calling me a thief," I said.

"No, on second thought, I withdraw that." For the first time,

I noticed what mean little eyes she had. "You're too yellow to steal. You're nothing but a cheap, two-timing gigolo, and I rue the day I ever set eyes on you."

With that, of course, anybody would blow their cool, and I walked out, leaving her in hysterics. And now, rereading her note, I pieced it all together. Her conscience must have bugged her, else she wouldn't have parted with this much bread. Well, good riddance, I reflected. Things could be a damn sight worse; I had a plane ticket home and over a grand in my kick, so there was no sense crying the blues. I'd spend a couple of weeks in Europe looking over the zook and, if nothing better turned up, breeze on back to New York. So down I go to the travel agency in the lobby to book my flight, and that's where I catch my first glimpse of Shasta Allahjee.

Let's face it—beautiful women are a dime a dozen in the Far East, but this one was so terrif my knees started knocking together. The face was Ava Gardner at nineteen if you combined her with, say, an Oriental Catherine Deneuve; and the casabas—well, Elke Sommer was a dried-up old prune in comparison. The clerk waiting on her must have dug my reaction and tipped her off, because she turned and gave me a sort of shy, inquiring smile as if to say, "Do I know you?" Whatever it meant, I had the answer and moved in fast.

"Pardon the intrusion, Miss," I said. "I forget exactly where we met, but your name's on the tip of my tongue. It's something like Venus—now, don't tell me—"

The clerk was one of those creeps that like to play the big shot. "This is Shasta Allahjee, our best-known film star. You probably recognized her from the many hits she's appeared in."

"Of course. How stupid of me," I said. "I've admired your work for years, Miss Allahjee. I'm in the movie game, too— Gary Goodspeed, the independent producer."

She thought that was quite a coincidence, but there was a bigger one in store the next day, when she boarded the west-bound plane to Istanbul and Rome and found what independent producer in the adjoining seat. I'd done my homework the night before, reading up on the local movie scene in their fan magazines, and my patter sounded pretty hip. Almost every picture they make in India—and they make thousands—is about Shah Jahan's love for his wife, Mumtaz Mahal, and how he built the Taj Mahal in her memory, and, from what I could gather, this doll was starring in all of them. So I poured on the Jap-a-lac, raved about her talent, and predicted she'd cop all the Oscars if she ever came to Hollywood.

"Curious we ran into each other like this," I said. "I've just been scouting locations and personalities for my forthcoming twelve-million-dollar epic, the story behind the Taj Mahal, and it strikes me you'd be perfect casting for the female lead."

"No, no—out of the question, I couldn't consider it." She seemed kind of nervous and upset. "I have too many commitments, people pushing me this way and that. Please, don't let's discuss this topic anymore."

Well, that was copacetic with me, since I was only using it for openers, so I chatted awhile about my impressions of India—the quaint customs, the colorful temples, the succulent food buzzing with flies, and the deep wisdom that we in the West could learn from their philosophy. After lunch, I got on a more personal tack, commenting that her skin and chest had the same texture as Audrey Hepburn's except hers was more exciting because much younger. She didn't deny it—just sat there curled up, with her eyes closed, drinking it in, and I knew I was making real headway. Then, at Istanbul, a peculiar thing happened. As we start off the plane toward the airport lounge, I hear shouts from the visitors' platform on top. Two guys in Indian turbans are up there waving cans of film at us and yelling something.

"What's with those jaspers?" I said. "What do they want?"

"Never mind," she said, grabbing my arm. "Back on board —quick!"

Well, up the steps we scrambled, and for the next twenty minutes she had the shakes but good. I managed to calm her down after a while, but she wouldn't explain why she panicked. Whatever it was—a religious hang-up or just plain nerves—I made it work for me and began ladling out the schmalz again. I sympathized with her about how tough it is to be a famous screen star—the lack of privacy, no home life, the kooky types demanding autographs and donations, and all the leeches, like agents, lawyers, and tax experts, that cling to your talented personality. She wound a scarf around her ears and moved to another seat to make out she wasn't interested, but I could tell I was getting through to her. In the meantime, I did some fast thinking. If her destination was Rome, so was mine; it was worth a detour to knock off such an exotic cooz. So right after we touch down I grab my twin-suiter from the baggage claim, and when she gets into a bus marked "Hotel Flora" I sprint ahead in a cab to the Via Veneto. From the gasp she let out as I greeted her in the lobby, you'd have thought I was a ghost.

"Hi there, Miss Allahjee," I said, all cool savoir-faire like Ray Milland. "You staying here, too? Look, why not have chow with me tonight and go for a row on the Tiber?"

That's where the missionary work I did on the plane paid off; she gives out with a smile, says O.K., and we fix a meet in the bar at seven-fifteen. Well, I'm in there on the dot, bright-eyed and bushy-tailed, knocking back an ice-cold Mart, when, zingo, another pair of jokers like the ones in Istanbul—or maybe the same two; I can never tell those handkerchief heads apart— bust in, also hugging cans of film. The only other party in the bar is an old crone covered with diamonds, juicing it up with her fancy Dan in a corner, so the gooks head for me and ask am I waiting for a lady of Indian extraction.

"That's right," I said. "I've got a date with an Indian lady extractionist—we take turns yanking out each other's teeth. What the hell business is it of yours?"

Before they can frame up a rejoinder, Shasta appears in the doorway looking sensational in a solid-gold sari, with all her accessories quivering like jello. She does a big take at the sight of the two, and backs out in a hurry; the whole thing was so quick that neither of them spotted her. As soon as they fade, I call her room, and after about eighty rings she answers, sounding good and scared.

"We'll have to call it off tonight, Mr. Goodspeed—sorry. . . . No, I can't explain—I'm leaving for Switzerland early tomorrow morning. . . . No, no, I couldn't possibly. Goodbye and good luck."

Even Don Rickles would quit after that, but not Gary Goodspeed, boy producer. I got hold of the concierge, greased him with a few hundred lire, and booked myself aboard the flight to Geneva she'd reserved. Fifteen minutes out of Rome, I took off my dark cheaters, strolled forward, and dropped into the seat beside my star of India. This time, I'm the one who gets handed the big surprise. She doesn't bat an eyelash—that's how great an actress she was.

"Look, honey," I said. "I've been studying you ever since Bombay, and I've finally figured it out. You're on the run. Some kind of a secret brotherhood—assassins or what, I don't know—is tailing you. Yes or no?"

She stared at me a long while, wrestling with herself whether to spill, and then gave in. "Gary," she said, and I felt my toes tingle even though my real name is Julius, "can I trust you?"

"*Trust* me?" I began. "I'd climb the highest—"

"Never mind the climbing and swimming," she cut me short. "Just listen. I've been—well, I've been a naughty girl. Those men you saw yesterday weren't assassins—they're movie producers. Which is the same thing, I suppose," she admitted. "But they're not trying to kill *me*—only my career. On account of I didn't finish their pictures, you see."

"I don't follow. How many pictures didn't you finish?"

"Seventeen," she said. "All of them about Shah Jehan and Mumtaz Mahal." Her voice broke. "And now they're threatening to sue me, to blacklist me, to attach the few things I own—a sweatshop, a noodle factory, four or five hotels in Kashmir." She fought back a sob. "Think of the publicity, the humiliation. I'll never be able to face my fans again. They'll pelt me with rancid ghee, draw mustaches on my glossies. Oh, Gary, what's to become of me?"

"Take it easy, sugar." I patted her arm, leaving the rest for a future session. "After all, you shook off four of your producers—"

"The others'll catch up with me in Geneva, Paris, and London," she said hopelessly. "You don't know Indian vengeance like I know Indian vengeance."

"Yes, yes," I said, thinking hard. "Wait—wait one second.

Suppose we could get the whole caboodle together in London and combine . . . Yes, by God, it would—it'd work! Now, listen closely, Shasta, here's what we'll do . . ."

"Well, gentlemen, that's the proposition," I finished, and stood up. There wasn't a sound out of the seventeen of them crowded into that suite at the Dorchester—Sikhs, Hindus, Muslims, all with their eyes glued on me like cats watching a mouse. "Let me recap it for you so you'll understand. If you bring suit against my client, it'll take five years to move through the courts, and the damages, even if you win, will be peanuts, chicken feed—*bubkess.* On the other hand, if we combine all your footage into one film, we'll have a real blockbuster that'll blow 'em out of the back of the art houses—the longest and sleepiest picture since Satyajit Ray's trilogy. Yessir," I said. "We here in this room may be inaugurating the most important breakthrough in anesthesia in the annals of medical science. Think it over. I'll be in the bedroom with Miss Allahjee, where I belong."

Well, they gibbered and jabbered, and finally agreed, and the rest is history. The picture, I don't have to tell you, goaled all the critics—even Jonas Mekas. They said it was a milestone in the cinema—a little repetitious in spots but a celluloid monument rivaling the Taj Mahal, the movie of the year. It sent Shasta Allahjee on to Hollywood and stardom, and all the thanks I ever got was that she threw me out when she caught me and her stand-in naked in the shower. So I'm back in Altman's luggage section again, and that's where I stick from here in. The next time anyone wants a matched ensemble for a world tour, let Fishmouth handle her. Gary Goodspeed, *geboren* Julius Wolfbane, has learned his lesson.

Hail, Hail, the Ganglia's All Here

"Absurd! Ridiculous!" scoffed Inspector Hesseltine. "I've never heard such pure, unadulterated tommyrot!" He put down his wineglass, folded his arms, and glared at me. "Are you serious, Novotny?"

"I was never more so in my life," I returned steadily.

"You actually sit there and contend that the whippersnapper you refer to, whose existence none of us has dreamed of hitherto, possesses powers of detection superior to our own? That this . . . this stripling can solve problems that have addled the keenest brains on five continents?"

"I mean precisely that."

"Humph," he said, lifting an ironical eyebrow. "What, pray, is the name of this prodigy?"

"S. G. Pefelman," I replied, "and he is only eleven years old."

The four of us had just finished dinner at Pietro's, in Soho—Hesseltine, of Scotland Yard; Armand Dulac, of the Sûreté; Colonel Bialy, of the Turkish police; and I, Rupert Novotny, chief of New York's detective force. Over the years it had been our custom, whenever we encountered each other in London, to forgather at Pietro's—who else has such a deft hand with chicken tetrazzini?—and quaff his delicious Frascati while exchanging shoptalk. Our conversation that evening had ranged over a variety of subjects when now, suddenly, my companions and I found ourselves at odds.

"But tell me, *mon cher* Novotny," Dulac asked, "zis leetle marvel of whom you speak—what ees so *extraordinaire* about heem?"

"His logic—his reasoning," I said. "It's fantastic, incredible. The man—I should say the boy; he hasn't donned longies yet— is a veritable thinking machine. Present him with a scrap of evidence, the merest soupçon of a clue, and presto, he arrives at a solution it would take any of us weeks to evolve."

"Come, come, man," Hesseltine expostulated. "You apparently believe that this unlicked cub is gifted with the same attributes as that fictional creation of Conan Doyle's, Mycroft Holmes."

"And so he is," I declared. "Like Sherlock's legendary brother, he rarely appears in public, has no intimates, shuns publicity. I myself have never seen him, though I've spoken to him on the phone."

"How then can one be sure he exists?" queried Colonel Bialy.

"Oh, he's real enough," I said. "We know, for instance, that at the age of five he was the youngest graduate in Harvard's history, that at six he had earned his doctorate, after which he spent two years at Oxford, Cambridge, the Sorbonne, Salamanca, Tübingen, and Uppsala, and that he has since applied himself to certain researches in mathematics and philosophy that may revolutionize the whole structure of Western thought. There are, in fact, those who maintain that not since the days of Tom Swift has there been a youth with so much gray matter."

"Hmm," Hesseltine commented skeptically. "This is all very well, Novotny, but fine words butter no parsnips. Can you give us a concrete example of Pefelman's astuteness?"

"With pleasure," I said, extracting my card case. "In one master stroke, he unraveled the mystery contained in the following newspaper account, and so expertly that my department was left with egg on its face. The affair, as summarized in the *New York Times,* read thus:'HIGH-VOLTAGE WIRING IS STOLEN OFF POLES. New Paltz, N.Y.—Thieves have taken 4,000 feet of copper wire strung on utility poles along a rural road north of this Ulster County community. The Central Hudson Gas and Electric Corporation said the line carried high-voltage current to serve a 4-H Club camp and a nearby summer colony on Plutarch Road. . . . Frank W. Shay, manager of Central Hudson's Newburgh District, said that as salvage material the copper wire would not bring an extremely high price in today's market, although the price of copper is up.' "

"Pouf," spoke up Armand Dulac. "Zat ees no grand problem. You send a couple of gendarmes to ze local junk dealers, you find ze wire, and you trace ze robbers."

"It wasn't that simple," I said. "Failing to apprehend the miscreants, the police appealed to us, but we, too, were baffled. Then the press raised a hue and cry, the Commissioner got on my back, and, with my job at stake, I put in a call to Pefelman. As luck would have it, he was not there."

Tense with excitement at my swift-paced narrative, Colonel Bialy moistened his lips. "Where was he?"

"Well, a voice—his housekeeper, I suspect—informed me that he had gone down to the candy store for some Necco wafers."

"What ees eet, zis sweetmeat?" Dulac demanded, mystified.

"You know, those powdery, colored discs," I explained. "To be honest, I lost my temper and retorted that Mycroft Holmes never went down to any candy store for Necco wafers. In whatever case, when I reached Pefelman and presented the riddle his response staggered me. He asked whether some carnival or circus had passed through New Paltz at the time of the theft."

My three colleagues gazed at me openmouthed. Colonel Bialy was the first to find his tongue. "What did he mean?"

"Ubangis," I said. "Those African women with platters in their mouths and long necks. He hypothesized that they had stolen the wire for necklaces, and, sure enough, we arrested a pair in Binghamton a few days hence with the loot encircling their throats."

"A remarkable piece of deduction, by George," observed Hesseltine thoughtfully as we bade each other good night. "Thank goodness Pefelman has allied himself with the forces of justice, for had he chosen a career of crime the world today might have seen the emergence of another Professor Moriarty or Fu Manchu."

It was perhaps a fortnight later that I received a call from Scotland Yard, and even before Hesseltine's voice flickered over the wire I had a premonition of its nature. My hunch was correct. The British authorities had become increasingly perplexed at the behavior of a mysterious housebreaker, to the extent that questions were being asked in Parliament.

"Between ourselves, old boy, the Government's got the wind up," Hesseltine confessed. "Do you think that perhaps that little chap of yours might shed a ray of light on this tenebrous matter?"

I signified I would be glad to intercede for Hesseltine, and he read me the London *Times* report of the business. Headlined "BURGLAR LEAVES 'SAUSAGE MEN,'" it stated: "Police are searching for a burglar who leaves a sausage with button eyes, a drawing-pin nose, wire mouth and limbs, and hair of modelling clay at every house he steals from. He also leaves a message and uses a special method of entry, but details are being kept secret. He has stolen several hundred pounds from houses in the Staines, Ashford, and Sunbury areas of Middlesex." The message left by the intruder, Hesseltine went on to reveal, ran, "You've tried the rest, now try the best—Stourbridge's Sausages, Best by Test," and in each case he had entered the premises through the chimney.

"Have you ruled out the possibility of espionage?" I inquired. "Offhand, I'd say the message was a code of some sort."

"I agree, but none of our cryptographers, and they are the topmost in their profession, has managed to break it," he said. "Anyhow, we should be unspeakably grateful if your man could help us solve the conundrum."

When I phoned Pefelman, I was again greeted by his housekeeper, who divulged that he had stepped out to purchase some chocolate Bolsters. This time, I kept a tight checkrein on my temper, and, obtaining the phone number of the candy store, rang through to him. He listened intently as I relayed the details.

"The chimney, the chimney," he deliberated. "Did any of the victims remember hearing sleigh bells?"

"I don't think so, else Hesseltine would have said," I rejoined. "Why, could that be an important clue?"

"Only in combination with certain other factors, like reindeer tracks, vestiges of a white beard in the chimney, et cetera. However, you can assure your friend at the Yard that there's no question of robbery. It's some sort of advertising campaign."

"For sausages, maybe?"

"That's difficult to say. Remember, we're not dealing with ordinary burglars here—these are advertising men."

"But if not robbery, why were hundreds of pounds in cash stolen?"

"A red herring, calculated to divert suspicion," Pefelman theorized. "I daresay all those pilfered will be recompensed in due time."

And, as subsequent events proved, he was one hundred per cent right. Everybody in the Staines, Ashford, and Sunbury areas of Middlesex who had been plundered, as well as many who had not, received a handsome check, and at year's end Stourbridge's Sausages paid a banner dividend to its stockholders.

Far and away the most dazzling display of Pefelman's deductive powers, however, was yet to come. Readers will no doubt recall the news item that burst like a bombshell some time ago in the pages of the New York *Post*. It read: "Flint, Mich. (AP)—The Flint Public Library has recovered a book that was 41 years overdue. Fines due on the book, E. Phillips Oppenheim's *The Great Impersonation,* totaled $758.75. The library received the book in the mail from Frank McPherson, of Petoskey, who said it was among a collection he bought recently. Library officials said they were unable to determine who checked out the book."

"A call for you from Flint, Michigan, Chief." The speaker

that hot August morning as I sat immersed in paper work was Fugazy, my able second-in-command. "It's the head of the public library there, Miss Robin Vermilyea."

I groaned inwardly, though there was no sign of a groan outwardly. "Damnation, that nasty business of the overdue fines again. Didn't you tell her I referred the matter to Pefelman as promised?"

"I did, sir, but she insists on talking to you."

"Very well." I reached into the cradle beside my desk and uncradled the phone. "Novotny here. I trust you're calling to report progress, Miss Vermilyea."

"Yes. Thanks to you, Captain, the culprit responsible for the outrage has been laid by the heels," she imparted. "I just wished to say how adorable Mr. Pefelman was. He sounds just like a little boy." She giggled. "Is he—er—by any chance single?"

"As far as I know. I doubt whether he's interested in marriage, though."

She sighed. "Oh, he's that way."

"What way?" I said coldly. "The guy's only eleven years old."

"Gracious, he's practically a child, isn't he? Anyhow, I must tell you what happened. I phoned him at that store you mentioned, where he was in the midst of buying some candy corn. After I told him the facts, he instructed me to insert an ad in our papers that went, 'Will the party who left a substantial amount of money in a library book call in person at 4 P.M. next Thursday?' "

"How many people showed up?"

"A hundred and twenty-five. And, as Mr. Pefelman directed, we had a newspaper photographer take a group shot of the whole caboodle. Then I told them if everybody would subscribe six dollars and seven cents to avoid becoming a laughingstock, this would total the $758.75 due on the Oppenheim book. You should have seen them swarm around pressing money on me."

"But how did you cotton on to the person who had kept the book?"

"I'm coming to that. Just as Mr. Pefelman shrewdly forecast, one individual remained behind when the rest left—a miserly old curmudgeon named Russel Schrimpf, the richest man in Flint. Under questioning he broke down, confessed he was the blackguard we sought, and offered to make restitution by donating a new extension. We accepted with one proviso; namely—"

"That it be called the S. G. Pefelman Wing," I hazarded.

"Well, I swan! How on earth did you ever guess?"

"My dear Miss Vermilyea," I said. "Some people call it luck, others instinct—in my trade, it's part of the day's work. Once in a while, though, Nature lavishes these, plus genius, on one mortal. I'm sure you know who I mean."

"Yes," she said softly. "He's a wonderful, wonderful human being. May Heaven preserve him, wherever he is."

"That I can tell without asking," I said. "He's either in or en route to the candy store."

Grifter, Stay 'Way From My Door

I was bent over the frozen-food bin at the supermarket that morning, trying to decide whether the baby limas were less likely to poison me than the baby parsnips, when an all too familiar voice sounded in my ear and Rudy Horlick smote me playfully between the shoulder blades. In a township as rich in bores as ours, it would require instruments as yet unknown to science to determine who was the most odious, but Horlick ranked close to the top. He was tedium personified, ennui raised to the nth power, the Grand Sachem of all nudnicks, and I knew as I saw his widening grin that I was a gone gosling.

"Hey, what's this?" Horlick brayed. "Are you still here? I thought you left for Europe weeks ago. Listen," he said, plainly uninterested in any explanation I might furnish, "what gives with that spread of yours while you're away? You renting it?"

I shook my head, and he stared at me incredulously. But this was unthinkable, he said, caught between indignation and pity. Didn't I realize what revenue the place could earn me, apart from the obvious advantage of protecting it from robbery? Look at the Hardacres, for example; the party occupying their house during their absence in Spain had repainted all the bedrooms, installed a barbecue pit, and planted a hillside of rare Dutch bulbs. The Softacres, similarly, had drawn a refined elderly lady so smitten with their home that she had added an

24

extension costing eleven thousand dollars that contained a play-room, a library, and a sauna. Of course, he continued, lashing himself up to a fury, he appreciated that plutocrats like me disdained such paltry sums, but he did feel that in these days, when housing was short, I might have the decency to provide shelter for those less fortunate . . . I scooped up my vege-tables just as his face was turning to the hue of a ripe eggplant and made for the checkout counter. When I looked back, he was still fulminating away, his eyes closed and his jaws clacking soundlessly.

Reviewing the enounter as I drove home, however, it struck me that, unspeakable though the man was, there was a grain of sense in his twaddle. A good trustworthy tenant, at even a nominal rent, would pay for the utilities and upkeep and automatically discourage thieves. The realtor I phoned in the county seat was most encouraging; she had, in fact, an ideal couple at the moment, a wealthy young businessman and his wife who were renting a house nearby but needed more stabling for their polo ponies. Could the Gonifsons, as they were called, view the place the next day? I signified my rapture at the prospect.

At two the following afternoon, a pearl-gray Daimler as elegant as any of the British Royal Family's whispered up the lane, bearing the couple in question and Mrs. Bushmaster, the realtor. Gonifson was a bronzed and virile chap with the whitest teeth I had seen outside of a TV commercial, his wife an effervescent, curvilinear package on the order of Toby Wing. For some puzzling reason, possibly because they had just at-tended the regatta at Cowes, both wore yachting outfits, but, taken with the Daimler, the total effect was impressive.

"Isn't this the most heavenly spot, lambie?" Mrs. Gonifson exclaimed, staring about her openmouthed. "So peaceful and unspoiled like. It reminds me of Tahiti when Gauguin first landed there!"

I interpreted this to mean that the couple had an artistic bent, and observed that over the years the premises had inspired oils, gouaches, temperas, silk screens, mezzotints, and silver-points too numerous to mention. Though suitably impressed,

Gonifson was more concerned with garage space for his motor. I held my breath as he whizzed into the wagon shed with barely an inch of clearance on either side, but he smilingly assured me that it was quite ample. As for the polo ponies, he said, there was no immediate crisis; he was shipping them to Hurlingham, where he was scheduled to play a match against Prince Philip shortly, and if, on his return, there proved to be not enough box stalls in my barn, he would put in a few at his own expense. I considered this a very generous offer, and thanked him warmly. He begged me not to give it a second thought. As he and his wife embarked on a tour of the house, Mrs. Bushmaster launched into a panegyric on the pair. In all her experience, she had never seen a housekeeper to equal Mrs. Gonifson. The residence they were currently occupying was spotless; it virtually gleamed. Regarding Mr. G.'s solvency, his words spoke for themselves, but I might care to know that whenever the couple were abroad they spent all their time between Windsor and Balmoral Castles.

"Boy, oh boy!" remarked Gonifson as they emerged from the house. "Where'd you ever pick up antiques like those? Gad, this place is a jewel box!"

"Yes, but it's cozy at the same time," his wife pointed out. "By that I mean you don't get the feeling you're in a museum. Oh, precious, I can hardly wait to move in."

Won over by their bubbling enthusiasm, I would have surrendered the keys on the spot except that Gonifson insisted on being businesslike; his references, he promised, would be forthcoming in the next mail.

When, unaccountably, none appeared after a week, I took the liberty of calling him. To my surprise, he sounded gruff, almost petulant.

"Yes, yes," he snapped. "My bank in Camden, the Hornswogglers' National, can vouch for me, and if you need a social reference call the Nifty-Gam Hosiery people in Barcelona, Delaware. . . . No, I don't remember the number. Just ask for Mousie there."

Inasmuch as Barcelona, Delaware, proved to be nonexistent, I was unable to raise the Nifty-Gam people and least of all

Mousie, so I got on to the man's bank. The clerk who answered was a bit nonplussed. There was no depositor of that name, but a substantial auto loan in five figures had been granted to a Mr. Wolf Gonifson to purchase a foreign car. I suddenly experienced the buzzing in the ears that afflicts those who have just been rescued from a millrace, and hurriedly rang up Mrs. Bushmaster.

"Oh, I've been meaning to call you," she said before I could question her. "That couple I brought over, you remember—the Gonifsons? Well, it seems the person they were renting from got back from Honolulu yesterday, and his house was empty. Every stick of furniture . . ."

For courtesy's sake I listened to the rest of her aria, but I already knew the score. When she had finished, I laid down new ground rules: henceforth, all prospective tenants were to be fluoroscoped, screened, and certified free of larceny. Three days later, Mrs. Bushmaster called to say that she was sending around a retired gentleman of unimpeachable character.

Mr. Fleischkopf, who had wisely refrained from Anglicizing his name to Meathead, was an affable old kraut with eyes that twinkled behind steel-rimmed spectacles. He explained he had been the foreman of a printing plant for many years, and now amused himself by operating a private press that accepted assignments from a few connoisseurs. Would I have any objection to his installing a small flatbed press, together with appurtenant tools, in the barn? None whatever, I blithely returned; the threshing floor, of centuries-old oak, could support half a dozen elephants trunk to tail, let alone some piffling machinery.

"What sort of work do you specialize in, Mr. Fleischkopf?" I asked him. "Limited editions—pamphlets—that type of thing?"

He chuckled. *"Ach, nein,"* he said. "More in the engraving line. Little portraits on green paper of our Presidents—Washington, Hamilton, all the different ones." He looked about the barn approvingly. *"Ja,* I think this is goot place here. Plenty privacy—no windows for snoopers to peek in."

I sympathized with his distaste for busybodies, for I, too, resent folk rubbernecking at me while I work. We exchanged handshakes, and I phoned Mrs. Bushmaster to draw up the appropriate lease. The next morning, as I was idling through a batch of flyers at our local post office, my eye was caught by a familiar face. The caption beneath read, "Hans Fleischkopf, alias Charlie the Barber, alias Juggins, alias Silk Hat Harry, alias the Pretzel Kid. Wanted for counterfeiting, mopery, and household theft. Warning! Fleischkopf is a smooth, plausible individual who conveys the impression that butter will not melt in his mouth, but he is extremely unstable. If crossed or thwarted in any way, he may plunge a knife into your *derma*."

I made for the nearest phone and dialed the realtor. "See here, Mrs. Bushmaster," I said agitatedly. "That client of yours has a record like Mad Dog Coll! Don't you handle anything but hoods?"

"Oh, I'm so glad you called," she burbled. "I *thought* there was something sneaky about him. But it's just as well—I have two of the loveliest gentlemen in my office right now. Portrait painters."

"Have you frisked them?" I asked. She assured me that their reputations were flawless. "Well, send them along," I said reluctantly, "but get this, girlie—if they're on the muscle, you and your agency walk the plank."

The Messrs. Smith and Brown, as they styled themselves, arrived in a sedan equipped with bulletproof glass and reversible license plates; their hands, dangling below their knees, resembled an orangutan's, though much less endearing. They ignored my invitation to inspect the house but made a swift circuit of the grounds to check the escape routes. My casual mention of a bank or credit reference elicited thin smiles.

"We don't fool around with banks, Dad," Smith growled. "All transactions in cash, you know what I mean? And anybody that don't, they're liable to wind up with their feet in a barrel of cement."

I swallowed, or, rather, attempted to; some sort of twig was embedded in my trachea. "Oh, sure, sure," I croaked. "Well, look around—I have to go lie down now. Did Mrs. Bushmaster tell you?"

"Tell us what?"

"Why, about my smallpox. They don't think it's contagious, but Christmas, you never know——"

The rest of my sentence was blotted out by the screech of rubber as their sedan raced down the lane. I went indoors, obliterated Mrs. Bushmaster's name from my Wheeldex, and called a couple in New York whom I regarded as my bosom friends. I was off to London at daybreak, I announced, leaving my house for them to use as they saw fit. So overwhelming was their gratitude at the confidence I was reposing in them, so infectious their emotion, that we burst into tears on the phone, and I was literally forced to hang up.

Four months thence, travel-stained if no wiser, I stood once again in the dooryard of my home and gazed about me. Except for a somewhat deserted air, the house was exactly as I had left it, without any visible blemish. Marveling at my acumen in entrusting it to intimates, I entered the kitchen, where the first of several surprises greeted me. Someone had hammered spikes into the wall, and from them suspended quantities of rusted Mexican tinware. In one corner, a sizable hillock of empty whiskey bottles lay shored up; in another, rivulets of soup had coursed down the stove front to congeal on the floor. From the refrigerator, the door of which hung open, there emanated a dizzying, noxious vapor. I plunged through it into the living room, and there beheld further carnage—broken glasses, cigarette burns, upholstery ruined by candle grease. Trying to estimate the extent of the damage, I finally gave up and sat with my head in my hands. All of a sudden, the phone began ringing insistently. I picked it up and heard the unmistakable voice of Rudy Horlick.

"Welcome home, stranger!" he bawled. "I saw you go through town and yelled, but you high-hatted me, you skunk. . . . Listen, I'm thinking of renting my place for the summer, and some folks that I understand lived in your house recently have given you as a reference. Their name's Chris and Libby Yahoux—what do you think of 'em?"

"Rudy," I said earnestly. "You've known me a long time, right? Let me tell you about those people. Rudy, just let me tell you about those people, will you please, Rudy?"

"For Chrisake, go ahead and tell me!" he bellowed. "I'm waiting!"

"O.K.," I said. "Well, they're the living end, is all I've got to say. Whoever made them, after he did so, broke the mold."

"Right," he said. "Then I'll certainly take 'em. Gee, I'm much obliged."

"On the contrary," I said. "Thank *you*. After all, didn't you get me into the whole thing?"

Around the Bend
in Eighty Days

I—Disquiet, Please, We're Turning!

Of all the fantasies cherished by the public about the craft of fiction, perhaps the most venerated concerns the moment of creativity—the instant at which, presumably, the divine spark infuses a writer and sets him frenziedly wooing his muse. The popular conception of an author, in fact, is almost total fantasy. The average reader imagines him as a rather Byronic, darkly brooding individual, an amalgam of Baudelaire, Robinson Jeffers, and MacKinlay Kantor, who sits in his study garbed in a smoking jacket and velvet tam-o'-shanter, his brow furrowed in thought as he puffs on a meerschaum, awaiting the flash of inspiration essential to the work of genius. Suddenly a lightning zigzag cleaves the gloom, narrowly missing the bust of Homer on the bookshelf: the Idea has been born. With a stifled cry— sometimes there is not even time for a stifled cry—the author seizes his quill and begins covering page after page of foolscap. Useless for wife and family to plead with him to take rest or nourishment; the all-consuming urge to create, the *furor scribendi,* is upon him and will not be stilled. E'en if it destroys him, he must press forward till he writes "Finis" to his master-piece.

The series of events that climaxed in the present narrative

31

had a somewhat different origin. They began on the sweltering summer morning in 1955 when Avrom Goldbogen—better known to the world of entertainment and various referees in bankruptcy as Michael Todd—first swam into my ken. I was seated in the dingy office on lower Sixth Avenue where I daily immured myself with an intractable typewriter, staring despondently at the rear wall of the adjacent apartment house. Three weeks before, the venetian blind veiling one of the windows had magically risen and I beheld, standing there in pearly nakedness, a lady of such flawless proportions that I was transfixed. She had obviously just emerged from the bath, to judge from the droplets of moisture that clung to her marble limbs, and the innocence of her pose, her sheer Eve-like rosy perfection as she stretched forth her arms and luxuriated in the morning sunshine, wrung my withers. Unhappily, as I was craning forward for a better view my head struck the windowpane. The impact startled her out of her reverie, and a second later the blind crashed downward, abruptly terminating my idyll. For weeks afterward, I kept expecting the vision to recur, but all I ever saw was an unshaven citizen in his undershirt, clearly an enforcer for the Mafia, glaring at me suspiciously through the blind, and I desisted.

I was sitting there, as I say, stirring the dead ashes of desire when the phone rang and a crisp female voice came over the wire. "This is Candide Yam, Michael Todd's beautiful Chinese secretary," it declared. "Mr. Todd just called me from the Coast. He wants to know if you ever read a work authored by Jules Verne entitled *Around the World in Eighty Days.*"

"When I was eleven years old, lambie," I said patiently. "I also read *Toby Tyler, or Ten Weeks with a Circus, Phil the Fiddler,* by Horatio Alger, *Sink or Swim,* by Oliver Optic—"

"My, you really *are* a well-read person," she said. "I don't get much chance to talk to people like you in this job."

"Then why don't we have lunch?" I proposed. "I know a quiet little drop here in the Village—a droplet, so to speak—where we can relax over a vodka Martini and chat about books and stuff."

"Slow down, brother," she said. "There'll be plenty of time for that when we're filmy."

"Filmy?" I repeated. My mood, instinct with romance, conjured up a vision of this exciting person, clad in filmy black negligee, forcing kumquats into my mouth and pleading for love, and I was suddenly on the *qui vive*. "Look, where are you? I can be there in ten minutes. The Plaza bar, the Drake—"

"No, no—*filming,* dear," she corrected, in a voice that rivaled little silver bells. "Like in a movie."

"What movie?" I asked, bewildered. "I'm not involved in any flick I know of."

"Oh, yes, you are," she said. "The Michael Todd production of *Around the World in Eighty Days*—that's why he wants you to reread the book. I'm sending down a copy by messenger in twenty minutes. Be there."

I hung up and, after a quick peek at the apartment window opposite to make sure my Lorelei had not reappeared, tried to recall what I could about Mike Todd. Having written for the theater sporadically in the past. I knew he had produced several shows of passing consequence, like *Star and Garter, The Hot Mikado,* and *Up in Central Park,* but his reputation, even by Broadway standards, was not fragrant with frankincense and myrrh. Playwrights who had dealt with the man showed a tendency to empurple; they castigated him as a cheap chiseler reluctant to disgorge royalties, a carnival grifter with the ethics of a stoat. My association with showmen of the type, notably Billy Rose, had taught me that, in Joyce's felicitous phrase— James Joyce, that is, not Joyce Matthews—they were as full of wind and piss as a barber's cat. Still, I remembered the enjoyment Verne's novel had given me in youth, and if, in my present becalmed state, the project looked as though it might yield up enough to keep the pot boiling there was no harm in discussing it with Todd.

The book, when it arrived, proved to be a children's version bound in gleaming yellow calf, with my name—misspelled, naturally—so freshly emblazoned in gold on it that a few grains sifted into my palm. In due course, Todd rang up my agent and offered even fewer for my services on the screenplay. There then ensued the usual choleric exchange of insults and recriminations that attends all negotiations in the film industry, and ultimately a figure was arrived at which, in the hallowed phrase, we could both live with. Todd was living with his, I found when I reached Hollywood a week later, in opulence; he occupied a luxurious villa at the Beverly Hills Hotel, subsisting chiefly on champagne and caviar and smoking Flor de Magníficos, which cost a dollar apiece—frequently two at the same time. As he wove a verbal tapestry about the production he envisioned, the wonders of the Todd-AO process, the stars he planned to inveigle into cameo roles, and the *réclame* that would accrue to everyone concerned, I took stock of this *luftmensch* to whom I had indentured myself. Squat, muscular, intensely dynamic, he was the very pattern of the modern major moviemaker—voluble, cunning, full of huckster shrewdness, slippery as a silverfish, and yet undeniably magnetic. In short, a con man, a *tummler* with a bursting Napoleonic complex. Forever in movement, he walked in a fighter's crouch, as if both to ward off a blow and dodge a summons. The key to his nature, as I was to learn in our association, was his mouth, which bore a marked resemblance to a rattrap. Those thin lips, I sensed, could be merciless, but at the moment they were busy weaving blandishments.

"We'll kill 'em, Jack," he predicted ebulliently. "It's going to be the picture of the century—we'll blow those civilians out the back of the theater. Rolls-Royces . . . town houses . . . emeralds and rubies the size of your nose. They'll be naming ships after us!" I was reminded of Walter Burns wooing Hildy Johnson in *The Front Page*. "O.K., now, get lost, and remember this, you bum—no hanging around the water cooler. We start shooting with a finished script six weeks from today in Spain."

To chronicle with any accuracy the arguments, intrigues, stratagems, and frustrations I was embroiled in over the next several months would be virtually impossible. One factor, however, was constant: Todd's utter, neurotic refusal to part with money. A compulsive gambler, he would toss away thousands on the turn of a card or the convulsions of dice, but when my stipend or those of my coworkers fell due Todd automatically vanished. Week after week, it took cajolery, pleas, and threats of legal action to collect one's salary. All the while, of course, our impresario lived like the Medici, running up awesome bills that he waved away airily on presentation. Whether they were ever settled, even after he hit the mother lode, was doubtful. His *chutzpah,* however, was indisputable, for, as became more and more obvious daily, his million-dollar epic was a classic shoe-string operation. In Hollywood, he held endless whispered consultations in corners with squat Neanderthal types who rested on their knuckles, underarms bulging as though harboring shoulder holsters. In Europe, these gave way to foxy-nosed characters in homburgs, reputedly Swiss and Austrian bankers, so suave that marzipan wouldn't melt in their mouths. The financial ramifications of any movie are cloaked in mystery; those of *Around the World in Eighty Days* were as impenetrable as the Mato Grosso. To this day, I venture to say, nobody knows where or how Todd promoted the wherewithal to make his chef-d'œuvre, or who got what share of the golden hoard. All I know is that my pittance was extracted only by deep surgery.

European filming began in a village outside Madrid, inaugurated with a Homeric quarrel between Todd and the director, John Farrow, that ended in the latter's dismissal. This stroke of luck raised everyone's spirits—so much so that the bullfight sequences starring Luis Dominguín and Cantinflas were completed ahead of schedule. The company then descended on London, where Todd installed himself in a pad at the Dorchester of such barbaric tastelessness that it must have been shipped piecemeal from Las Vegas to make him feel at home. As with everywhere he roosted, the premises instantly took on the aspect of Donnybrook Fair: phones rang wildly, coveys of actors, agents, and technicians boiled through the rooms, and the air was blue with cigar smoke and maledictions. Concurrently, shooting went on in Knightsbridge and Belgravia, while interiors—the Reform Club, Lloyd's, and Phileas Fogg's residence—were in progress at the studio. One consolation in the uproar was the presence of Candide Yam, Todd's handmaiden from New York. A fetching Celestial strikingly reminiscent of Anna May Wong, Candide inexplicably possessed a fund of colloquial Yiddish, and whenever the turmoil became overwhelming the two of us used to steal away to Isow's, on Brewer Street, and share the inscrutable wisdom of the East over a knish.

Complex as parts of the English production were, they paled beside one exterior, a crowd scene, shot in Paris a fortnight later. The physical action involved was trifling; Phileas Fogg and Passepartout were to arrive in a carriage in the Rue Castiglione and enter the offices of Thomas Cook & Son. Seeking to demonstrate the scope of his AO process, Todd bade his marshals make the scene as lavish as possible. Eight hundred extras were outfitted in the costumes of 1872, and various conveyances of the period—victorias, barouches, berlins, horse-drawn buses—were routed out of warehouses and museums. Since any glimpse of an automobile would have been disastrous, men were employed to clear the area the night before filming; cars were thrust helter-skelter into the streets fringing the Place Vendôme, much to the ire of their owners and the police, who subsequently touched off a lengthy investigation. In any case, by ten the next morning a juggernaut laden with cameras and technicians was positioned against the railing of the Tuileries, seven French assistant directors were rehearsing the crowd with a maximum of hysteria, and our principals had executed so many turns in their vehicle that they were dizzy. Then, just as the whistle blew for the take and the extras started moving, an altogether unforeseen hitch occurred.

Directly above the arcade at the bottom of the Rue Castiglione was a hotel with a number of heavily shuttered windows. Suddenly one of them opened and a fat man in lurid pajamas stepped forth into the sunshine, yawning and scratching himself. His gaze slowly traveled downward into the Rue de Rivoli and, on the instant, he turned to stone. His stupefaction was pardonable; he had retired in 1955 and awakened into a world populated by folk in crinolines and beaver hats. Todd, already overwrought because of the expense and time consumed in the take, suffered a paroxysm. He snatched up a megaphone and screamed at the interloper. "Get back, you dummy!" he shouted. "Can't you see you're on camera, you frog bastard? Close the blind!"

Though Todd's words were inaudible over the din of the extras milling about and the street noises, the man did withdraw, but only momentarily. In an *augenblick,* he popped back with an equally corpulent lady in a peach-colored robe, who reacted as he had. The two of them stood on the balcony gesticulating and chattering nineteen to the dozen while Todd raged up and down, smiting his forehead and inveighing against the French, his subordinates, and destiny. At length, a vassal was dispatched to hale the couple indoors, the multitude was regrouped, and the scene—valueless to the story but quenching Todd's thirst for spectacle—went into the can.

What with another costly crowd scene at the Gare du Nord, involving a number of French screen luminaries, the budget was becoming visibly distended, and Todd decided he had sufficient European footage. In one frantic morning, he organized a second unit to make process shots in India and the Far East, providing its members with tickets to Rangoon, yellow monk's robes, and begging bowls so they could scrounge enough rice to continue onward. Then, distributing a reckless largesse of smiles and handshakes to the technical crew, he raced off to California to do the Western exteriors, and our paths diverged for a spell.

Some six weeks later, I received a midnight telephone plea to join Todd in Hollywood, where he was preparing the Barbary Coast episode and a couple of others in the picture. I complied and, as I expected, was immediately plunged into a courtship unsullied by any hint of money. He urgently needed lines and situations, he confessed, for some exceptional stars he had acquired for cameo roles. I confessed, with equal candor, that I urgently needed bread for my dependents. His eyes took on a glassy, hypnotic stare and he began casting my horoscope. In it he saw yachts the size of the *Stella Polaris,* racing stables, seraglios full of milk-white lovelies surpassing Jane Russell.

Impressed though I was by his clairvoyance, I managed to retain my equilibrium and demanded cash on the barrelhead. He vilified me, rent his garments, and howled aloud, but eventually he consented to a deal on a piecework basis. Nightly in the weeks that followed, therefore, we would meet in a Beverly Hills parking lot, I clutching the pages required for the next day's shooting, he the pro-rata payment. At a concerted signal, we made a lightning exchange, leaped into our respective cars, and drove off.

Five months after the picture had opened and Todd's own picture was appearing on postage stamps, David Niven and I lunched at the Beverly Hills Hotel. As we reviewed the vicissitudes we had undergone in its making, he suddenly interrupted his discourse. "Bless my soul, I almost forgot," he said. "This reunion deserves a special celebration. Waiter—two more Martinis, please!"

"But why?" I asked.

"Because this just came through yesterday." He withdrew his card case and exhibited a check. "My final week's salary for *Around the World in Eighty Days.*"

The waiter, engaged in removing our empties, grunted sympathetically. "Well do I know the *boychick* of whom you speak," he said. "The fastest con in the West."

II—New Girdle, With Lots of Support

It was on a drowsy July afternoon in 1970, fifteen years after Mike Todd's siren song had lured me into working on his celluloid epic, *Around the World in Eighty Days,* that the novel itself returned to make a further impact on my life. I was sorting through a carton of mildewed books in a tool shed on my Pennsylvania farm, wondering what possible magpie instinct had impelled me to retain them, let alone buy them originally. Why, for instance, would anybody be interested in *Hoofbeats,* a novel by that early cowpunch William S. Hart, or a *pfann-kuchen* of Erich von Stroheim's entitled *Paprika, the Gypsy*

Trollop? The graphomania of Hollywood's great must have excited me at one time, to judge also from Errol Flynn's autobiography, *Beam Ends,* and a whodunit by George Sanders called *Crime on My Hands.* As literature, surely, these could be said to possess no enduring qualities, and their value even as mulch was questionable. Here, too, was a dithyramb by J. C. Penney, the chain-store magnate, acclaiming his own business acumen; a limp-leather copy of J. M. Barrie's *A Window in Thrums,* gnawed by squirrels; the complete sailing directions, in Dutch, for western New Guinea; an Emily Post manual for hostesses with some title like *What, No Fingerbowls?;* and an irascible memoir of the Sepoy Mutiny by a British diplomat aptly named Conniption Fitzroy. So when, in this unpromising cache, I came upon the book that had precipitated one of my weirder experiences in the picture business, revulsion gave way to nostalgia. Whatever my memories of Michael Todd, its *deus ex machina,* they had softened with time; I remembered only the pace and gaiety of Jules Verne's original story, its color and suspense, its ingenious dénouement. I sat down to reread it with anticipation.

I was not disappointed. Phileas Fogg was still as delicious a spoof of English *sang-froid* as ever; elegant, imperturbable, Olympian, he strode across the world displaying utter aplomb at every obstacle man and nature interposed in his path. Passepartout, dear man, was likewise intact, a faithful dog's-body whose artlessness the dastardly Mr. Fix continually played upon to subvert their project. Each episode of the story—the immortal bet over the whist table at the Reform Club, the elephant trip in India climaxing in the rescue of Aouda, Passepartout's debacle in the Hong Kong opium den, Fogg's race to Shanghai, the transcontinental dash across America, and the desperate, last-ditch voyage to Liverpool—heightened the momentum, irresistibly drawing you on, so that even though you knew the outcome you were enchanted. And as with other romances of Verne's, what was remarkable was his technical detail—the fidelity with which he described the locales his characters frequented and journeyed through. If his biographers were to be credited, he was no great shakes as a traveler; in fact, apart from a short trip to America in 1867, there were several countries in Europe he had never set foot in. Obviously, then, it must have taken a masterly job of research to write *Around the World in Eighty Days*. More out of admiration than a desire to check up, I turned back to the opening pages of the book, where Phileas Fogg's personality and daily routine were portrayed—and all unknowingly took my first fateful step into the wild blue yonder.

"In the year 1872," the text began, "No. 7 Savile Row, Burlington Gardens, the house in which Sheridan died in 1816, was occupied by Phileas Fogg, Esq." Sheridan, I was to discover subsequently in London, did no such thing; he expired in No. 17. Hard on the heels of this came another dogmatic statement: "Phileas Fogg left his house in Savile Row at half-past eleven and, when he had put down his right foot five hundred and seventy-five times before his left foot, and his left foot five hundred and seventy-six times before his right foot, he arrived at the Reform Club, a huge edifice, standing in Pall Mall, that cost quite a hundred and twenty thousand pounds to build."

Now, here was a poser. I understood Verne's desire to characterize Fogg as a precise, methodical person who lived by the clock, but how did he know how many steps were required from No. 7 Savile Row to the Reform? Had he himself ever walked it? (I did, ultimately, with a pedometer; it took one thousand two hundred and forty-seven steps—six hundred and twenty-three with the left foot, six hundred and twenty-four with the right.) A suspicion slowly dawned that this classic would bear closer investigation. I read on, and almost immediately fetched up against a real howler. Describing Fogg's habitual behavior at the club, the text said, "If he took walking exercise, he invariably did so with measured step on the inlaid floor of the front hall, or in the circular gallery under a dome of blue glass supported by twenty Ionic pillars of red porphyry." My mouth fell open. This was balderdash, absolute poppycock. Any member of the Reform Club—and, by an odd coincidence, I happened to be one—knew that the gallery was not round. It was square, or nearly so, and the glass in the dome above was colorless. Furthermore, far from being supported by

Ionic pillars of red porphyry, the pedestals were of blue-veined white marble with dies of broccatello panels, the column bases of white statuary, the fluted shafts of light Siena scagliola, and the Corinthian capitals richly gilded. Verne was talking through his hat.

Well, there I was on the horns of a dilemma, and you can see why. I could replace the book in its moldering carton, lock the shed, and pretend to myself that these fallacies never existed. On the other hand, did I have the moral right to do so? Generations of readers had accepted the story as gospel; millions unborn would read it and never question its accuracy. Was it not incumbent on me to dig deeper—to ascertain whether the book had any basis in fact or was merely a chimera sprung from the brain of a great romancer? I spent a sleepless night pondering the difficulties inherent in the problem, and by daybreak vanquished them. Within a fortnight, I had disposed of my worldly goods, flown overseas, and stood on English soil ready to press my researches. Quixotic? Headlong? Possibly. But then such is my nature. There are those—and, after all, wasn't Fogg one?—who never do things by halves.

As instinct had whispered, I found all too soon that Verne never let truth stand in the way of his racing imagination. There was, for instance, the detail in his very first chapter about "the Club's waiters, solemn-faced men in dress coats, with molleton under the soles of their shoes." And what, pray, was molleton? The skin of a swan with the feathers on, said the *Shorter Oxford English Dictionary*. Doubtful whether swanskin, with or without feathers, made for ideal footgear, I took this to mean that the Reform waiters had crept about in flannel (a secondary meaning of the word) so as not to disturb elderly members snoozing over their freshly ironed copies of the *Times*. I therefore went to the club and canvassed all the waiters in turn, ranging from a bearded boy of nineteen to an octogenarian whose grandfather had also served there. Not one, significantly, had ever heard of molleton, though the oldest dimly recalled that Sir Moishe Foxglove had once worn on his chest a piece of flannel saturated in whiskey to conquer a cold.

What with tracking down the necrology on Sheridan, pacing Savile Row, and canvassing waiters, my sojourn in London thus far was interesting but not fruitful enough for me to rush into the Royal Geographical Society and denounce Jules Verne as a schlep. It did have one positive result, however. The only possible way to test the veracity of the book, I decided, was to try to duplicate Fogg's journey, in the same time span, using the same transportation. The scheme, admittedly, had drawbacks. In this complex and troubled age, people didn't career around the globe with two woolen shirts, three pairs of stockings, and twenty thousand pounds in a satchel, buying ships and elephants when they got into a bind. Half the countries you needed to get through didn't want you—indeed, would relish the chance to emasculate you; the other half demanded visas, inoculations, liquor permits, documents certifying you free of rabies, Hinduism, and *Spirochaeta pallida*. I clearly needed a wizard travel agent, and I found him in Mr. Honeyball.

"A cinch—a piece of cake," announced Mr. Honeyball. He was a suave hippopotamus in gray broadcloth, the very image of Sydney Greenstreet, seated in a tiny hive off Bishopsgate in the City. "It's hardly a trip to Blackpool, mind you, but I think our worldwide connections can swing it. What did you say your name was—J. Pierpont Perelman?"

I disclaimed connection with any tycoon figure, explaining that I was merely an obscure eccentric who sought to re-create Fogg's exploit as set forth in the book. My purse was as slender as my waist, I added, with a significant glance at his own, and I would be grateful if he bestirred himself. Time was of the essence.

"Well and truly spoken, sir," he said. "You're a man after my own heart." I half expected Joel Cairo to slink in, bearing a phony falcon wrapped in newspaper. "I'll get on to my chaps in the Baltic Exchange, and we'll have you on your way in a jiffy."

Exactly who the chaps were or what Balts they exchanged I never learned, but in short order Mr. Honeyball phoned me on a distinct note of jubilation. He had solved the first and most difficult aspect of the trip. Inasmuch as the Suez Canal was closed and maritime traffic beyond it immobilized, a sea journey to India such as Fogg had made was, of course, out of the question. Nonetheless, he added triumphantly, there was still one way left to transit the Near East by surface. "Try this on for size," he proposed. "You go to Istanbul by ship, cross Turkey and Iran by rail and motor, and sail down the Persian Gulf to Bombay. How does that grab you?"

I judged from Honeyball's idiom that he had glimpsed a few American movies lately on his telly. "Real heavy, man," I said. "But why not Beirut by sea and overland through Syria and Iraq? Isn't that a much shorter route?"

"It is, but the Iraqis won't give you a visa, because America's selling arms to Israel," he said. "That doesn't surprise me, though. Those little brown buggers are just out of the trees."

"What about the elephant situation in India?" I inquired. "Don't forget—I need a good pachyderm to cover the area between Kholby and Allahabad where the railway gives out."

"You're still opposed to buying one, like Fogg did?"

"No, I'd prefer a second-hand rental, if it hasn't too many miles on it. Do they have any?"

"I'm afraid we've a bit of a problem there," Honeyball admitted. "We sent a message in a cleft stick to Kholby, and it seems there's no such place, and, worse yet, no elephants. I wonder if Jules Verne could have made that up."

"That doesn't surprise me, either," I said. "Well, I'll just play it by ear when I get to Bombay. What other hang-ups?"

"Just one," he said. "As yet we haven't been able to find you a balloon."

"Look, Buster," I said. "Once and for all, let's get something straight. There's no mention of a balloon in the book. Todd lifted that from another *guzma* of Verne's, *Five Weeks in a Balloon.*"

"Fancy," he said. "Now, why did he do that?"

"Because it wasn't nailed down," I said. "O.K., Mr. Honeyball, hustle along the tickets, so I can hit the road."

The contrast between Fogg's preparations a century ago and mine became increasingly marked when I began kitting out for the journey. From the evidence at hand, my model had worn but one suit in the many climes he traversed, and if he encountered any dry cleaners in his dizzying progress Verne did not think it worthy of mention. Vivid memories of the temperatures in Asia, though, and the sketchy hygienic facilities everywhere I was scheduled to roam made me overfastidious. By the time all my impedimenta were assembled, however—the winter garments, tropical gear, footwear, toiletries, purges, febrifuges, emollients, and insecticides—panic gripped me. I foresaw myself floundering along the equator, red-faced and perspiring, wrestling this pyramid of luggage through customs sheds and chaffering with greedy porters. What to do?

At that juncture, the simplest, the most obvious of solutions flashed over me. Fogg had had his valet—why not I? Why not minimize the rigors of the trip with a cheerful, trustworthy aide capable of sharing my burdens and disentangling the innumerable complexities ahead? If I could find such a person, I mused . . . And then, in the magical way it sometimes does, inspiration came. Not a *man*servant but a Passepartoute—a big husky doll, preferably with a creamy skin and green eyes, who could lift a valise or rub my back if the occasion arose. I remembered how, when my strength flagged during a TV special several years before, Julie Newmar had picked me up like a feather and borne me to our rehearsal hall high above Ratner's Dairy Restaurant, on Second Avenue. No doubt Big Julie's commitments nowadays precluded global travel, but perhaps somebody of her proportions was available. I hastened to the Yellow Pages for a likely employment agency. Unsurprisingly, they knew twenty young females willing to take a trip around the world free gratis, and my phone began ringing wildly.

Sally-Lou Claypool was her name, out of Pass Christian, Mississippi, and a toothsome cupcake she was—six feet one, with a figure that fractured the senses, a lovely contralto voice, a casque of shimmering jet-black hair, and a degree in home economics from Tulane that immediately set visions of popovers dancing in my head. Immaterial that our eighty-day trajectory would include scant time for baking; I knew instantly that this was the one. She was the last of the candidates I interviewed—New Zealanders, Scotswomen, Yugoslavs, Lebanese, and Finns. All had something to offer, some quite boldly, but Sally-Lou led the field.

"Are you strong?" I asked. "I don't need a Percheron, but there'll be lots of suitcases, grips—"

"Feel," she said, and doubled her arm. "Daddy says I'm just like a boy."

Daddy was obviously myopic; still, I thought it best to reassure myself, and squeezed. Withal it was iron-hard, the surface was like satin. Yes, Sally-Lou seemed well-qualified. In what I hoped was a crisp, executive manner, I delved into her past. Except for a brief absorption in a discus thrower at Cal Tech, she found most men boring, but admitted that latterly she had been fascinated by mustached writers with little steel-rimmed glasses. But, I inquired, could she adapt herself to the many contingencies in store for us? Was she sufficiently flexible?

"Oh, I can curl up anywhere—honest," she assured me, her great eyes shining. "And you know, I really eat very little for a big girl. You don't think I'm *too* big, do you?" she went on anxiously. "I guess it's because I'm—well, so ample."

It was this candid recognition of her femininity that won me, and we sealed the bargain instanter. The next fortnight was a crowded one. Honeyball was busy completing the intricate mosaic of the journey, cabling worldwide for reservations with splendid disregard for expense. I flew daily from doctors to bankers, immunizing myself equally against foreign bacilli and the money changers lying in wait. Sally-Lou lost herself in the boutiques of Chelsea and Carnaby Street, buying armfuls of dresses in the morning and swapping them at night. The rumor of my undertaking, which at first had awed my acquaintances, slowly began losing its novelty, and something akin to resentment became evident on their faces. Why was I still waffling around London when I should be racing across the deserts of Rajasthan on a camel? The phrase "I say—haven't you left yet?" echoed so often in my ears that I wondered if I ought not hide in Wales or Portugal till departure. Phileas Fogg, plainly, was no fool; whether credible or not, he had left England within three hours of the wager at the club. It looked as if I were stricken with a mild case of anticlimax.

At long last, on leaden feet, the moment arrived. A handful of intimates—more jovial, if less solvent, than the quintet of biggies who had seen Fogg off—bade us Godspeed with a bumper of champagne at the Reform. They were all palpitant with curiosity about Sally-Lou. The women's eyes glittered as they took inventory of her chassis and accoutrements, and a distinct buzz, as of hornets, rose above the chatter. One lady, in tendering me a farewell gift box, observed sweetly that it was an editorial comment on my companion. I opened it in the hansom cab that conveyed us to Charing Cross. It turned out to be cheesecake.

At a quarter of nine precisely, aboard an identical Dover express on which Verne's mythical creatures had left to girdle the globe, I leaned out the window and watched the station lights recede into the darkness. And, as one always does, I asked myself the inevitable question—would this singularly bizarre enterprise have happened had I not strayed into that tool shed in Pennsylvania? Well, no doubt the answer lay in the last line of the haunting quatrain Jimmy Durante used to croon in the old Parody Club back in 1928:

> A boy sat under the Anheuser
>   Busch,
> The rain, 'twas coming down in
>   Schlitz,
> He rose a sad Budweiser boy,
> Pabst yes, Pabst no, Pabst yes.

III—The Turkey Trot: One Step Forward, Two Steps Back

The very embodiment of Barbarella, Daisy Mae, and Modesty Blaise, she stood there atop the Spanish Steps in Rome that frosty March morning, as heedless of the arctic blast sweeping the Piazza di Spagna as though it were a zephyr—Sally-Lou Claypool, handmaiden of my lightning peregrination of the globe. It was a magnificent sight. And to the *vitelloni, paparazzi,* and other layabouts transfixed by her dazzling smile, Sally-Lou's shorts, Roman-legionary boots, and halter embossed with the masks of Comedy and Tragedy were exactly what they expected of unfettered American girlhood. Their awed exhalations made little jets of steam in the air. *"Sontuoso! Provocante di saliva*—mouth-watering!" they said. "This graybeard, *evidentemente,* must be her father." One bolder than the rest sidled up to me, touching his cap. *"Scusi, Signore,"* he apologized. "I run a small export business to South America. Is the lady for sale?"

For an instant, the rogue's impertinence tempted me to box his ears, but since they were obscured by a luxuriant growth of hair, I had no time to hunt for them. Uppermost in my mind was the obligation to adhere to Phileas Fogg's schedule, and thus far we had done so slavishly, employing the very same transport. In record time, we had breasted the Alps—indeed, surpassed them, if the reaction of fellow-passengers on the *wagonlit* was indicative; jiggling and swaying, we had whirled through the Mont Cenis tunnel down the boot of Italy, and now, within a few hours, we would embark at Naples on the M/V *Bellezza Turca* for the Golden Horn. I was, in fact, discoursing on the vanished glory of the Ottomans as Sally-Lou and I proceeded toward the Via Veneto to join some friends for an apéritif.

Sally-Lou's eyes misted over reminiscently. "Wow, do they turn me on—do they ever!" she said, sighing.

"What?" I asked, perplexed.

"Ottomans," she said. "This Turkish boy had one in his room at Tulane when I was taking home economics."

At Doney's, thickly crowded with its usual mélange of tourists and bunco artists, Earl Griggs and his Italian wife, Lucia, bade us a heartwarming welcome. A bit too effusive, almost; Griggs, an ebullient press agent turned movie producer, was deeply concerned lest Sally-Lou catch cold, and, commandeering his wife's stole, insisted on tucking it around her. None of his byplay escaped Lucia, whose face paled with such jealousy that I was afraid she might plunge a hatpin into his *gedeirim*. As it turned out, the means were not far at hand, for Griggs shortly produced a slender bamboo walking stick from under his chair.

"You got any kind of protection on this trip of yours?" Griggs demanded.

I replied that I had an insurance floater and a St. Christopher's medal.

"Child's play," he snorted. "What happens if you run into a Burmese dacoit, or that Thuggee sect out in India? Now, this is what we call a *bastone animato*—a sword cane." With a twist of the handle, he unsheathed a gleaming, handsomely chased blade inscribed with the legend *"Non ti fidar di me se il cor ti manca."* "That means 'Put not your trust in me if your heart is faint,' " he explained. "It's all yours, Marco Polo. Wear it in the best of health."

Flourishing the cane in the streets of Naples the next morning, I found it to be a real boon; I could slash irritably at cars threatening to run me down, beat off importunate shoeshine boys, and generally designate myself a *cavaliere inglese* who brooked no nonsense.

The *Bellezza Turca* was a small five-thousand-ton vessel out of Genoa, calling in at Piraeus, Izmir, Istanbul, and Venice. She carried mainly cruise passengers—stiff, poisonous Prussians of the kind George Grosz impaled with his pen, dusty French bank managers fiddling with their pince-nez and little change purses. Their wives were as typical; evenly divided between fat *Hausfrauen* and beady-eyed spiders, they sat in the midship lounge endlessly crocheting doilies and gossiping to Chopin rendered by a wild-haired trio. Our presence gave them something to gossip about. Whenever Sally-Lou sashayed past, usually trailed by several young officers, the ladies would freeze in their chairs.

"Dégoûtant," they said to each other. *"Schrecklich!* Why does not the captain interfere?"

The captain had his own problems, as it happened. The voyage was a stormy one, and, for a man with a skinful of ouzo, steering the craft through the Strait of Messina and the Cyclades was like trying to pressure a pinball machine. I rewrote my will twice the night we bumped through the Corinth Canal, figuring that by breakfast I would be sacked out with Phlebas the Phoenician among the sea anemones and the amphorae.

Once in calmer waters, bingo and similar tedium prevailed aboard, and I sought to while the time away as Fogg had throughout his journey—at the card table. The night before our arrival, failing to scare up any pigeons, I laid out a game of solitaire in the lounge and smiled invitingly at passersby. Nobody gave me a tumble, but eventually an elderly Frenchman wearing a beret and clearly afflicted with palsy drew near. Excusing himself for his inadequate English, he suggested we play piquet, bezique, or the like for a few sous a point. Touched by the old chap's frailty and Old World charm, I assented. Apparently, the pastime had a beneficial effect on his ailment, for he very soon ceased quaking. *Par hasard,* he asked, did I know a game he had learned at the lycée called Noir-Jean, or blackjack? More to humor him than anything else, I offered to let him teach me, whereupon quite unexpectedly, he produced a green eyeshade and rolled up his sleeves.

At 5 A.M., I tottered out on deck and dropped over the side a leatherette folder that had once contained express checks. From the haze shrouding the Sea of Marmara, the spires of Istanbul's mosques were just emerging, and, from my own personal haze, so was the realization that I had been cleaned like a spring chicken (*nettoyé comme un poulet de printemps*). I kept an eye peeled for my seducer in the bustle of debarkation, but by then he had undoubtedly changed his makeup. And when, somewhat later in Kuwait, I heard that Chicago Eddie LaFong, that king of thimbleriggers, had been working the Near East, I understood why I had been suckered.

With only eleven hours' leeway before catching the night express to Erzurum, there was barely time for me to discharge a couple of essential errands, so, manacling Sally-Lou to a lamp-post in the Istiklal Caddesi, I plunged into the hurly-burly of Istanbul. My first objective was the Topkapi museum, to ascertain whether a person suspended by his ankles could really abstract a jeweled dagger from a showcase, as portrayed in the movie of that name. Three guards I interrogated deemed the exploit sheer flapdoodle, assuring me that their feet were like two blocks of ice at all times. An assistant curator, who was selling halvah from a tray in the forecourt, corroborated their opinion. "Stealing with the hands, yes," he acknowledged. "We do it all the time. But hanging upside down from the feet? It's a *bubba-meiseh*—mine are like two blocks of ice the whole time." The revelation would have made a sensational news story, but rather than disgrace Eric Ambler, who had conceived the idea originally, I chose to remain silent.

My second mission involved the fulfillment of a lifelong dream. Ever since 1925, when I first saw mention of it in Aldous Huxley's *The Tillotson Banquet,* I had coveted a Levantine decoration known as the Turkish Order of Chastity, Second Class. Now that I was based in London, I felt that this insignia would vastly increase my social standing, opening doors to salons and other chambers previously denied me. Much to my elation, I was able to track one down in the recesses of the Grand Bazaar—well worth the sixty-seven quid I shelled out for it.

When the midnight choo-choo left for Erzurum, it already bore one disenchanted customer. Mr. Honeyball's sales pitch in London had led me to expect a version of the Orient Express, full of mysterious veiled charmers redolent of patchouli, and double and possibly triple agents in black monocles smoking endless Sobranies. In the event, it proved to be a slow train through Arkansas, bulging with country folk and their turbulent possessions, and a miasma of hippies bound for Afghanistan. As calisthenics, two nights and days of jolting across the Turkish hinterland by rail were doubtless beneficial to the tripes; as tourism, they were an ordeal. The train crept through snowy mountain defiles at a snail's pace, pausing every few seconds at villages whose only resource seemed to be the unquenchable gaiety of children capering along the tracks. The poverty everywhere was appalling, the incidence of soldiers and fortifications sinister. Considering that a military coup was in progress, as we heard later, everything was as quiet as the grave, and equally somber. Even more so, though, was the weather; the farther east we went, the more prevalent the snow became—a disquieting portent, for at Erzurum a car was scheduled to ferry us through the mountain passes into Iran, and one day's delay could cause us to miss our vital steamer connection beyond at Kuwait. Altogether, the situation was not conducive to optimism, nor was the train cuisine, a cheerless mixture of goat cheese, leathery Wiener schnitzel, and bread resembling Michigan peat moss. My companion, lost in dreams of the hush puppies and fatback she had been reared on along Mississippi's Gulf Coast, began to weave alarming fantasies. "Do you know what I'd like this minute?" she queried as we gnawed away at our schnitzels the last night. "A couple of shots of bourbon and a big platter of chicken swimming in gravy, with beaten biscuits, hominy grits, and a side order of black-eyed peas. Then I'd cut me a huge chunk of pecan pie and stretch out in the hammock . . ."

Heavy snow blanketed Erzurum the next morning, and the sky was laden with the promise of more. My heart sank when I queried the hotel staff about the state of the overland route southward into Iran. Other than a jeep and a badly battered lorry, no vehicles had come through from Tabriz in four days; their occupants reported apocalyptic drifts, buses and cars and camions snarled in blizzards still raging. Under different circumstances, one could have waited for the roads to clear, but time was now our enemy—unless we reached the Persian Gulf pronto, the British Mideast liner S.S. *Choleria* would sail without us, knocking our forward arrangements into a cocked hat. A decision was imperative, and once again the hoary precept that there is more than one way to skin a cat was demonstrated to be hogwash. I squared my chin (insofar as nature would permit) and ordered our driver to fetch us at daylight.

Midway through the First World War, at the age of thirteen,

I wrote an essay that won first prize in a contest sponsored by a magazine called *The American Boy*. It was entitled "Grit," and it extolled the valor of those taxi drivers who had stemmed the Prussian horde at the Marne. Grit, I explained, was raw courage in the face of overwhelming odds, fortitude under well-nigh unbearable pressure—in a word, pluck. Had anyone scraped away the snow from a black sedan stalled in the mountains of eastern Turkey some five decades later, he would have seen a man fresh out of pluck. Whatever illusions I had previously entertained about my durability had flown, and henceforth I was content to regard myself as a pantywaist. Nine hours of crawling up almost vertical inclines in a whirlwind of snow, teetering on the edge of chasms, and skidding down icy gorges into eternity had reduced me to the consistency of calf's-foot jelly. To Sally-Lou, on the other hand, the nightmare we were embroiled in was sheer heaven; refusing to comprehend the gravity of our plight, she whinnied with delight as our wheels spun us halfway to kingdom come. But now, with two mountain peaks unscaled between us and the Iranian border, they had ceased to spin, and our driver's prognosis was bleak in the extreme. What with traffic immobilized ahead and darkness falling, no plows would be operative until morning. Tabriz, therefore, was unattainable, as were Tehran and Khorramshahr, farther along. To spend the night in the car in such intense cold was suicidal; ergo, the only solution was to retrace our steps.

Among my many speculations as we drove back to Erzurum with tire chains beating out an obbligato against the fenders, one was recurrent: How would Phileas Fogg have solved this particular dilemma—or, rather, how would Jules Verne, seated in his cozy study in Amiens, have solved it for him? Genius though he was, Verne would have been stumped. And yet, so indomitable is the human spirit, so deeply ingrained the grit that stemmed the Prussian horde at the Marne, that somehow we muddled through. Thirty-six hours later, Passepartoute and I ascended the gangplank of the S.S. *Choleria* in Kuwait. It had taken superb logistics on my part, and a peck of money.

"Goodbye, goodbye!" the baggagemen called from dockside, waving the baksheesh we had lavished on them. "May you live a thousand years and a trolley car grow in your stomach annually!" Before us stretched the Persian Gulf, most historic of waterways to India and Africa; already the spicy scent of the Middle East, compounded of open drains openly arrived at and Texas oilmen, permeated our nostrils. Ahead of us, in the little-known Trucial States and sheikhdoms bordering on the Gulf and, above all, in fabled Muscat and Oman, lay adventure unimaginable. I drew a deep breath, brushed a small, many-legged Arab off my sleeve, and went down to unpack.

IV—Dip in Hot Water and Fry Till Acerbic

Under a midday sun crueler than an obsidian knife, the British Mideast liner S.S. *Choleria* crawled slowly down the Persian Gulf from Bahrain, bearing twelve hundred deck passengers of mixed Indian nationality, an American traveler easily distinguishable from Phileas Fogg and accompanied by a female attendant, and a cargo of Basrah dates, apricot kernels, dried fish, and old bicycle frames. Far away to the south, in the shimmering heat, lay the hazy shoreline of the seven Trucial States—Abu Dhabi, Dubai, Sharjah and Kalba, Ajman, Umm al Qaiwain, Ras al Khaimah, and Fujairah—and beyond it the illimitable, half-charted wastes of Saudi Arabia. Truly a scene out of the *Arabian Nights,* I reflected as I stood on the flying bridge shielding my eyes against the glare; all it lacked was the mythical roc to swoop down and whisk me worlds away, ideally into some air-cooled Manhattan delicatessen where the fragrance of pastrami and new dill pickle could replenish a sorely tried spirit. An involuntary sob burst from my throat. Fain would I have traded my soul to the Devil for a chopped-chicken-liver sandwich on rye, yet no smell of brimstone heralded the approach of the Prince of Darkness to offer me a deal. Nowhere in that immensity of sea and sky could one detect so much as a speck of sturgeon, a poppy-seed roll—only the boarding-house reek of Brussels sprouts, intermingled with fried plaice, that meant lunch was imminent. Simultaneously, the gong resounded along the lower decks, and, girding myself for the purgatorial hour ahead, I made for the companionway.

There are, unquestionably, people who would relish an eight-day voyage in Islam with three Scottish mariners fixated on golf. There are also crackpots who like to explore caverns infested with bats, who bathe in Sheepshead Bay in February, and who flagellate themselves with the films of Vera Hruba Ralston. None of these forms of masochism stimulates me; in fact, the mere mention of golf causes me to break out in hives, evidently because I once worked in my youth as a caddie. So it was hardly remarkable that the spoon clattered in my plate when Captain MacMurdo launched into a long, infinitely detailed account of a tournament he had played at St. Andrews during his last home leave. Mr. Broomhead and Mr. Splint, his chief officer and engineer, regarded me with concern.

"Are you all right?" Splint inquired. "What are all those red bumps on your face?"

"Hives," I mumbled. "Childhood allergy. Psychosomatic, they say, but I know different."

"Well, I hope it isn't the food," said Captain MacMurdo, frowning. "Don't you like the meals on this ship?"

"No, no—I adore them," I protested. "I could eat Brussels sprouts and fried plaice till the cows come home." Frightened lest he clap me into irons for insubordination, I shoveled in a huge mouthful of the stuff, which gagged me.

"Hmm," MacMurdo commented. "You need looking after, man. Where's your nurse—that lassie you came aboard with?"

"Nurse?" I asked, arching my eyebrows. "I'm afraid you're laboring under a misapprehension, Captain. The truth is, she's my former governess—my nanny."

He froze, a sprout impaled in midair on his fork. "Don't be ridiculous," he snapped. "Why, you're twice her age—maybe three times. She's a robust young woman."

"Yes, she *is* well-preserved," I acknowledged. "Nevertheless, she happens to be eighty-six years old. It's a rather unusual case of rejuvenation. Would you like to hear about it?"

Needless to say, he was agog and begged me to elucidate, so I elucidated. Sixty-five years ago, I explained, my family, grown fantastically wealthy as a result of rediscovering the Lost Dutchman mine, had engaged Sally-Lou Claypool to care for me, and she had done so with doglike devotion. Never married—she often observed wistfully that she could not hope to find another Apollo like her young master—she had grown gray in the household, one of our innumerable staff, until she became too infirm to work. Then, by sheerest chance, I happened to leaf through Gertrude Atherton's celebrated romance, *Black Oxen,* which dealt with the magic transformation of an aging Hungarian noblewoman into a vibrant, desirable beauty of thirty. What better recompense could I make to my old nanny for a lifetime of unstinting service than the gift of youth? Forthwith, I took her on a round of the foremost clinics in Europe, to every geriatrician of note, including Dr. Paul Niehans, in Switzerland, and Dr. Anna Aslan, in Rumania, the two of whom had wrought the miracle my auditors now saw. What did it matter that the cost of the treatments would have erected a high-rise building with a pool on top and garage facilities for two hundred tenants? I did not begrudge it. My motto was: If you've got it, spread it around.

Captain MacMurdo's eyes were wet when I finished. "You're a wonderful, wonderful person," he said. "If there were more people like you in this world, I don't know what would happen. Well," he said, rising, "I better have a dekko at those little clocks and dials on the bridge ere some treacherous reef consign us all to Davy Jones's locker."

I drifted out after him and took a leisurely turn around the deck, where half a dozen Arabs, our fellow-occupants in cabin class, lay dozing in the heat. I bade them a courteous *"In cha Allah"* as I passed, and they inclined their heads gravely in response. Curious how a single phrase like that can often accomplish far more than a decade of diplomacy; I was told afterward that within a matter of hours peace mysteriously descended over the strife-torn Middle East—foes embraced, hatchets were buried and swords beaten into plowshares, lovers were reunited, and birds sang again. Although I was unaware of it at the time, it was pleasing to learn that I had played a vital part in defusing a potential powder keg. These are the small by-products of global travel that can be so enriching, but I claim no credit for myself. I just happened to be in the right place at the right time.

It was also my privilege, since I had never before sailed these waters, to observe for the first time how the Indian proletariat sails them. Most of those aboard the vessel—Hindus, Gujratis, and Tamils—were migrant workers from the Kuwait oil fields, with a sprinkling of Baluchistani mercenaries who had fought in the endless tribal wars along the Gulf. They were colorful folk, each family with its flowered tin trunk and bedrolls, and the luckier ones were camped out on the afterdeck under tarpaulins. The remaining eleven hundred were packed like sardines in the three lower decks, in dark corridors and along-side cargo holds where the temperature reached truly spectacular heights. I permitted myself a few mild strictures on the comfort and sanitation there as Mr. Broomhead and I stumbled through on a guided tour.

"Ah, yes," he said with a bland smile. "But you see, they're used to it—they've never known anything else."

"You mean if they'd lived at Claridge's or the Waldorf before, this would be a deprivation?"

"That's right. Besides, it probably gives 'em a sense of security to huddle together like that. Look at that cute little chap—snug as a bug in his mother's arms. Reminds me of my own bairns in Auchtertochtie—except for the color, that is," he added hastily.

"How's the food down here?"

"Well, I've never tasted it myself, but it's good hearty fare—plenty of seeds and that sort of thing. Of course, they don't get anything like the Brussels sprouts and fried plaice we do."

So, I mused, there *were* some compensations, arduous as was their lot. A day or two later, I tried in a small way to alleviate it. I brought down several copies of the *Reader's Digest* abstracted from the ship's library, urging them to read such inspirational essays as "Nephritis Can Be Fun" and "Paul

Getty—Misery in the Midst of Plenty." Additionally, I made a short talk entitled "The Twilight of the Raj," in which I pointed out that there was pie in the sky, that Britain was shortly withdrawing from the Gulf, and that in their next incarnation they, too, would occupy suites at Claridge's and the Waldorf. All present joined in vigorous applause, acclaiming me both a humanitarian and a jolly good fellow, and we parted fast friends.

As it steamed southward toward Bombay, the *Choleria* called in at Doha, Dubai, and Abu Dhabi, ports that prior to the discovery of the rich oil deposits in the region had been sleepy little harbors for dhows trading to India and East Africa. Now, suddenly, they had become bustling entrepôts; overnight, banks and commercial offices had mushroomed on sandpiles, tankers bearing remote foreign flags lay in the roads, and everywhere cement dust and the clangor of construction were overpowering. For some indefinable reason, all this brouhaha intoxicated my Passepartoute; whenever we docked, she sprinted ashore to haggle daylong in the bazaars, returning laden with camel saddles, yashmaks, incense burners, and filigreed daggers. Her purchases were invariably borne by a couple of liquid-eyed, unshaven admirers who hoped to filch a few tins out of the ship's stores. Failing to do so, they fastened on me with tales of a cousin in Hingham, Massachusetts, in whose carpet factory they had been promised jobs if I loaned them the fare. When I declined, they shrugged with true Arab fatalism, spat on my shoes, and slunk off, vowing revenge.

Amid the jagged gray peaks of a coastline as inhospitable as I had ever seen, a cluster of white buildings swam into view one breathless morning. Muscat, capital of the legendary sultanate of Muscat and Oman, had nothing to do with the renowned grape; indeed, any grape exposed to its furnace heat would have shriveled in a twinkling. Until recently, foreigners, except for a few British military advisers, had been ruthlessly excluded from the area, but now its gates were creaking open, thanks to oil, the universal solvent, and we were favored with a morning's tour of the town and its environs. Whatever expectations of romance I had nursed were shortly dispelled. Despite the number of picturesque tribesmen visible in the souks, festooned with pistols and scimitars, everybody else was in a hell of a state—ragged, malnourished, disease-ridden. I saw none of the rich, poetic imagery the *Rubáiyát* had promised; not only were the loaf of bread and jug of wine nonexistent but even the bough. It was a Muslim version of Appalachia, and it seemed unlikely that these Omanis would soon be tooling around in Cadillacs, as our guide, a young English whippersnapper fresh out of Cambridge, fluently assured us.

Two days later, at Karachi, the Arab world was astern and we were descending on Mother India, which was already groaning under insoluble problems. All my acrid memories of Indian bureaucracy revived when Passepartoute and I disembarked for a look around the city. Countless heads were scratched, pencils chewed, passports fingered. Our money was counted and recounted, hands were run over us to detect cameras, weapons, concealed packets of nose candy. I watched the pompous little toad who was examining the documents I had filled out in sextuplicate, longing to unsheath my sword cane and flick the buttons off his tunic, but I mastered the impulse and sweated silently. His eyes bored into me. "You failed to fill out this space with your grandmother's maiden name."

"I'm sorry. Magda Lupescu, care of Poste Restante, Bucharest, Rumania."

He wrote it down, laboriously. "Why do you wish to enter West Pakistan?"

"Purely for shopping. This lady with me wants to buy some hair spray. Having done so, we shall continue onward to Bombay."

"Not with the hair spray. That must be deposited with the authorities prior to embarkation. Read Section 5."

"I'm not allowed to. My doctor has forbidden me to read Section 5."

"In that case, your stay here is limited to four hours."

"That's the best news I've had in donkey's years. Thank you very much."

"You're welcome. Now pass along, Mr. Lupescu. There are people sweating behind you."

By the time our circuit of Karachi was complete, I realized that besides retracing Phileas Fogg's footsteps I would do well in future to emulate him in another respect. "The thought of going ashore to see the town never occurred to him," Jules Verne wrote, "for he was one of those Englishmen who, when traveling, leave their servants to do their sightseeing for them." What with the swarms of humanity, the apocalyptic noise and turbulence in those fetid streets, and incipient sunstroke, I succumbed to vertigo and fell into a cartful of mangoes, occasioning a fearful tohubohu. A vast crowd collected as the stallkeeper put on a performance worthy of Jacob Adler, the Jewish tragedian. His name, curiously enough, was Abou ben Adler, and his tribe did increase, uncles and nephews streaming in from nearby alleys to swell his lament. He called on Heaven to strike me dead—not, however, without a whopping reparation for damages to his wares and peace of mind. I finally mollified him with a fistful of Maria Theresa thalers I had picked up in Muscat. The contretemps had one redeeming aspect, though. We got back to the ship in time to miss lunch.

A quarter century had elapsed since I had last seen Bombay, and, incurable sentimentalist that I am, memories crowded in on me the morning of our arrival. I remembered such monumental heat, discomfort, and muddle that I had knelt down in the lobby of the Taj Mahal Hotel and sworn that wild horses tied tail to tail would never force me back there. It was gratifying to find that nothing had altered. The air was just as stifling, the traffic as demented, and the inhabitants in precisely the same state of flap. The sole difference was that it was now impossible to kneel in the Taj lobby, where an archeological dig or some similar lunacy was in progress, but I renewed my vow upstairs on the floor of my room, and, much refreshed, phoned the travel agent in charge of our forward arrangements.

Mr. Mookerjee presented himself within the hour, a small, woebegone lemur of a man with a briefcase full of bad news. "I am floundering in the depths of despair, my dear sir," he announced, wringing his hands. "Unexpected obstacles are popping up in your path. Only last night, I am saying to my wife, 'What shall we do about dear Mr. Perelman? How will he be responding to the change in his plans?' And she is saying . . ."

The burden of the message, when I finally stanched his flow of rhetoric, was stark. No steamers eastward from Calcutta were available for weeks to come—in view of which we would have to sail from Madras. Unfortunately, between Bombay and Madras not a single passenger elephant of the type that had served Fogg and Passepartout was to be found; these existed only at Jaipur, seven hundred miles north of Bombay and separated from Madras by the full width of the subcontinent. Hence, if I was still intent on covering some portion of India by elephant, it meant a diversion of roughly three thousand miles within the next five days—a zigzag that would entail a flight to New Delhi, a round trip of four hundred miles by car to Jaipur, and a further flight from Delhi to Madras.

As the full import of Mr. Mookerjee's words sank home, I realized, not for the first time, how complex was the exercise I had so lightly undertaken, and why Fogg had carried twenty thousand pounds in his carpetbag. My immediate impulse was to yield to hysteria, curse the Fates for their capriciousness, and, in passing, give Mr. Mookerjee a good poke in the snoot for failing to discharge the express instructions sent him from London. In the very breath, though, I spurned the thought. Under whatever circumstances, no matter what the provocation, the man on whom I was patterning myself had never lost his aplomb. Forthwith my face froze into a mask—composed, icy, imperturbable. Signifying with a nod that I accepted the inevitable, I dispatched Mookerjee to book our behemoth, and turned back to re-examine my face in a mirror. Yes, I was as cool as a cucumber—and perhaps it was that metaphor that suddenly secured my downfall. For "cucumber" meant "pickle," and pickle, in turn, awoke my dormant craving for the unattainable chopped chicken liver on rye. Out the window went Fogg and the Stiff Upper Lip. I threw myself on the bed, and, burying my face in the bolster, dissolved into floods of tears.

V—*In Vishnuland I'll Take No Stand*

The first long shadows of dusk were just deepening over Jaipur's Rambagh Palace Hotel in north-central India when an elderly Chevrolet saloon wheezed up its driveway, coughed to a stop, and deposited two passengers under the portecochère. Those who had witnessed my departure from the Reform Club in London twenty-three nights earlier, attended by a female valet and bent on reproducing Phileas Fogg's supposititious circuit of the globe, would have derived a grim chuckle from my present appearance. Dehydrated by four hours' jouncing over the blistering, eroded moonscape of Rajasthan, I was a mirror image of Walter Huston in *The Treasure of the Sierra Madre*—disheveled, sunken-eyed, temper honed to razor edge. Throughout the two-hundred-mile journey from New Delhi, the driver had given a virtuoso performance on his horn, tooting bullock carts, cyclists, and pedestrians out of his way, meanwhile delivering a FitzPatrick travel talk on India the Beautiful. Unfortunately, my sentiments about guided tours closely approximated those of Fogg. "Phileas Fogg had no desire for information," Verne's chronicle stated. "He was not traveling, he was merely describing a circumference. He was a solid body moving through an orbit around the terrestrial globe, in obedience to the laws of rational mechanics." My body was less solid because twenty-five years older than Fogg's, and the mechanics plainly irrational, for I had digressed widely from his route solely to include a ride on an elephant. To compound my irritability, moreover, Sally-Lou Claypool, my Passepartoute, looked as fresh as a daisy. Her lustrous eyes, her statuesque frame exuded rude health—a deliberate simulation of energy almost as if to proclaim the superior hardihood of her sex. It was pure women's lib in the middle of Nowheresville, and I didn't need it.

Providentially, the maxim that it's always darkest just before the dawn proved true. Before you could say "bo" to a goose—a formality demanded of everyone checking into the Rambagh Palace, whose lobby was crowded with geese—I was chambered in the very suite tenanted by the former Maharaja, the kind of spread Cecil B. De Mille used to conjure up at his most feverish. The bedroom, forty-five feet long and lit by twin crystal chandeliers, would have held a senatorial caucus; gold taps gleamed richly in the sunken marble tub and stall shower, ceiling fans revolved blessedly overhead. Recumbent in my bubble bath aromatic with the perfumes of Araby and Ind, I felt as sybaritic as Gloria Swanson in De Mille's version of *The Admirable Crichton;* in the ascending steam I saw the faces of Thomas Meighan, Lila Lee, Raymond Hatton, and Theodore Roberts benignly regarding me and healing my spirit. In such surroundings, one tends to become expansive, and when a fiercely bearded Sikh bowed in a bit later bearing the chota peg I had ordered, I was tempted to fling him a lakh of rupees with a princely gesture. Not knowing how many rupees there were to a lakh, though, I had to content myself with the princely gesture, but he was deeply grateful nevertheless. Many of these fellows rarely receive more than a kick for their pains.

"Many of us fellows rarely receive more than a kick for our pains, Sahib," he said, cringing. "Did you know that, revered sir?"

"So I am reliably informed," I said. "Watch out there—you're spilling the soda on the rug. Kurdistan carpets don't grow on trees."

"Forgive me, Your Highness," he stammered. "I forgot my lowly station. In my sottishness, I obtruded on your royal meditations—"

"Yes, yes," I cut him short. "Now buzz off and let me drink my whiskey in peace." Lucky for him he left when he did, else he might have got a kick for his pains. You have to know how to deal with these fellows.

A vague suspicion that we had fallen into one of Winsor McCay's Little Nemo fantasies began to haunt me shortly when Sally-Lou and I entered the dining room. Resonant as an armory and thirty feet high, it contained an infinity of tables, all deserted except for a trio of blue-haired Gorgons with plangent

New Jersey accents. The pair of Indian youths in snowy white drill serving us appeared to be sunk in a cataleptic trance that nothing could penetrate. They twice brought us steaming apple roly-poly as hors d'oeuvres, and insistently plied the ladies with mulligatawny soup, though they had long since concluded their meal. At length, they and the entire kitchen staff, in fact, vanished, presumably into a state of karma that disdained bodily sustenance, and we were forced to fall back on some dispirited graham crackers and cashew nuts gleaned from our luggage.

The much-heralded elephant trip took place next morning at the Amber Palace, another onetime royal abode, situated on a crag seven miles distant from Jaipur. Far below, in a huddle of booths displaying postcards and souvenirs, four or five jumbos were somnolently munching a breakfast of sugar cane while their mahouts bargained with a dozen Australian and German tourists. Our beast, a female named Gulab-Kali, or Rosebud, was decked out with a fair degree of splendor. In contrast to the sleazy side curtains on her fellows, she sported a red velvet saddle blanket, an embossed silver headplate, chain anklets and earrings, and fake wooden tusks. Though she wore no mascara or eye liner, her trunk was rainbow-colored with various intricate designs, and altogether, from the tip of her howdah to her three-inch painted toenails, she was a gorgeous bit of elephanthood. To add further panache to the scene, her mahout and two bearers were attired in gold tunics and turbans, one of the latter holding aloft a gold umbrella, the other a silver scepter. Impressive as all the panoply was, however, I was attacked by sudden misgivings. "Look here," I said to the overseer in charge of the troupe. "I don't mind a touch of Disneyland, but won't this gold fringe and stuff impede our progress through the bush?"

"What bush is that, gentleman?" he asked, blinking.

"Why, dash it all, whatever was laid on for us to traverse," I sputtered. "Mr. Mookerjee in Bombay promised us a first-class trip through impenetrable jungle as previously supplied to Phileas Fogg of No. 7 Savile Row, Burlington Gardens. Where is it, man? Speak up!"

He stifled a yawn. "No impenetrable jungles around here, Mister," he said. "This is Maharaja Special Pony Ride—two blocks up hill, five-minute tour through palace, two blocks down. A hundred fifty rupees, please, plus eight annas extra for popcorn."

Had my wattles not turned pink with rage and my voice become inarticulate, I daresay I could have hammered some sense into the rascal, but under the circumstances one had to accept the situation. We therefore ascended a stone upping block and disposed ourselves in the howdah, and, animated by a thrust from the mahout, Rosebud slowly shambled forward. She had hardly gone fifteen feet before I realized that of all the imbroglios I had ever got myself into this was the most terrifying. Each step involved a sickening circular lurch, exactly as though we were circus acrobats pinned to a sway pole. The sky was blotted out by a shimmering television test pattern, a vast nausea enveloped me, and I clung for dear life to the iron bar securing us in place.

"Stop! Stop!" I shouted. The mahout spun around, overcome by alarm. "Your animal's run amok—she's fixing to shake this entire shooting match off her back!"

"Don't be ridiculous," Sally-Lou said impatiently. "She's a perfect pet—aren't you, Rosebud?" She craned over and cooed into the creature's ear. "Come on, honey, turn around—that's an angel."

Rosebud, responding to her soft endearments, emitted a sound between a whinny and a bray and executed a curtsy, tipping the howdah into an angle steeper than the deck of the *Titanic*. Dizzied by the abrupt plunge, I slid into the bottom of the litter, from whose depths I just managed to croak out an offer of another lakh of rupees to return me to terra firma. The bribe had its desired effect, and in jig time I was an earthling again, scarcely able to credit my deliverance. Sally-Lou, of course, felt obliged to demonstrate how pusillanimous I was, and proceeded on the junket with a great show of bravado. I wrapped myself in a mantle of dignity and watched her go, my lip curled in a cold, contemptuous smile. To me her silly little heroics were so much swagger, designed to impress a few credulous natives. Brief and costly though the experience, it was of inestimable value to me. Hitherto, three principles exposited by Nelson Algren had ruled my life: Never play cards with any man named Doc; never eat at any place named Mom's; and never sleep with anyone whose troubles are worse than your own. To these I now added a fourth. Never again would I be tempted aboard a quadruped of any sort, however seemingly docile—not even those on a merry-go-round.

During the endless trudge back to New Delhi, the sweltering overnight stop there, and the successive transit to Madras, I had ample opportunity to reflect on the sea journey ahead of us. The prospect did not whet my appetite: Eight days across the Bay of Bengal on the S.S. *Moribunda*—somehow it had an ominous ring, a forewarning of disaster. Headlines persistently formed in my imagination: "FIERY HOLOCAUST SWEEPS INDIAN VESSEL" . . . "GIANT SQUID ENGULFS CROWDED LINER" . . . "SURVIVORS SOUGHT IN BAFFLING SEA HORROR. Penang (Reuters)—In a mystery rivaling that of the *Mary Celeste,* the steamship *Moribunda* was today found floating . . ."

"Are you worried about something?" Sally-Lou queried as a taxi ferried us through the sprawling inner suburbs of Madras to our hotel. "You look—well, so subdued."

"Not at all," I said lightly. "I'm as happy as a lark. I was merely speculating how Houdini ever got out of that box."

"Houdini?" She blinked at me. "I don't get it. Who was he—a Yoga, like?"

"No, just somebody they used to handcuff and stuff into a box that was then flung into the ocean. He always escaped in less than two minutes."

"Whatever made you think of that?"

"Er—nothing, really. Just musing about the voyage tomorrow," I said. "Gee, I can hardly wait for the food we'll be given on board—mutton curry and cold, greasy chapatties. I never can get my fill of cold, greasy chapatties."

"Listen," she said, pursing her lips. "I *told* you to wear a hat back there in Jaipur. You've had too much sun."

Oho, I thought to myself—more women's lib. Yesterday she

showed off her prowess with elephants, today she's a world-famous brain surgeon diagnosing people's ailments. Yet why should I be surprised? It confirmed what I had always noticed about women traveling in the East. Unable to withstand the crises, the hardships that men could, they took refuge in fantasy—became bossy, authoritative, self-pronounced experts—and thus lost all their femininity. A pity, because *au fond* they were decent creatures, and, if properly trained, as capable of loyalty as a good dog.

For those whose rarefied tastes thrive on the odor of imperial decay, there is much to savor in Madras—a museum stocked with cannonballs and tarnished uniforms from the days of the East India Company, an English department store the size of a mid-Victorian railway station where oatmeal and tinned pilchards are available, and a church containing the marriage certificate of Elihu Yale. Philistine that I am, however, such survivals act on me like a barbiturate, so strongly that when the *Moribunda*'s whistle sounded at last signalizing our departure from India, I was still too benumbed to express my gratification. What an experience it had been to rub elbows with its colorful inhabitants, to observe their customs at work and at play, to bask, albeit hurriedly, in its age-old culture. And what an eternity it would be, I prayed as I had twice in the past, before I set foot on its shores again. Others had managed to escape with only one trip to India, but some monstrous quirk always brought me back. How could anyone be such a schlemiel?

"Nagapattinam," I said as I lay gasping in my stateroom that fearful second afternoon of the voyage. "Naga-pat-ti-nam," I repeated, rolling the syllables over my tongue. I wanted to remember this place where, ever since daybreak, the *Moribunda* had stood offshore in the breathless heat loading onions from swarms of tenders tied alongside. Baskets and bundles of onions by the thousand were swung aboard in the nets; the shriek of the winches, coupled with the boatmen's cries and overspread by the stupefying smell, boggled the mind. It was inconceivable that we should be piling up this avalanche of onions to discharge on Malaya, unless perhaps as an act of vengeance. But then, as I was soon to discover, everything about the ship was inconceivable—the roach-ridden cabins, the rats that nibbled the soap in the washstands, the total disregard for lifeboat drill, the Indian rock and roll that blared eternally from the public-address system. The premonitions I had had about the food, as it turned out, were unjustified. I *was* able to get my fill of cold, greasy chapatties, as well as of the handful of Westerners who clung together on the crossing. There were seven of them at our table—a honeymooning Canadian couple, two faceless Scottish spinsters bound for Australia, a pair of deracinated hippies, and a loose-wristed Illinois aesthete fresh from a *Wanderjahr* in Katmandu. Since we lacked any common bond except revulsion for our victuals, dialogue on the whole was sparse, and Wildean epigrams of the sort that used to dazzle the Domino Room of the Café Royal could be counted on the fingers of one hand. Still, now and then the conversation became cultural, as when, one evening, the Canadian benedict began extolling Jacqueline Susann's *The Love Machine*.

"She's really gifted," the Canadian declared, his adenoids shining in admiration. "She has this marvelous grasp of feminine psychology—it's uncanny." He turned to me. "Now, you're a writer. Which one do you think is more talented—Jacqueline Susann or Harold Robbins?"

"Gosh, who can say?" I protested. "It's like trying to compare Balzac with Tolstoy. I mean, they're two colossi. And then there's Henry Sutton, who wrote *The Exhibitionist*—that makes three colossi. I wouldn't know which is the greatest."

"I believe she's the most successful," his wife stated. "How much does she make a year?"

"Twelve dollars," I said. I was ready to jump overboard.

"You can't be serious," she said incredulously.

"I am, my dear—I never joke about such things." I got up. "Excuse me," I said thickly. "I—it must be the chlorine in the drinking water. I need a breath of air."

But even as I said it I knew the futility of any hope of relief as the *Moribunda* inched its way across the Indian Ocean day after day under the remorseless sun. Time lost all meaning; everything was submerged in the unceasing pandemonium of rock and roll, the hum of roaches chewing the bedclothes, and the drone of the engines. Mealtime was a charade, a formal ritual in which we participated like actors eating make-believe food on the stage. Even the waiters joined in the dumbshow, exhibiting the viands and whisking them away in the same swift gesture. Intentionally or not, the *Moribunda* had evolved a consummate reducing diet—indeed, an almost hazardous one, for when I surveyed my face in the flyblown looking glass in my cabin I was reminded of the leaflet for J. Collis Browne's Compound, a specific greatly favored in England which I had brought with me. Describing the inroads of dysentery on British troops during the Boer War, it stated sonorously, "Gaunter and gaunter grew the soldiers of the Queen." "What lovely hollow cheeks you have, Mr. Gaunter," I told myself. "A few more days aboard this ship and they'll be using that head of yours for a tobacco jar."

Luckily, boundless as is the capacity of the human body for punishment, the Bay of Bengal does have limits. Two days after rounding the Andaman Islands, immortalized by Conan Doyle in *The Sign of Four*—a locale singularly apropos in the circumstances—we steamed into Penang, a stone's throw from Singapore, our destination. I leaned on the ship's rail, watching the harbor coolies unload our pungent cargo and wondering if they realized what we had gone through to deliver it. Could they possibly encompass the privations we had endured, the fiery holocausts and giant squids we had eluded? Perhaps I should go down and enlighten them—even take up a small collection in my behalf. It was a temptation, but I dismissed it. Once, many years before, I had set foot in this port and been trapped there for five weeks—an episode beside which the voyage of the *Moribunda* was peaches and cream. And so, as the effluvium rose over the green hills of Malaya, I said "Aloha" to Penang with a schmalz worthy of FitzPatrick, and buoyantly went back to the rock and roll.

VI—*For Sale or Rent: One Pair of Seven-league Boots*

Early one mid-April afternoon of that year, Ah Sim Gee, a sleek young Chinese businessman returning to Hong Kong, emerged from Kai Tak Airport briskly swinging his dispatch case and looked about for a bus to carry him into town. None was in sight, but his quick eye detected two travel-worn foreigners, a lady and a bespectacled gentleman with a russet mustache, boarding a nearby taxi, and while unable to descry the name on their luggage tags, he sensed that it might be E. Z. Pickens. He bounded toward the car, wrenched open the door, and settled himself beside the driver. "Excuse me for bursting in like this, good people," he apologized. "I could see that the weight was unevenly distributed in your cab, and I was afraid it might overturn in transit."

"Very chivalrous of you," commented the gentleman, whose craggy features unsurprisingly matched those in my passport. "In the circumstances, I suppose, one could hardly ask you to fork over your share of the ride."

"So I figured," said Ah Sim smoothly. "Now, friends, as to your hotel accommodations. The night clerk of the Highland Fling in Repulse Bay is my cousin, so I can promise you a truly palatial suite at half price."

"You *are* a Good Samaritan," I said. "Unhappily, the Golden Bamboozle, which is already reserved, would be desolate if we failed to appear."

"No problem," he assured me. "The concierge there is my uncle. Next, the matter of clothes. Where, you ask me, does Cary Grant get his suits at a fraction of what they would cost in Savile Row? Why, at the Wideawake Tailors in Des Vœux Road, my grandfather's renowned establishment. He also operates another emporium on Icehouse Street, featuring stereo systems, mutton jade, and the largest selection of cheap, machine-made gewgaws in the Orient. Here is my card, Mr. Pickens—the Setting Sun Import-Export Corporation of Macao. And if, by the way, you or the lady should require anything in the way of plastic dentures," he added, extracting a tongue depressor from his pocket, "I am equipped to take your measurements right now."

I bared my teeth to indicate how superfluous I found his offer, to say nothing of his society, and eventually, as the cab wove through the noisy, congested maze of Kowloon, our incubus persuaded himself to clam up. Once aboard the vehicular ferry to Hong Kong Island, he disappeared—not, however, without engaging Passepartoute, my companion, in an extended colloquy on the afterdeck. What its purport was I could not imagine, but the longer it lasted the more suspicious I became. After all, it was at this very stage of Phileas Fogg's journey that his nemesis, the detective Fix, had enticed the former's servant into an opium den, hoping to delay Fogg until a warrant arrived for his arrest. Was this plausible Chinese hatching a similar scheme, I asked myself uneasily. Sally-Lou and I were booked to sail to San Francisco two days hence on the *President Wilson,* and though I could envision no possible motive for him to prevent our departure, I frankly disliked the cut of his jib. As it turned out, my apprehensions were groundless; he was merely pressing her to visit his mother's noodle factory in Wanchai, which she quite properly refused to do. And small wonder, for, as everyone knew, the noodle factories of Wanchai were well-known recruitment centers for the white-slave traffic.

Incurable romantic that I am, I somehow expected to find Hong Kong as exotic as it had been when I first saw it in 1947, but the transformation a quarter of a century had wrought was staggering. Skyscrapers elbowed each other all the way up the Peak, masses of humanity surged through the narrow, traffic-choked streets, nowhere was there any escape from pestilential racket and confusion. From my tiny bedchamber atop the Golden Bamboozle, costing a prince's ransom, I looked down fifteen stories into an immense excavation advertised, a sign said, to hold the tallest building in Asia. I could believe it; the spoon in my coffee cup danced to the ceaseless thump of the pile drivers. Downstairs, in the lounge, the clangor was even more disheartening. Scores of tourists, festooned with cameras and shopping bags, milled about, gleefully displaying to each other the booty they had amassed—the electronic gadgets, batik shirts, sandalwood fans, carved-ivory tusks and balls and book-ends, all the sleazy gimcracks Chinese ingenuity could contrive to dazzle the foreign devil. Deafened by the hubbub, I wandered all forlorn through the Bamboozle's arcades, yearning for some human contact in this soulless discount center, and then, amazingly, my plea was answered. A face loomed out of the crowd, a hand wrung mine, and there stood my old and valued friend Jeffrey Proctor.

Since we persisted in interrupting each other, it required considerable time and whiskey to update our activities over the last dozen years, but neither of us begrudged it, and the bar of the Press Club was an ideal haven for the purpose. I had known Jeffrey in a number of phases—as a Broadway publicity man, a writer for television, and a journalistic jack-of-all-trades who nowadays, he disclosed, had achieved executive status in a worldwide record corporation. The particular link in our past, though, was the ravishing Candide Yam, Mike Todd's Chinese secretary, whom he had known and adored in the tempestuous period I spent with Todd, and hence my present exploit had a special relevance for him. He besought me to recount the stages of the journey thus far, and with what enthusiasm I could summon up I sketched in the highlights.

"Well, I must say you're a glutton for punishment," he commented. "Tell me something. Under that lighthearted exterior of yours, do I detect a note of disenchantment?"

"Ridiculous," I said. "Whatever makes you say that? The truth is, it's been the most stimulating—"

"Yes, yes," he broke in. "Never mind the bromides. This is your old friend Doctor Proctor—you can level with me. You're a bit fed up, aren't you?"

"I certainly don't know where you got that impression," I said haughtily. "Naturally, there've been difficulties—it's only normal in a trip of this magnitude—"

"Of course," he soothed me. "Look, I'm not criticizing you or anything. All I said was, I think you've had it. And God knows I'd feel the same way if I were in your shoes—especially during the next three weeks."

His shaft had struck the target with such accuracy that I was momentarily stunned, but I had to pretend innocence. "What—what do you mean?"

"Why, the Pacific crossing—from here to San Francisco. Didn't you see that mob in the lobby of the Bamboozle—those imperious blue-haired dames from Santa Barbara, those old pirates with the liver spots? They're going to be your shipmates for nineteen days, Charlie. Cocktail parties every night so the ladies can show off their formals . . . bingo galore . . . square dances and tango contests . . . loads of galas with paper hats and confetti. Oh, yes, and don't forget Honolulu—the leis and the tin ukuleles, all that yakka hoola hickey doola. Listen, old chap," he said, glancing at his watch, "I've got to run, but I just want to leave one thought with you. Phileas Fogg wouldn't have sailed on the *President Wilson* if he'd had any alternative."

By what clairvoyant process Proctor had so unerringly read my mind I shall never know, but in that moment the forebodings that had oppressed me dissipated and I breathed again. The man was dead right. The moment had come for one of Fogg's improvisations. Mentally, I stepped off the *President Wilson* and into the first available jet liner. I felt like a man reborn.

Nineteen hours afterward, Sally-Lou Claypool and I sat in the boarding area at Kai Tak Airport, our impedimenta piled about us, each of us waiting for our respective aircraft—hers westward to Britain, mine to Tokyo, Los Angeles, and New York. Unaccountably, none of the drama I feared my decision might evoke, the possible tears or recrimination, had manifested itself. My handmaiden had displayed an astonishing composure tinged, almost, with delight—a reaction that thoroughly baffled me until the reason emerged under close questioning. Quite unknown to me, it appeared, an incorporeal third party had been accompanying us along the route—Dan Cupid. The discus thrower at Cal Tech with whom she had confessed an earlier infatuation at the time I hired her had re-entered her life. Currently living in London, he had been wooing her assiduously throughout our journey—indeed, had proposed by cable in Singapore, importuning her to curtail the trip and join him at the altar. Needless to say, I was overjoyed that my change of plan should be hastening Sally-Lou's future happiness, and I sensed, as she picked up her things and prepared to go through the gates, that she was struggling to express her gratitude. "Well, this is it, I guess," she said awkwardly. "It could have been worse, but I don't see how."

"It could have been longer," I said. "Still, half a loaf is better than none, isn't it? I'll always remember you, Passepartoute."

"And I'll never forget you, no matter how hard I try," she promised, and was gone. A lovely yet curious person, I reflected, gazing after her. How odd that we had traveled so many miles, shared so many perils, and parted with so little emotion. Still, there was one peril I had avoided, I thought with a sigh of relief. If Cupid had loosed his arrow at me instead of the discus thrower, things might have been very different. With my genius for seeking out trouble, the two of us might have wound up on the Mississippi Gulf Coast, battered by hurricanes and subsisting on a diet of catfish, fatback, and greens.

Tokyo to Los Angeles, Los Angeles to New York—a blur of images superimposed on each other, movie dissolves that left no residue except an immense thankfulness for the wings annihilating the distance between them. What did it matter that the food in the plastic tray before me was as bland as the captain's smile, the attentions of the stewardess as mechanical as the Muzak?

By the time I arrived in New York, though, I realized that some lingering sense of noblesse oblige still gnawed at me: I owed Jules Verne's hero the final sentimental gesture of completing the pattern as he had, by sea, and, in a quixotic, last-minute decision, I traded in my plane ticket for a cabin aboard that majestic ocean greyhound the *Queen Elizabeth II*. It was a singular but in the end worthwhile experience, for it convinced me as nothing else ever could have of the existence of magic. Somehow, all the blue-haired ladies from Santa Barbara, all the elderly pirates with liver spots I had eluded on the *President Wilson* had mysteriously hurtled across the world to enliven the passage. They held cocktail parties morning, noon, and night, danced the tango in paper hats, and generated such jollification that the crossing became one endless gala. Not a cashmere sweater or a sliver of Waterford glass remained after they had finished stripping the ship's boutiques; it was bargain time on our floating supermarket, and their cheeks flamed with fever as they shopped. And when the mighty vessel drew into her berth at Southampton, terminating the longest five-day voyage in memory, I felt that I had paid my debt to Phileas Fogg.

On a Saturday evening in May a fortnight later, I stopped by the Reform Club to pick up my accumulation of mail. It was my first visit there since returning to England, and the club was deserted, everyone who could having fled to the country to enjoy the fine spring weekend. I was about to depart, leaving the great silent edifice to its sole tenant, an elderly member dozing in the library, when I heard voices issuing from the cardroom. I looked in and beheld a quartet of players clustered about a bridge table.

"Oh, excuse me," I apologized. "I hadn't meant to interrupt your game."

"Nonsense," one of their number called out. "We've finished —come and join us, won't you? We're just having a nightcap and a bit of a discussion."

"Yes, do," said another, pulling out a chair for me. "It's about that American member of ours who set off around the world a while ago."

I froze on the threshold. "Why, what about him?"

"Nothing, really," he said. "We were just wondering whatever became of the chap. Do you have a theory, by any chance?"

"I've got more than that, gentlemen," I said, reaching for the doorknob. "I've got the answer. He was lost, completely and utterly, from the moment he conceived the idea, but somewhere along the way, thank God, he managed to find himself. Thank you for your hospitality, friends, and good night."

I came down the club's magnificent staircase and paused before the grandfather clock in the foyer. It read a quarter to nine—precisely eighty days, by a coincidence, since I had last looked at it prior to my leavetaking. Surely there was a moral here, a conclusion to be drawn if one had the wisdom. Well, I had the wisdom, all right—the very few grains I'd acquired in those eighty days—but I was saving it up in case ever again, Heaven forfend, I felt the tiniest compulsion to travel. I made a deep obeisance to the clock, collected my hat, and went forth into Pall Mall.

Pipe All Hands—Chimeras
Dead Ahead!

Where did one learn for the first time that Indian rajas often gave dinner parties on the Riviera at which liqueurs were distributed to the guests in solid-gold toy trains speeding over silver tracks? That Anna Held's damask complexion resulted from bathing daily in forty quarts of asses' milk? That the eye of the common fly, if magnified to the size of a soup plate, resembled the telescope atop Mount Wilson Observatory? Well, the answer to these rhetorical questions is yet another—where else but in Hearst's *American Weekly,* whose pages, teeming with the latest society scandals and oddities of science, exercised a profound educational influence on my generation? Yes, and it was in those very pages, moreover, that I was spellbound by Professor Hugo Münsterberg and his fantastic experiment at the Harvard Law School.

Hugo Münsterberg was a psychologist internationally celebrated except on Elmwood Avenue, in Providence, where I read about him at the age of twelve. In the course of lecturing a class of future lawyers on the unreliability of eyewitness evidence, he prepared a demonstration. A young man would rush in, he explained, quaking in terror as a pursuer hard on his heels pointed an object at him. There would be a brief dialogue between them, followed by action. The lights would then be extinguished for a moment and then turned on again, and the class would be asked to write down what had ensued. The events described thereupon took place. The first youth, as he ran, agonizedly called out, "Don't shoot!" The other, who was extending a banana, shouted, "You betrayed my sister! Boom!" Down went the presumptive seducer, the room blacked out, and the spectators fell to work recording their impressions.

The results were noteworthy. Eleven in the class stated that the avenger had borne a revolver, five that he was brandishing a dagger or dirk, and three that the weapon was a serrated bread knife. Four were unable to describe the weapon, though one recalled seeing a flash of yellow. The witnesses' accounts of the verbal exchange were equally confused. Some had distinctly heard the phrase "You brute!," others "You're afraid of my sister!," still others merely a string of profanity. Not one of the twenty-three, the Professor summarized, accurately reported what had occurred, despite having been briefed beforehand, so it was patent how little credence should be given such evidence in a courtroom.

The foregoing nugget of jurisprudence would have vanished irretrievably into limbo were it not for an article I came across a while ago in a regional publication called *On the Sound.* The writer, one Rudolph Chelminski, had set himself the formidable task of describing *La Belle Simone,* a ten-million-dollar yacht owned by William Levitt, the building tycoon. Apart from such luxuries as a marble spiral staircase, a shower with gold spigots, a leather-paneled elevator, a master stateroom with mirrored ceiling and a bulkhead cunningly devised to swing open at the touch of a button, the vessel, in its owner's words, was more or less a replica of his home on Long Island: "For instance, you know how in hotels there's the third tap for ice water? Well, we put that in here. What I did was to use my house-building experience." All in all, it justified his quietly prideful confidence to Chelminski: "I like to call it my Taj Mahal." Granted that Mumtaz Mahal's tomb contains no third tap for ice water and Levitt in his photographs appears less soulful than Shah Jahan, but otherwise the sentiment is dashing and incontestable.

The specific paragraph that waylaid me, though, dealt with the scene confronting the writer when he boarded the craft. It ran: "The gangway has a pleasing springboard effect to the tread. As we make the first yard a white-jacketed figure with black hair tied up in a coquettish ponytail bars passage to the poop deck. This is Dr. Greenberg, the ship's physician, who is identifiable by the badge on his chest. 'Dr. Greenberg,' it says. Dr. Greenberg is a young interne in surgery spending the season aboard for a lark. His ponytail attests to progressive ideas, but he still orders visitors to remove their shoes (parquet decks) and follows one pace behind to make sure they do not lift any ashtrays."

The instant I read that, I pricked up my ears—there was something radically wrong here. Why should Levitt, a chap affluent enough to spend millions on a vessel, engage a mere interne as ship's doctor? After all, the well-being of the two persons he loved most—his wife, Simone, and himself—was at stake, and either might be felled by a spar or snuffed out in a twinkling by *Salmonella enteritidis*. No, it was unthinkable that people chronicled as buying their wine from Alexis Lichine and their frillies from Irene Galitzine would scrimp on their medico. But hold on, the thought struck me abruptly—perhaps Chelminski had been deceived. Perhaps, overcome by excitement at beholding so fabulous a craft, he had fallen into the precise psychological state of those Harvard students of yesteryear and was reporting what he *thought* he saw rather than the actuality.

It was a fascinating speculation, and, filling my pipe with shag from a rug at hand, I tried to reconstruct the true course of events. The element that promised to be most fruitful, I decided, was Dr. Greenberg's onus to prevent ashtrays from being stolen. Surely so inconsiderable a theft would never perturb anyone, unless—and here an intriguing hypothesis began to take shape—it chanced to be immensely valuable, a collector's dream. Suppose, then, for the sake of argument, that of a sunny spring morning in London Levitt has issued from Claridge's (where he doubtless stays) and is being driven officeward in his Rolls. Infused with energy by the fine weather, he alights near Shepherd's Market and orders the chauffeur to follow in the car. (The rich often do this, as is well known.) Suddenly, through the dusty window of a small antique shop, he espies a priceless ashtray of mutton-fat jade among the Toby jugs, Staffordshireware poodles, and other bric-a-brac. Entering, he asks an old man in a yarmulke behind the counter where he acquired it.

"This?" The merchant fingers his cap. "Why, in a yarmulke store. Where else?"

"No, no—the ashtray," comes the impatient reply.

"Oh, that I bought from a lascar newly arrived on a ship laden with rich silken stuffs, with ivory, apes, and peacocks from fabled Samarkand and Ind."

"Hmm," Levitt comments skeptically. "Was he swarthy? All lascars have to be swarthy."

Assured that the seller's swarth was beyond cavil, Levitt purchases the ashtray and leaves—only to be held up at knife point by the chauffeur, who is not a chauffeur at all but the accomplice of the lascar, the real chauffeur being trussed up as neatly as a fowl back at Claridge's. Thanks to a vigilant police constable, however, the miscreant is collared and removed to the bridewell, there to receive his just deserts. Levitt, shrewdly foreseeing that his treasure will be a target for light-fingered guests aboard his yacht, hires a robust butcher from Smithfield Market to guard it; and it is he whom, clad in white coat and apron, Chelminski erroneously took for a surgical interne.

At this point, a lesser investigator might have succumbed to self-congratulation on his astuteness. Fortunately, I am not prone to hubris, and, heeding the Malay proverb *"Banyak djalan"*—which is to say, there are many roads or solutions to an enigma—I re-examined Chelminski's words for another rationale to Greenberg's identity. Straightaway, I was rewarded with another theory. It lurked behind the phrase "he still orders visitors to remove their shoes (parquet decks)." Implicit therein is the assumption that the mere touch of a visitor's shoe might profane *La Belle Simone*'s decks. Very well—what religion makes the removal of shoes mandatory on entry to hallowed places? Why, Buddhism, to be sure, and instantly the whole thing becomes crystal clear. Unknown to his business associates and even his intimates, Levitt has embraced that faith, and what more natural than that he should hire a zealot—in this case, a Burmese dacoit—to watch over his salt-water home? It all fits in—the crisp white jacket, the black hair exotically coiffed. . . . Had Chelminski bothered to glance down, he could not have failed to notice the *longyi*, the characteristic sarong worn by all Burmans, but he was too dazzled by his surroundings. Just because the badge pinned to the fellow's chest said "Dr. Greenberg," the poor innocent swallowed the bait and took him for Greenberg. Still, knowing what we do about Burmese dacoity, it was lucky for him that he didn't press the matter, else he would have had his weasand slit from ear to ear.

In my triumph at having evolved two cogent interpretations of the scene at the gangway, I fell into an error committed by even the most skilled of logicians: I assumed that a third was impossible. It was not until I had painstakingly reread the entire paragraph word by word that I detected the reason. In spite of the repeated use of the masculine pronoun to describe the interne, his ponytail was pointedly characterized as "coquettish." Was this a slip of the pen, or—far more significant—a clue to the real sex of the *soi-disant* "Dr. Greenberg"? But of *course*, I exploded as the truth dawned on me. The white-coated guardian of *La Belle Simone* wasn't a male at all—she was Consuelo Münsterberg, by an incredible coincidence a great-granddaughter of the renowned psychologist himself! A junior at Vassar, she and Peaches Yaroslav, the two brightest students in their class, have been neck-and-neck rivals for the post of editor of the influential *Vassar Economic Review,* the palm to be awarded to the author of its most stimulating editorial. Consuelo has chosen for her subject "Henry George and the Single Tax," and who better qualified than Levitt to be interviewed on this abstruse subject? Bewitchingly garbed in a laboratory coat inherited from her famed ancestor, the intrepid creature had smuggled herself aboard the yacht and lurked on the poop, primed to charm her unsuspecting quarry. Small wonder, then, that Chelminski, already mommixed by the floating palace he had set foot on, should fall prey to Consuelo's dimples and misinterpret what he saw. Who are we to criticize him? A man would have to be made of stone.

The first mauve flush of daylight had streaked the eastern sky over Sarasota as I concluded my reflections, and, watching Old Sol gild the distant roofs on Siesta Key, I experienced a thrill of pride that I had brought these two young people together. Would Consuelo and Chelminski find happiness with each other? Would Levitt, mayhap touched to the core by their devotion, in a supreme act of self-abnegation relinquish his yacht to them—marble staircase, gold spigots, the whole caboodle? A suspicious drop of moisture very akin to a tear splashed on my wrist, sentimental idiot that I am, and obedient to another old maxim, "Sufficient unto the day are the rhetorical questions thereof," I stole away to my bed.

Mad About the Girl

When a man of threescore and five suddenly announces to family and friends that he's fallen in love, his auditors react either in outrage or with shocked incredulity. If he persists in his folly, as he usually does, their procedure is standard: they summon a lawyer who calls in two shrinks, they sign a writ, and away he goes in a butterfly net. There are cases, however, and mine is one, that are much more complex. At an age when most of my contemporaries are wheezing over a Crokinole board or pitching horseshoes down at St. Petersburg, I seem to be hung up on a baby gorilla in Switzerland. Her name is Quarta, she's fifteen months old, and she's so sweet you could eat her with a spoon.

In a way, this crush of mine was inevitable; I've been hooked on genus *Gorilla gorilla,* both coastal and mountain, for half a century—ever since 1915, in fact, when I first read Paul du Chaillu's dithyrambs on the great apes. Apart from Gargantua and M'Toto, his mate, who were essentially sideshow exhibits, the earliest gorilla I developed a fixation for was Bamboo, the magnificent male at the Philadelphia Zoo in the mid-1930's. Bamboo, whose adult weight was 450 pounds, stood seventy inches in his stockinged feet, and when he beat his chest, the thunder was audible miles distant in the badlands of Bucks County where I dwelt. How hypnotic his effect on me was I didn't realize until I overheard a furtive phone call of my wife's late one night. "Please listen, Doctor," she was pleading. "He's walking around in a crouch, resting on the second joint of his fingers. . . . No, no, not the knuckles—he's always done that. I'm frightened—I don't know what it means."

I knew, though; I was identifying with Bamboo, so closely indeed that I began haunting his cage and smuggling in sacks of fruit that set his keepers whispering of a possible liaison between us. Eventually I made a clean break—I took a furnished room near the Zoo so I could be close to him. Wives don't understand that sort of thing, and mine, like Mrs. Strickland in *The Moon and Sixpence,* drew the banal conclusion that I was entangled with a woman. She sent an intermediary (oddly enough, Herbert Marshall, the same one who played the role in the movie) to remonstrate with me. The message I sent back was unequivocal. I had no artistic aspirations like Gauguin or designs on any hominid, I assured her. I was merely infatuated with an anthropoid ape and I proposed to spend the rest of my life pitching woo at him.

Well, I got over my *Schwärmerei* in time, but the major attack came three decades later. In the fall of 1968, intrigued by rumors in the French press of a zoological phenomenon in Switzerland, I journeyed to Basel to see it. According to the grapevine, Achilla, a lowland gorilla from the Cameroons, had borne and reared three infants in captivity—a feat still unequaled at any zoo—and was, moreover, so tractable and well-adjusted that she permitted humans to feed and fondle her young. The report was understated, if anything. She had recently produced a fourth baby—aptly named Quarta—and as she sat in the cage cuddling it, the benign maternal expression on her face beggared all the religious art in the Uffizi and the Pitti Palace. But this was no static tableau confronting me through the bars. Just as I stood there with my faculties, so to speak, rooted to the floor, a zoo attendant materialized bearing a dish of gruel and seated himself knee to knee with Achilla. She handed him her baby, sniffed the gruel, and began sipping it reflectively. Quarta, having meanwhile wolfed a tidbit or two proffered by the keeper, fell to nuzzling his cheek. When, however, he arose with a pretense of abducting the child, there ensued an instant of suspense such as Hitchcock never dreamed of. Achilla slowly lowered her head and measured the distance between them, her enormous biceps tensed for the spring. A bead of icy perspiration rolled down my forehead, almost obscuring it. With a reassuring pat, the attendant restored Quarta to her mother and departed. A sob of relief escaped my lips. At the sound, Quarta turned and gave me a look, in Ring Lardner's matchless phrase, that you could pour on a waffle. From that moment I was hers, body and soul.

Owing to beastly luck with the cards, I was unable until recently, a year later, to revisit my nymphet, now installed in a new habitat that was clearly a model of primate care, and she was transformed. No longer a puny starveling barely able to creep, she had grown into a fur-clad dynamo forever in movement, somersaulting and careering around in sheer exuberance, scaling platforms that appeared inaccessible, unraveling the burlap bags strewn around her cage, and altogether ravishing every heart. As for her parent, though Achilla had lost none of her immense dignity, I perceived in her a patience, a resignation worthy of Job; she allowed the tot to tweak her pompadour and bite her feet, play the vibes on her spine, and generally bedevil her in a manner no human mother would have tolerated.

"Corpo di Bacco!" I suddenly heard an impatient female voice in my ear. "If I were she, I'd give that youngster a good poke in the snoot. She's a nuisance, eh, *caro?"*

I wheeled and beheld a shapely lady resembling Sophia Loren, who, except for the topless frock she wore, was clad in the height of fashion. Jewelry, bag, and all her accessories were chic beyond words and one might have been tempted to accept the gambit, but frankly, I was too absorbed in the gorillas to bother. Through the door of the cage adjacent to theirs, a formidable figure was advancing stiff-legged—Stephy, the 23-year-old mate of Achilla who had sired all her progeny. Up to the present, he had been denied access to her area for fear that jealousy of the baby might provoke a conflict. The very reverse seemed to be the case. He circled his kinswomen warily, almost fearfully, and made a minute, ponderous study of some peanut hulls and banana skins they had rejected. Then, with a bone-cracking yawn that revealed a mouthful of the most chilling dentistry since Cesar Romero's, he curled up and went to sleep.

That continuity is the chief ingredient in every successful courtship is a maxim I long ago learned from authorities like Casanova, Lou Tellegen, and Count Boni de Castellane. The better to ingratiate myself with Quarta and her duenna, therefore, I sent them a fancy steamer basket of stem ginger, glacé fruits, and bonbons from Basel's leading greengrocer, and posted myself before their enclosure to watch the result. To my chagrin, they betrayed not the slightest notice of their benefactor; I might have been any stagedoor John honeyfogling some fly chorus girl with a nosegay of wilted flowers. The pair ate all the delicacies as well as the basket and proceeded to pelt Stephy with left-over cashews. The poor, henpecked paterfamilias, shielding his face in a corner, only once gave vent to his feelings. Driven beyond endurance by the exasperation W. C. Fields felt for Baby LeRoy, he waited till Achilla's back was turned and dealt his offspring a lightning smack on the *tochus*. Instantly, all hell broke loose; Achilla swung the child under her belly for safety and baring her fangs, leaped at his throat. Stephy, his whole four hundred pounds quaking in terror, scuttled into his den to cower there the rest of the afternoon. Every so often, whimpering pitiably, he licked a small laceration in his thumb.

After ogling my affinity for three days without a flicker of encouragement, I finally adopted the one expedient left to me—the tactic Myles Standish used in his plight. I sought out Dr. Ernst Lang, the curator of the zoo and world-renowned for his knowledge of the behavior and breeding of the great apes. "Look here, Lang," I said bluntly. "I'm a plain man and I've a mind to speak plainly. I've lived hard and I've played hard, and I've taken my fun where I found it. But I've made my pile and the time has come to settle down."

"Dégagez la farine du maïs de votre bouche" (Take the mush out of your mouth), he said. "What are you driving at?"

"Well," I said. "I realize I'm a lot older than Quarta, but I feel that the two of us would make a wonderful life together in those Pennsylvania boondocks, if you could see your way clear." I put up my hand hastily. "Oh, I can tell what you're thinking, sir, that it's just another Peaches and Daddy Browning romance, but it's not, I promise you. I worship the ground she waddles on, I honestly do—she's straight, and clean, and fine. I know she doesn't love me right now, but she will in time, as sure as my name is Paul Getty."

"There, there, man, no need for tears," said Dr. Lang kindly. "I'll be glad to intercede, but it's really up to someone else. You'll have to speak to her father."

"How's that?" I asked, recoiling. "What do you mean?"

"Why, just go into his cage and pop the question," he said, taking my arm. "I'll be glad to let you in, and to carry you out when you've finished. We often perform this service for old dotards with your symptoms."

I shook him off. "I—er—maybe I ought to talk it over with my wife," I stammered, and edged toward the exit. "I mean, seeing I'm right here in Switzerland where you have so many shrinkers, it would save time, if you follow me."

"I don't intend to," said Dr. Lang. "Just close that glass door when you leave, if you please. We've got to watch out for drafts with these primates."

And there the whole thing might have ended, pure Graham Greene—a solitary, apeless figure in a waterproof drearily trudging toward the railway station in the autumn rain—had it not been for an incredible twist of fate. For who should I encounter there outside the zoo but the Italian signorina with the lovely accessories, just returning to find her umbrella. Do you know, we looked all over Basel, in every blessed bar and *Nachtlokal,* and never found it? But that, as Kipling often said, is another story.

Razzle-dazzle in
the Rib Room

If we didn't believe there were enough people to appreciate the difference then we wouldn't have covered the walls of our El Padrino Room with suede. . . . But we think there are certain people, lots of them perhaps, who appreciate the subtle touches—the special amenities —so we have just built a very special addition to our hotel to accommodate those certain people. . . . Our double rooms have 1½ bathrooms. The water closets are enclosed. And if the phone rings while you're in the bathroom, you can answer it right there. We'll even shine your shoes. Merely leave them outside your door in the hall before you retire. And where the Beverly Wilshire's subtle amenities leave off—we offer everything else you have naturally come to expect from a fine hotel. . . . A ballroom with a 1,000 capacity, nine separate meeting and party rooms. And, of course, suede on our El Padrino Room walls.—*Adv. in The New Yorker.*

I'd been down in Palos Verdes that whole morning, trying to locate a missing widower whose children were afraid he was blowing his bankroll on a lady evangelist with green eyes, and it was three o'clock before I got back to Beverly Hills. I didn't mind, though; by then the luncheon crowd at Bienstock's deli had evaporated—all the TV producers and agents and other highbinders that infest the joint—and I was sitting in a booth, geared for a nice, cozy sandwich behind my newspaper. The place was nearly empty—just a couple of skinny blondes buzzing in a corner, and a fat man with his head in his hands staring into a coffee cup. So there I was, eyes pinned on an interview with the surfing champion of Redondo Beach and my choppers locked into the Irving Lazar Special—sturgeon, pastrami, whitefish, Fiddler's Creek turkey, corned beef, pastrami, whitefish, chopped liver, and coleslaw—when a voice sounded in my ear. The fat guy was bending over me.

"Excuse me butting in," he apologized. "You wouldn't be Manny Tremayne, the private investigator, would you?"

"Not if given my choice," I said. "I'd much rather be Lieutenant General, His Exalted Highness Asaf Jah, Muzzaffar-ul-Mulk-Wal-Mumilak, Nizam-ul-Mulk, Nizam ud Daula Nawab, Mir Sir Osman Ali Khan Bahadur, Fatem Jung, Sipha Salar, G.C.S.I., G.B.E., Nizam of Hyderabad and Berar."

"I—I don't get you," he said, blinking.

"One of the richest men in the world," I said. "Still, if I were, I wouldn't be sitting here eating the Irving Lazar Special, because he cooled six years ago. So I guess I'm better off being Manny Tremayne. What's bugging you, my friend?"

His eyes suddenly grew shifty. "Who said anything was?"

"Look, chubby," I said. "You've got a problem of some sort or you wouldn't be draped over me like a Virginia creeper. Go ahead—spill it."

"Here—in a delicatessen?" he asked. "I thought everyone in your line had a crummy little office with a desk containing a bottle of booze and a beautiful, hardboiled secretary."

"I haven't found a desk big enough to accommodate both," I said. "So until I do I'm operating out of my hat." I extended a glassful of toothpicks. "Help yourself and tell me your troubles."

"Well, it's like this," he began. "I'm Sam Forthright, owner-manager of the Beverly Moonshine over there on Wilshire. We've been making a lot of changes lately."

"Yes, I noticed you blocked up your front entrance a while ago."

"We put it in the back," he explained. "You see, we cater to a type person who appreciates subtle little luxuries like that, the finer things of life which your hoi polloi don't. For instance, we installed toweled walls in the bathrooms so a guest can dry himself by rubbing against them. That way they don't have to fumble around with soap in their eye."

"What do you do, redecorate each time a new arrival checks in?"

He nodded. "It runs into money, but our clientele are connoisseurs that we strive to baby their whim. We give them conveniences they don't even have at home—disposable shoehorns, free jars of cocoa butter in case someone needs it."

"Who needs cocoa butter?" I asked.

"Search me," he said. "I never tried it myself, but the survey we made showed that people like to have it around. Anyhow, that's beside the point. The reason I spoke to you is, some kind of psycho—we can't find out who or why—is carving up the walls of our new rotisserie lounge, the El Ribino Room. Is it vandalism? Is it spite? Maybe some competitor—"

"Whoa there, Forthright," I stopped him. "Easy does it. Suppose you go back to the beginning."

It took the whole jar of toothpicks and all my patience to worm the story out of him, but I finally got the highlights. In remodeling the Beverly Moonshine, Forthright had incorporated a pet notion of his, a facility where patrons could watch spareribs barbecued to soft music and consume them in tasteful surroundings. The walls of this El Ribino Room, as he conceived it, were to be upholstered in dark-brown toweling that diners could wipe their hands on and that would in time exude a rich, meaty aroma to tempt even the most jaded palate. His decorators, however, had vetoed the fabric and persuaded him to use suede, which, according to tests they quoted, absorbed the pungency of meat cooking and had a patina no towel could equal.

"So they put in the suede," Forthright continued. "It cost me a bundle, but people liked the feel of it, and it was a nice conversation piece. Well, around two weeks ago, parts of it began disappearing. First a little square, next a whole foot, then a big triangle. All these shapes were cut out with a scissors, maybe a razor blade, and it happened during the night, after business hours. We tried gluing in patches for a while, but the color didn't match and I had to reupholster a whole section. No damage for three days; then it all started again. Yesterday we found a piece snipped out in the form of an arrow, and today a string of dots and dashes." His voice rose. "Never mind the expense of the thing—it's the aggravation I can't stand. Somebody's got it in for me! They're trying to drive me crazy!"

"Now, now, calm down," I said soothingly. "Have you reported this to the police?" He mumbled something about adverse publicity. "How about your employees? Anyone who might possibly bear you a grudge?"

"Nobody—I'm like a father to them. They worship the ground I walk on. I can't bear to fire anybody—I always do it through a subordinate. And if I have to fire a subordinate I can't do that, either. I call in another subordinate."

"Well," I ruminated, "I could be wrong, but chances are this isn't an inside job."

"Then what is it?"

"An outside job. You follow?"

"Yeah, now that you explain it," he said. "I guess there are tricks in every trade, eh?"

"Not too many in mine," I said. "Most of my best cases were the result of patient, plodding investigation. O.K., Forthright, I'll look into it. Reserve a table for me in the El Ribino Room at ten tonight."

The bar off the Moonshine's rotisserie was packed to overflowing when I got there, but I found myself a niche where I could rest a glass and study the action. Except for a few young swingers, it was a middle-aged crowd—well-heeled, suburban, and mainly out-of-towners. Five in a group near me, Southerners from their accent, were exclaiming over the hotel's amenities.

"You know the door of the medicine cabinet?" one man was saying. "Well, ours has a mirror set into it. I thought I'd seen everything, but this is a brand-new wrinkle."

"We've got a phone in the corridor right outside our room," the woman next to him boasted. "If a call comes in, you don't have to run down to the lobby in your nightdress. You just pick up right there."

"The shoes are the part I can't get over," said another man. "I put them in the hall last night before retiring."

"And they were shined this morning, were they?" someone asked.

"No," he admitted. "I took them in again—I was too nervous."

When the guy with the medicine cabinet began repeating his spiel, I finished my drink and drifted into the El Ribino Room. A couple of hundred diners were jammed into tables surrounding a stainless-steel barbecue pit, where three chefs were dishing out the ribs, and, what with the candlelight, the smoke, and the chocolate-colored walls, the patches in the suede weren't too noticeable. I could understand, though, why Forthright's morale was shot; who wouldn't be spooked at the thought that someone was waging a vendetta against him? I'd almost finished the meal when a suspicion so vague that I couldn't define it began nagging at me. I glanced around at the table behind mine, the one in front—and suddenly it jelled. At least one person at each table had some article made of suede—a jacket, a handbag, gloves. A very odd coincidence—or was it more than a coincidence? I decided to find out. The waiter, a heavy-set bird with a Chester Conklin mustache, came shuffling over at my signal. I extracted a five-dollar bill, tore it in two, and handed him half.

"Lots of suede around here, Max," I said casually. "If a person needed some fast suede—never mind why—who would he have to see?"

His eyes buttoned on to the remainder of the fin in my hand. "Depends," he said, licking his lips. I flattened my palm and he swished his napkin across it, enveloping the gray-green morsel. "He might have to contact Mr. Big in the Yellow Pages."

He didn't need to tell me any more; I knew what he meant. I got up, left a sawbuck to cover my check, and blew. The phone book in the lobby listed three firms that specialized in cleaning and repairing suede. Just as I was going to ring them, though, some instinct warned me to call Information instead. My hunch paid off: none of the three stayed open evenings. I went home, showered and shaved, brewed myself a pot of coffee, and set out Tartakower's version of the Ruy Lopez gambit. By the time I played it through, Sam Forthright's problem wasn't any clearer, but I knew what I had to do.

At eleven-thirty the next morning, I pushed open the door of a fancy little boutique on Rodeo Drive called Portulaca Leathercrafts. A robust, white-haired party rotating an unlit cigar in his teeth was bent over the counter adding up a pile of sales slips. He didn't look up as I entered, but both the pencil and the cigar stopped moving.

"A waiter at the El Ribino Room in the Moonshine," I said softly. "Kind of a heavyset bird with a Chester Conklin mustache. He thought you might fix me up with some suede elbow patches for this coat I'm wearing."

"He gave you a bum steer, sonny," he whispered. "He meant one of those cut-rate joints on La Cienega—Joey Lustgartner's, or the Hide & Hair."

"I've been there," I said. "They dummied up on me." I scratched my chin with the ten-case note folded between my fingers, let it float down gently onto the counter. His pencil shot out, speared it, and tucked it under the slips.

"It's an outside chance, but it could cost you," he said dreamily, his eyes still fixed on the papers. "The stuff you want is scarcer than a hound's tooth. Sixty clams is a lot of loot for two little patches."

"Not if you're as fond of the garment as I am." I stripped off the jacket, tossed it on the counter. "When do I collect it?"

"Two, three days—less if I get lucky. Phone me late to-morrow."

"You won't get any luckier than Manny Tremayne," I told myself as I shut the door behind me. It was the second time in twenty-four hours a hunch of mine had paid off, and, if my guess was right, a certain hotelkeeper I knew was due for a dandy little surprise by the weekend.

I spooned in the last few drops of Royal Hawaiian chicken hazelnut pudding with seltzer sauce, leaned back, and regarded Sam Forthright across the table from me in Bienstock's deli. He was haggard with anxiety, quaking to hear the report I'd promised him on the phone, and I hesitated, unsure how he'd take it.

"Listen, Tremayne." His jowls were loose, but he spoke tightly. "Don't play games with a human being—I'm desperate. If I told you what we found in the El Ribino Room this morning—"

"You don't have to," I said. "Two oval holes in the suede, each about six inches long." His face fell apart. "How did I know that, you ask? You'll dig in a minute or two, but first I want to tell you a story. Once upon a time, there was a hotelman in Beverly Hills called Sam Forthright, who had a silent partner named Maury Fabricant. And this silent partner had a wife—a beautiful, passionate, headstrong woman named Ginger."

A dark red flush overspread his forehead. "There's nothing between me and Ginger Fabricant!"

"Nobody said there was," I quieted him. "Stay with me a second. Now, let's suppose that this couple worked out a scheme—a fiendishly simple yet foolproof scheme—for muscling Forthright out of the hotel. Posing as one of his decorators, Ginger Fabricant phoned and influenced him into using suede rather than toweling on the walls of his rotisserie."

"I—I thought there was something familiar about that voice," he broke in. "But who would suspect Maury—Maury, who I trusted like my own brother—"

"Wait. I'm not finished," I said. "Having tricked him into investing in the suede, the couple now systematically set out to ruin it, hoping to induce a nervous breakdown in Forthright, which would cause him to relinquish his share of the partnership. They made one fatal error, though—they were too greedy.

They fenced the parts they cut out, and who do you think was the fence?" I shoved a typewritten sheet at him. "This is a photocopy of the lease on the Portulaca Leathercrafts boutique, at 226 Rodeo. Recognize the signature?"

" 'Ginger Fabricant,' " he murmured. "My God. That cinches it, all right."

"No, merely confirms it," I said, and stood up. "Here's the real proof. Do you notice anything odd about this jacket?"

He studied me intently. "The seams, I think. It—it looks like you're wearing it inside out."

"Right. And when I reverse the sleeves, as I'm doing now, what you see are two elbow patches that exactly match the holes in the El Ribino suede. There's a chemical analysis of their meat content in the breast pocket, Forthright. That ought to give you all the evidence you need."

For an hour after he had left, I sat there pondering the strange quirks of fate that shape one's life. What if I hadn't gone into Bienstock's deli that particular day and ordered the Irving Lazar Special? Or what if there had been no Bienstock's to begin with and hence no Irving Lazar Special? The more I thought about it, the more I realized that if there had been no Irving Lazar it would have been necessary to invent one to name the special after, and thus help me to solve a complex and haunting puzzle. And that, for a shamus with a few untarnished ideals in this dirty little world, was some consolation.

Ready, Aim, Flee!

To the best of my recollection, which is porous, I think I originally met the firebrand Mark Silver in connection with a yeasty publication named *Mickey Finn,* which a handful of idealists projected back in 1927 in the Village. In those days, it was almost impossible for people wielding brush or pen to forgather down there without founding a magazine, and this one was evolved by a group of us who customarily ate in a restaurant opposite the Jefferson Market Courthouse. By and large, we were an unprosperous lot, barely managing to scrape along on contributions to *Life, Judge,* and *College Humor,* and the prospect of having our own forum—an American version of *Simplicissimus,* as we conceived it, where we could discharge our bile at the Establishment—excited us. The immediate task, we agreed, was to enlist a few more kindred spirits in the enterprise, and we busily set about inviting whatever talent we could recruit to a meeting at which the style and purpose of *Mickey Finn* would be clarified.

Of the dozen folk who showed up at the meeting, at least half were unashamedly, aggressively political—writers and artists whose work appeared in *The New Masses,* the *Daily Worker,* and the *Freiheit*—and they formed a very cohesive body. While the rest of us were bombinating away, proclaiming that the journal would tilt at social pretense, greed, and hypocrisy, they listened woodenly, now and again exchanging contemptuous smiles. Then one of their number, a shockheaded, pugnacious character who introduced himself as Mark Silver, the *Daily Worker* columnist, spoke up. The evils we deplored were piffling; our real target, he announced, would have to be the capitalist system. Into the hush that followed there intruded the sound of hackles rising. So the Brillo boys figured to turn our sheet into a propaganda organ, did they? The battle lines were drawn, and we smote them hip and thigh. The dispute became really acrimonious when the choice of an editor was broached.

"Who needs an editor?" Silver asked derisively. "Pin the cartoons and articles on the wall and let the majority decide which ones to print. That's the democratic way."

The hubbub this evoked had hardly subsided when a nattily dressed stranger arrived at the meeting. An advertising executive who had offered to promote backing for the venture, he was en route to the opera and was wearing a dinner jacket. The effect of his garb on the radical splinter group was volcanic. Its members rose to their feet outraged, surveyed him disgustedly, and stalked out. The advertising man, obviously appraising us as a bunch of losers, shrugged and followed suit. That sealed the fate of *Mickey Finn*.

Over the next couple of years, I saw occasional mention of Mark Silver in the press—once concerning an agitprop play he had written that had a brief run, and again as author of a novel dealing with the plight of immigrants on the lower East Side. The book proved a best seller, enabling him, according to an interview I read, to buy a chicken farm somewhere in Pennsylvania. I suppose it was petty of me, but I conjured up a vision of ten thousand Rhode Island Reds, in Russian smocks, pinning their eggs on the wall so that they might democratically choose those to be sent to market. In any case, I didn't give it very much thought, and I certainly never dreamed that my future would be intertwined with Mark Silver's.

I was quite mistaken. Late in the autumn of 1932, my wife and I were living in a so-called club hotel in the East Fifties managed by her brother, Nathanael West, then an aspiring novelist, who had turned the place into a sort of Fort Zinderneuf, a refuge for writers from the rigors of the Depression. At one time, so many literati were domiciled there on his largesse that the lobby took on the aspect of Yaddo or a book-and-author luncheon. For example, burly pipe-smoking poets with thick orange neckties—nobody has ever ascertained why poets affect cravats with the texture of caterpillars—stood around swapping meters; the girl at the newsstand, if asked for the sports final, was likely to gaze at you unseeingly and reply with a quatrain from Emily Dickinson. One evening, as I was descending in the elevator, the operator halted the car between floors and swung around with a determined gleam in his eye. I thought he was about to glom my wallet, but when he spoke it was in the rich Stanislavskian cadences of a Group Theatre actor. "Excuse me, sir," he said deferentially. "The housekeeper told me you wrote something for Broadway or Hollywood, I forget which. I'm scripting a play, too—on a Biblical theme—but I got stuck in the second act, in the obligatory scene. Could you recommend a good book on construction, or would you advise me to go back to the Bible?"

I advised him, and thereafter used the stairs. To return to Mark Silver, however, it was during this period that I began to detect glowing references in my brother-in-law's speech to Bucks County, Pennsylvania, where he had recently spent several weekends. His eclogues on its Arcadian peace, its flora and fauna, and its architecture verged on rhapsody, and inevitably it developed that he had seen a wonderful buy—an eighty-three-acre farm embodying all these features. This was, it turned out, the farm Mark Silver had bought, apparently as a homestead for an indigent brother and his family, who strove to raise chickens there with signal unsuccess; and now, to compound his troubles, Silver was enmeshed with a tigress in New York who was threatening a breach-of-promise suit. To help him escape to Mexico, which he deemed the ideal expedient, he was willing to sell the property for a token down payment and illimitable easy installments. In West's view, it was the biggest steal since the theft of the Mona Lisa from the Louvre.

The house was uninhabited and in rather sorry condition when my wife and I inspected it a few days later; judging from the pots on the stove and cutlery encrusted with verdigris, Silver's kinsfolk had departed as abruptly as the crew of the *Mary Celeste*. Also, a tour of the outbuildings disclosed that the family, after the poultry debacle, had turned their hand to carpentry. Dozens of modernistic plywood bookcases, smeared with bronze radiator paint and weird tropical colors, stood piled in the sheds. Long after we acquired the place, as we seemed destined to, these monstrosities harassed me; whenever I tried to chop them up for kindling, the springy wood repelled the axe and perforated me with splinters. I eventually made a gigantic bonfire of them, nearly burning down the barn in the process.

Throughout our first year of ownership, we often pondered the mystery of the Silvers' precipitate flight without reaching a solution. Then we began to hear tantalizing rumors about some drama that had occurred on the farm—some near-fatal episode involving Mark Silver and a famous New York playwright. Nobody was sure of the details—who the playwright was or exactly what had happened—but there had been gunplay, it was said, and the real facts had been hushed up. Ultimately, I managed to piece the story together, and though the principals never revealed it in their lifetime (and could hardly do so afterward, save on the Ouija board), the truth can at last be told.

The affair commenced one Sunday morning as a real-estate agent named Mrs. Grundig was piloting Mr. and Mrs. George S. Kaufman up the Delaware Valley to show them a couple of farm properties. It had taken considerable persuasion for Kaufman, a stubborn city dweller, to agree to the junket; as they rode along, he accused his wife, Beatrice, of suffering from a milkmaid complex like Marie Antoinette's, adding that he loathed the out-of-doors, that rural living was full of pitfalls, and that nobody had ever incurred a hernia lifting a sandwich in Reuben's. His wife, however, was enraptured with the countryside. The greenery worked on her like adrenalin, and the farther they progressed into the bush the more ecstatic she became, until Kaufman, despite himself, began to thaw. He surreptitiously took a deep breath, and, to his surprise, the fresh air did not produce the convulsions he had expected.

Meanwhile, up at the Silver farm in the rolling hills beyond Erwinna, a curious demonstration was going on in the yard. To an audience composed of his brother, his sister-in-law, and their five children, Mark Silver, a man who could not open an umbrella without puncturing someone's lung, was explaining the intricacies of handling a shotgun. Why he was doing so is inexplicable. The class war he was constantly ululating about in his column was not that imminent, nor could he have hoped to convert his listeners into Nimrods, rich as the region was in game.

"Now, people," he said, balancing the weapon on his palms, "pay close attention. This is what we call a sixteen-gauge shotgun. Note the double barrels."

"Double barrels," his nieces and nephews dutifully echoed.

"These little iron things sticking up along the barrels," he continued, "are the sights—to help you aim, as you'll see later. But first, the part back here. That's called the breech, and the wooden end, which fits against your shoulder, is the stock. Now, watch what happens." He slid the gun onto his forearm and jerked open the breech. "This is known as 'breaking' the gun. You all understand everything so far?"

"Yes—yes!" the youngsters chorused. "Go on, Uncle Mark!"

At that point, roughly, the car bearing the Kaufmans and Mrs. Grundig was passing through an especially bucolic patch of landscape a quarter of a mile distant from the Silver farm. A turbulent creek, along whose banks several cows peacefully grazed, bisected a meadow edged by fields of ripening grain. Off in the distance stood a quaint covered bridge, a clump of weeping willows, and a hay wain that any fool knew had been designed by Constable. Beatrice Kaufman was spellbound. "Oh, George, have you ever seen anything so divine?" she said.

"Lovely," he said grudgingly. "But it could get pretty lonesome out here. No newspapers, nobody to play cards with. I'm no bird-watcher—"

Stuff and nonsense, his wife interrupted crisply. Given such idyllic surroundings, all the intimates would flock down weekends, would rush to acquire homes close by; Moss Hart, she reminded him, was avid for a country retreat near any they might discover. Sensing that Kaufman was starting to capitulate, Mrs. Grundig loosed her sales pitch. The Silver property they were approaching was, admittedly, unimproved. Nevertheless, its potential as a showplace, a gentleman's estate combining privacy and beauty, was unmatched in her experience. Within five minutes, she promised, their dazzled eyes would behold as breathtaking a scene as mortal man had ever looked upon.

Simultaneous with her prediction, the circle of relatives large and small absorbed in Mark Silver's lecture up at the farm watched in awe as he fumbled forth two stubby cardboard cylinders rimmed with brass.

"Now, you know what these are, of course?"

"Bullets!" one of the older boys sang out.

"*Shells,*" his uncle corrected. "Shotgun shells. And here," he went on, inserting them into the appropriate chambers, "is where we load them. The next step is to close the breech, like so." He locked the mechanism smartly. "O.K., we're ready for business. I lift up the gun and hold the stock firmly against my shoulder. Remember what I told you about these little irons on the top here—the sights? The idea is you line them up with whatever you're aiming at." He squinted along the barrels to illustrate, then lowered the weapon. "Before you fire, though, I better explain about this jimjick here, the trigger. A lot of crazy people think that all you do is grab the gun, point it, and pull the trigger—boom! No sirree—there's more to it than that!"

Only the Prince of Darkness himself could have arranged the timing, for, coincidental with these words, Mrs. Grundig's car lurched off the county road into the farm's private lane and began ascending the steep wooded hillside surmounted by the Silvers' fieldstone house. By now, Beatrice Kaufman was wellnigh speechless with delight. This view was just what she had always dreamed of, she exulted—a noble expanse of tilled earth and woodland, sun glinting on faraway barns and silos, and, tying it all together, the ribbon of the majestic Delaware.

"Wait till you see the barn here, Mr. Kaufman," Mrs. Grundig was chattering. "You could turn it into the most beautiful studio."

"I wasn't planning to produce any movies," he countered.

"Then make it into a guesthouse," she advised. "There's

room enough for servants' quarters, a six-car garage—even a bowling alley."

Before he could ask where the pinboys would come from, his wife had a question. "Is anyone living here at present, Mrs. Grundig?"

"I'm not sure," said the agent, "but we'll know in a minute. The place is right over this next rise."

Mark Silver again braced the shotgun against the curve of his shoulder, canted its barrels downward, and, raising his voice to make it distinct, issued a final injunction to his kin. "Bear in mind," he stressed, "you don't *pull* the trigger—you squeeze it. A long . . . slow . . . squeeze. Just like this."

Suiting the action to the words, he squeezed. There was an apocalyptic, shattering roar mingled with shrieks of terror as the assemblage scattered. For a moment, a pall of dust and smoke obscured the spot, and when it dispersed, Irving Silver, Mark's brother, lay revealed on the grass. He was clutching his left instep, where the charge had struck it, and was howling inconsolably. Such, then, was the tableau that greeted the Kaufmans as they disembarked, thunderstruck by the explosion: a disheveled fellow with a shotgun frozen over his recumbent victim, six bystanders of assorted sizes caterwauling in the shrubbery. Hypnotized, they saw Mark Silver slowly react like the great Jewish tragedian Jacob Adler to the enormity of his deed. He emitted a heartrending cry, flung aside the shotgun, and raced up the lawn toward Kaufman, who shrank back ashen-faced at his approach.

"Cain and Abel!" Mark Silver bellowed, smiting his forehead. "Woe is me! I have slain my own brother!"

Swifter than Ford Sterling and his Keystone Cops, the callers leaped back into their car and went hurtling down the lane, hell for leather. How long the Silvers lingered is uncertain, but they let no grass grow under their feet. As for Kaufman, it was donkey's years before he could be induced to revisit Bucks County. "Yes, I know that neck of the woods," he was wont to observe grimly. "I'd stay away from it if I were you. The fratricide is something terrible. It's like a page out of the Old Testament."

I Have Nothing to Declare but My Genius

One morning half a century ago, give or take a decade, the Beelzebub occupying the desk behind mine in grade school surreptitiously affixed a steel pen point to the toe cap of his bluchers, thrust his leg under my chair, and kicked upward. Given more room, I might have executed a two-and-a-half forward somersault like that wizard of the trapeze, Alfredo Codona; instead, biting back my tears, I flung myself on my persecutor (whose name, oddly enough, was Frankie Torquemada) and tried to eviscerate him with a slate pencil. Neither of us, as it turned out, emerged the victor. He was sentenced to clap erasers for a week, I to transcribe fifty times on the blackboard the rubric, *Lives of great men all remind us/We can make our lives sublime/And, departing, leave behind us/Footprints on the sands of time.*

How the world could possibly be enriched by a legacy of sandy footprints I never understood, any more than I did the omnipresence of Rosa Bonheur's *Horse Fair* in every classroom, but like the pen point, Longfellow's precept must have sunk home, for thenceforward the lives of the eminent became a lodestar to me, a lamp unto my feet. Ultimately, the quest for sublimity carried me into a number of strange places—none of them stranger, however, than two panegyrics I recently ran across, a biography of Kipling and a prose poem in the *Holly-*

wood Reporter. We've all seen flapdoodle in our day, but man, these are vintage. I haven't experienced such gooseflesh since W. W. Jacobs' *The Monkey's Paw.*

I read Charles Carrington's *Rudyard Kipling* last winter in an appropriate Burmese setting—the Strand Hotel in Rangoon, where "Mandalay," the ballad beloved of every basso profundo in vaudeville, is said to have been composed. Now, nobody objects to idolatry in moderation; a pinch or two of hero worship can often season a fat book. Carrington's veneration for Kipling, though, was so glutinous that it threatened at times to clog his fountain pen. Some inkling of the schmalz quotient can be gleaned from the following passage:

> Rudyard had a gift for penetrating the undertones of conversation. His own French was fluent though inaccurate, and powerfully helped out by gestures; his skill at extracting the sense of what was said to him was uncanny. Not only could he fall into casual talk with some patois-speaking peasant in France, and come away after five minutes, equipped with minute technical knowledge of his farming methods and family history; there were occasions when he achieved the same result in Spain and even Czechoslovakia by signs and gestures, without pretence of knowing the language at all.

Was Carrington an eyewitness to these remarkable demonstrations? Were they confided to him by the aforesaid peasants in their quaint patois? It seems much more likely that the source was the great romancer himself, whose ego, I would have said, was unmatched up to the time Norman Mailer came along. I would have said so, that is, until I read the dithyramb in the *Hollywood Reporter* about Sidney Sheldon.

Sheldon, a television writer and producer, had just concluded a whopping $1,800,000 pact with Screen Gems to supply them with five pilot films, and he was snapping his suspenders in the presence of Sue Cameron, a reporter. By his own admission, Sheldon is a sequoia in the literary field:

> "When I'm working on a series I can write three scripts a week. I write one Saturday, one Sunday, and one

during the week. I have two secretaries and they get all the typing done. I feel guilty sometimes when I think about other writer friends of mine who really have to sweat to get scripts out. Luckily with me it just flows. I love to write," continues Sheldon, who has finished the five pilot scripts, a suspense play he will do in London, and 960 pages of his new novel. "I dictate 30 to 50 pages a day on it. I love to write so much that I have to stop myself from writing seven days a week." Sheldon's previous novel, *The Naked Face,* will soon be made into a motion picture and, naturally, he has already finished the screenplay.

As if the foregoing were not conducive to heartburn, Miss Cameron thereupon launched into an emotional little eulogy. "Sidney Sheldon is a rare man," she wrote. "He loves his work, his family, and his whole life. He is a gentle, sensitive man, who follows through on everything." " 'I see myself as a storyteller,' " he told her, adding, in an uprush of genealogy, " 'It all started with the cavemen sitting around campfires telling stories. Those are my ancestors.' "

By a fluke that almost wrenched the long arm of coincidence from its socket, I stumbled not long ago on evidence of someone whose feats bore a close kinship to those of Kipling and Sheldon. Rummaging through a carton of books in a downtown auction room, I unearthed a ring binder wherein this person— an author of mixed Irish and French ancestry named Patrick Foley de Grandeur—had kept a fragmentary journal. At a modest outlay of $1.75, I acquired the diary and an annotated copy of Stekel's *Frigidity in Women,* from the former of which I reproduce the extracts below. Extracts from the latter are still thawing on my windowsill.

November 17

Awoke feeling rather bushed this A.M.; I had stayed up past midnight dictating final 340 pages of *Bustmonger,* the novel I outlined yesterday. A story loosely based on the career of Hugh Hefner should do well these days that readers are wallowing in nostalgia. Managed to work in one or two quite effective scenes, esp. Joycean interior monologue where Hefner-type character recalls dynamic influence in childhood of Sears Roebuck corset ads. (*Note to myself:* Change denouement. The idea of cheesecake photos igniting his circular bed so as to fricassee Hefner too subjective. How about death struggle atop Niagara Falls between Hef. and publisher of *Penthouse,* à la Holmes and Prof. Moriarty?)

Spooky phone call this afternoon from my agent, Winnie Kochleffel. She apparently sensed I was doing yarn on Hefner theme, though I hadn't breathed a word to anyone, and acting on hunch, sold its paperback rights to Signet for $400,000. Some kind of ESP, doubtless; I remember reading that Tolstoy and V. Hugo had similar power of thought transference. I don't put myself in their class, to be sure; still, neither of them ever sold paperback rights for 400 big ones.

Started to write a novella or two after dinner, but frittered away the evening at the piano, unaware that my tape recorder was switched on. On playing it back, found I had unconsciously composed a whole jazz suite, a Ferdie Grofé type of thing. Nothing spectacular, yet the untutored ear might well mistake it for middle-period Gershwin. Funny how a person gifted in one medium can so easily distinguish himself in another. I felt quite pleased with myself.

November 29

Knocked out a couple of whodunits before breakfast to limber up for the day's work. I have to chuckle when I read about Simenon's astonishing ability to sweat out a thriller in eleven days. I could do one in as many hours if I cared to write bilge, but fortunately, I have *some* standards. What with mail and phone calls, I taped only 250 pages of another work with overtones of nostalgia, *A Child's Life of Peter Bogdanovich,* before rushing off to dentist's appointment. Why do I pay a cluck like Gluckstern an arm and a leg when I'm perfectly capable of filling my own teeth? (*Reminder:* Look through Yellow Pages for secondhand dental equip't—drill, spittoon, etc. Might be sizable tax deduction—discuss w. Tony Fiduciari, my accountant.)

A weird subway encounter on return home. Sat next to fine old bearded patriarch who was reading Yiddish newspaper—he unable to speak English, I to understand his patois. Thanks to my facility for mime, however, within three minutes I elicited his origins, profession, and artistic prejudices. He hailed from Vitebsk, the Russian province where Marc Chagall was born, and was a kosher baker, specializing in macaroons. Seemed to be well-versed in Chagall's work, though unimpressed by same. "So what's all the *geschrei?*" I interpreted him as saying. "Anybody can scribble a junkman flying in the sky or a donkey. By me is Norman Rockwell an artist, Max Parrish. They paint cherries, grapes, nectarines you could pick right off the canvas." Prior to descending at Columbus Circle, he fished out a macaroon and insisted I try it. It had a distinct odor of moth flakes. "Sure, from laying in my pocket all winter," he gestured. "I put some crystals in there to keep away the mice." When I got off at Herald Square, I was stunned to find my wallet missing. The policeman to whom I reported the loss cut short my description. "Yep, that's him, all right," he said. "Cooney Lemel, the smartest dip on the IND. Kiss your wad goodbye, Mac, you've been ripped off by an expert."

Too upset afterward to resume serious work, so I dashed off a trayful of short stories and pastiches, donned a smock, and got out some modeling clay, which I find therapeutic whenever I'm overwrought. So totally immersed did I become that it was nearly dawn when I surfaced, and there before me was the figure of a reclining female nude indistinguishable from the best of Maillol or Despiau. (Or Rodin, for that matter, whom, between myselves, it evoked rather than these lesser fry.) The moment I realized, however, that the reputations of all three might be diminished if my effort came to light, I decided to destroy it. It was the only decent thing to do, and I feel confident posterity will agree.

December 5

A busy morning—phones ringing, the clatter of typewriters struggling to keep up with my output, such pandemonium that all I accomplished was a 90-minute TV special, "The Romance of Bauxite," and the script of a porno flick to be filmed in the Ajanta Caves. Every ten minutes Winnie Kochleffel rang up with some proposal more fatuous than the last—an updated version of *Die Fledermaus* to star Truman Capote, a juvenile for ages six to nine about Sweeney Todd, the Demon Barber of Fleet Street. The chaos was climaxed by the arrival of a delegation from the top echelon of CBS, headed by William Paley. They were all babbling like a pack of kindergartners, so incoherent that I was hard put to understand them, but I finally deciphered their pantomime. I could hardly credit my senses: they want me to handle all future writing for the network—sitcoms, reportage, talk shows, documentaries, anything involving words—in return for ten per cent of their gross. Judas Priest, what do they think I am—superhuman?

December 9

A red-letter day, mingling jubilation and triumph. The mail brought a communication from France's former Minister of Culture, addressing me as *"Cher Maître."* Inadequate as is my French, it read in translation: "One has long enough been acquainted with your eminence in the belletristic sphere. Now we are overturned to uncover you as a painterly ace, having possessed ourselves of two masterworks the most fabulous from your palette. Lady Rumor has it that these are but joys of the spirit, dashed off as refreshments between labor. *Basta!* (Bastard.) To us they are uniquely flavorsome, gorgeous celebrations of the Post-Impressionist style, reducing the daubs of Vuillard, Seurat, Signac, and Pissarro to artistic pimples. You shall hang in the Jeu de Paume, by blue, or else I scrawl the names of my fellow-Academicians in every vespasian in Paris! Welcome to the company of the immortals. I embrace you. André Malraux."

I used to wonder what it felt like to be a Renaissance man, a Leonardo da Vinci, enshrined with the gods on Olympus. Now I know.

December 21

Eureka—the capstone of my endeavors has fallen into place, the dream I have so long nurtured is realized at last. After two days of unremitting toil, my masterpiece, the chef d'oeuvre that will render the name of Patrick Foley de Grandeur imperishable forevermore, is complete.

For years, just as a diamond-cutter seeks a Kohinoor worthy of his mallet and chisel, just as a fishmonger sorting whitebait envisions the marlin he will mount on his wall, so have I scratched my noggin for a subject to inspire Calliope, my muse. To rewrite Balzac's *Comédie Humaine?* Harold Robbins and Irving Stonehenge have anticipated me. To retrace the endless neurotic embroideries of Proust? Jacqueline Susann has delved into the feminine soul—with a manure fork, true, but the damage is done. And then, in a blinding flash, the scales fell from my eyes. *Shakespeare!*

What I have done to Shakespeare, in the apt phrase of Ruskin's *Stones of Venice,* shouldn't happen to a Doge. I have taken all his high-flown rodomontade, his euphuistical bombast and sesquipedelian twaddle, and distilled them into tales comprehensible to the veriest moron, to the most benighted redneck, to even a rock fan. Fifty years from now, I prophesy, hard hats swilling their beer in the taverns of East New York will be tearfully quoting my lines, the dingy metaphors and crapulous elegiacs of the Bard long forgotten. Singlehandedly, I have like written finis to the age of the egghead, man. This I guarantee.

Only one scintilla of Angst clouds my gratification. Twice during the past three days, a person in a white jacket has rung my doorbell. When I queried him on the second occasion about the net he was carrying, he said he was a lepidopterist, desirous of showing me some rare butterflies. I mistrusted his insincere smile, to say nothing of the foot he tried to interpose in the door. As I dictate this, he is lurking across the street, clad in a trenchcoat and scanning my windows intently. Something tells me I'm going to have trouble with that man.

Summertime, and the Living Ain't Easy

Back in the summer of 1959, and thanks to some Italian highbinders for whom I was writing a screenplay in Rome, I occupied a suite at the Grand Hotel there that only an ingrate would cavil at, but I caviled morning, noon, and night. Tasteful and commodious though it was, my lodging overlooked the Piazza Esedra, where a café loudspeaker endlessly brayed forth the strains of "Ciao Ciao Bambina" above the roar of tourist buses arriving and departing at the C.I.T. terminus. To compound the bedlam, the Grand was building an annex on which a corps of stonemasons clambered about singing "Santa Lucia" at the top of their voices, and whenever they paused to rest waiters in the hotel's outdoor restaurant dragged iron tables across the marble floor, generating a screech that penetrated one's marrow. The only surcease I ever got was on Wednesdays, when a squat little troglodyte sped in on a Vespa from the studio, bringing my emolument in cash—a wrinkle obviously devised to circumvent taxes. The two of us used to count it together, and, curiously enough, I was never conscious of the noise outside while counting.

A methodical person by nature, my daily routine that summer rarely varied. From eleven to one, I dictated to a secretary in a patois that mingled pidgin English with Hollywood script-ese, since none of the five girls I successively worked with—a

Yugoslav, a Greek, a Hungarian, and two Italians—was proficient in my own tongue. While I carefully spelled out all
polysyllabic words, they frequently came back to me in un-
recognizable form. "Raoul has a strange idioniscanary—a
fondness for snakes," one of the girls indited, and another
transcribed my characterization of our breezy ingenue thus:
"Babette enters. She is a vivastic creature of nineteen." (As for
the content of the screenplay, and how I wove drama from the
relationship of Raoul and Babette, that needn't concern us. The
less said about it the better.)

My midday meal was never a problem; I always took it at
Babington's tearoom, at the foot of the Spanish Steps, passing
Gogol's commemorative table in the Via Sistina with eyes
averted because I felt he was reproaching me for desecrating
our profession. Though the bacon and eggs at Babington's were
no culinary triumph, my real motive in eating there was to
eavesdrop on its American patrons, whose behavior toward
each other fascinated me. Screened behind a copy of the *Rome
Daily American,* I overheard tourists exchange taunts about
their travels—patronizing at first—that became increasingly
spiteful. The object of the jousting, apparently, was to humiliate
one's adversary, to make him feel that whatever he had visited
in Europe was picayune.

"You say you were in Belgium," a woman would address her
neighbor. "Did you get to Bruges? . . . You *didn't?* Ho ho!"
A crow of derision. "Well, if you didn't see Bruges, you didn't
see Belgium."

"We went all over Holland like you did, though," the other
would retort defensively. "Did you see Leyden?"

"No, we saw Amsterdam, Rotterdam—"

"Big deal!" the first would cackle. "If you didn't see Leyden,
you didn't see Holland. You might as well have stayed in
Ashtabula."

For some unknown reason, these skirmishes had a tonic
effect on me, and I strode back refreshed to the Grand for
another spell of dictation until the cocktail hour. I generally
drank my Americano in the main lounge rather than the bar
because after a couple of them I felt expansive, and the lounge

gave me more room to expand in. It was a hundred and seventy-five feet in breadth—I paced it off on several occasions—and it contained two full-sized palm trees, not to mention a thicket of rubber plants concealing a string quartet. It also gave me a better vantage point to observe Mrs. Shaughnessy when she crossed the lobby on her way to dinner.

Mrs. Shaughnessy was a wealthy recluse of eighty-odd who, according to the head concierge, hadn't set foot outside the hotel in seventeen years. Six feet tall, as ramrod-straight as a Grenadier Guardsman, she had a cloud of snow-white hair framing what must have been a surpassingly lovely face, powdered and rouged in the fashion of the early twenties. She usually wore a long pastel-colored sheath of shell satin and flourished a major-domo's cane tipped with an ivory knob. Promptly at six-thirty every night, she issued from the elevator and swept toward the dining room, looking neither right nor left. She was the Grande Époque personified, all of Proust and Edith Wharton rolled into one, and had I had a groat's worth of sense I'd have scraped acquaintance to elicit her secret. The perfect opportunity presented itself one evening in the white-and-gold dining room when I caught her studying me from behind a pillar. At the moment, however, I was too busy eavesdropping on a trio at the next table, a Maryknoll father with a skinful of Chianti who was coaching a Brooklyn contractor's wife and daughter for a papal audience. I sometimes think my whole life would have changed if Mrs. Shaughnessy and I had met. Granted our backgrounds were dissimilar, but if a Frenchman with a penchant for snakes can find happiness with a vivacious girl of nineteen, as my screenplay conclusively proved, we too might have reached an accommodation. Ah, well, *che sarà, sarà.* . . .

Evening at the Grand Hotel was the most difficult part of the day; lacking companionship and unversed in Italian, I soon became satiated with reading, exhausted all the available movies, and emptily wandered the streets to fill the interval between dinner and bedtime. A chance encounter with a play-girl out of my remote past augured well but proved an unsettling experience. Halfway though a meal at her mother's flat, the old lady launched into a panegyric to General Franco that inexplicably became a tribute to benzine as a universal cleaning agent, and I fled the pair convinced that they were loonies. Shortly afterward, an English couple took me to a party in a vaulted cavern on an island in the middle of the Tiber. We arrived to find half a hundred people standing hushed in the darkness, listening to a veal-faced young diplomat from the British Embassy sing Negro work songs in the most excruciating dialect since Octavus Roy Cohen laid down his pen. I thought the depths of indignity had been plumbed, until he rose to sashay around in a cakewalk pleading for shortenin' bread. Thereafter I buried myself nightly in the pages of Motley's *Rise of the Dutch Republic,* which, although not sparkling, at least didn't give me gooseflesh.

With the approach of Ferragosto, the holiday fortnight at the end of August, the hotel's guests shrank to a minimum, and as most of the staff also went on vacation, there was an acute shortage of help. I grew aware of it when the manager accosted me one morning with profuse apologies to ask if I would consider some extra work. I had just finished my script and was anticipating a period of leisure, so I told him that I had no appetite for writing.

"I don't mean that," he said. "I mean helping out around the hotel. We need somebody for little jobs—you know, to carry luggage, walk a dog, hook up a lady's dress. Not a steady position—only till the other fellows come back."

"Why don't you take on a relief bellhop?"

"It's unfair to hire a man for just two weeks," he replied. "Now with you, you're not making a career out of it. You pick up a few thousand lire, we shake hands, and goodbye."

"But I've never done that type of thing," I protested.

"What of it? You have as much brains as these other boneheads."

"We-e-ell," I said dubiously. "Maybe I could, but mind you, I'm not going to put on a uniform."

"Who's asking you to?" he said. "Besides, you couldn't get into the ones they wear. That's some bay window you got, Mister."

"Don't I know," I said sheepishly. "It's all that pasta you folks serve."

His lips compressed. "There's no law says you have to make a pig of yourself," he snapped. "Well, I can't stand here jawing with you all day. Go report to the front desk." He plucked the cigarette from my mouth. "No smoking on the job, Charlie. *Andiamo!*"

I soon discovered how ill-prepared I was for the work I'd undertaken. It wasn't a question of stamina; after I handled a few satchels and got the kinks out of my system, muscles dormant since childhood toughened, and I moved with the precision of a well-oiled machine. The real trouble was my lack of servility—I just couldn't learn to fawn. Some lah-de-dah *principessa,* say, would send for you to come up and scrub her back, and you were expected to bow and scrape if she tipped you a hundred lire. Sixteen cents for wielding a loofah in a steamy bathroom where a person could contract double pneumonia or worse. And the errands that people thought up, nobody would believe. They wanted a tin of oxblood shoe polish, Jewish rye bread with caraway seeds, a new reed for their harmonica, God knows what, and if you signified by so much as a lift of the eyebrow that they were cuckoo they flew into a tantrum. In a way, those two weeks were a valuable experience; they taught me how unreasonable and tricky some human beings are. It was, in fact, an episode involving an American stockbroker named Worthington Toushay that almost cast a pall over my last few days at the Grand.

Mr. Toushay, listed in the hotel register as a partner in the Boston firm of Parry, Thrust, & Toushay, was a benevolent white-haired gentleman resembling the late Warren G. Harding, who often sent down for drinks and was extremely liberal with his tips. Late one afternoon, when I brought in his cocktail, I found him fussing with the mechanism of a shallow black box some ten inches long by six wide.

"Is that a radio, Mr. Toushay?" I asked, mystified. "I've never seen one with rollers like that."

"No, it's something quite new in the States," he said. "It's called a 'money machine'—it converts small bills into those of a larger denomination. Like to see how it works?" He drew a dollar from his wallet and fed it into the rollers. "Now, you twist the rollers on this side, and out comes the result on the other." As he did so, a crisp new twenty emerged before my astonished gaze.

"That's impossible," I said. "It must be a trick of some sort."

He laughed indulgently. "Quite the opposite, I assure you. They're selling like hot cakes at home. Everybody has one, though naturally they're still rather expensive. This type retails for about sixteen hundred dollars, I believe."

"Does it take only small bills?"

"Not at all—if you put in tens, it produces fifties, twenties get you a hundred, and so on. I understand certain individuals have become fairly wealthy by this means, but to me it's only an interesting toy, since I happen to be independently rich. . . . What did you say?"

"Nothing," I said hastily. "I—I was just swallowing. Look, Mr. Toushay—"

"Yes?" he said, peering at me over the rim of his spectacles.

"I was wondering if you could—I mean, as you said, a man as well fixed as you doesn't need a gadget like this. I'd be willing to take your hands off it—I mean, take it off your hands—"

"But my dear boy, how could you afford it on your salary?"

"Oh, I'm not really a bellhop," I said. "Let me explain . . ."

Well, once he grasped who I actually was, his qualms vanished, and to make a long story short, he consented to let me have the machine for fifteen hundred. Inasmuch as he had several business appointments the next day before flying to London, I procured the sum in traveler's checks and met him on the stroke of noon at Ciampino Airport. The package he handed me seemed unusually heavy and I asked him why. He gave me a conspiratorial wink.

"You'll see when you undo it," he said, with a fat chuckle. "Well, that's my flight they're calling. *Arrivederci,* Clyde, and keep your nose clean."

The loudspeaker was still blaring out "Ciao Ciao Bambina" as I leaned on my windowsill that evening and watched the C.I.T. buses rumble through the Piazza Esedra. So what if that white-haired muzzler had nicked me for fifteen hundred clams with a paving block done up in brown manila paper? What if a couple of illiterates incapable of judging a work of art had flung my script into the wastebasket and were threatening to sue? Was I any the lesser man? Not by a long chalk, for out of their chicaneries I had acquired a ripeness, a tolerance for human frailty rarely granted the average mortal. I inhaled a deep draught of nighttime air curiously freighted with the scent of patchouli that trailed from Mrs. Shaughnessy, lay down with Motley's *Rise of the Dutch Republic* covering my face, and sank into a dreamless slumber.

Meanwhile, Back at
the Crunch . . .

Late of an autumn afternoon in 1946, a bustle of activity uncharacteristic of Philadelphia enlivened the corridors of the Warwick Hotel in Philadelphia. The door of Suite 1713 kept flying open to admit a procession of waiters, each bearing a dozen ponies of Scotch, and one might have deduced a joyous brannigan on foot within. The atmosphere of high wassail, however, was illusory, for in fact Hyman Bellwether, the occupant of the suite, was preparing a last-ditch stand reminiscent of the Alamo. A Broadway producer whose sorcery had enmeshed a number of us—a composer, a lyrics writer, myself, and another librettist—in a moribund musical comedy, he was making a desperate effort to stave off inevitable disaster. The show was a turkey, its three-hundred-thousand-dollar budget and its creators exhausted, and everyone connected with it knew that as sure as God made little green tumbrels they would roll on Saturday night. The one exception in the morass of pessimism was Bellwether himself. With an obduracy verging on the imbecile he believed he could pull the chestnuts out of the fire if the investors furnished enough oxygen to keep the curtain up a few days longer. What mesmerism he employed heaven only knows, but somehow he had managed to lure our backers, two wealthy New York matrons and their husbands, to the War-wick, hoping that his eloquence, reinforced by massive injec-tions of the grape, would loosen their purse strings.

My colleagues and I were grouped in the suite, cold sober and awaiting the arrival of the Maecenases with visible angst, when we became aware of a mysterious bit of voodoo in progress. Humming some unmemorable ditty from the show, Bellwether was transferring the sixty ponies of whiskey supplied by the hotel into three empty bottles, his Piltdown forehead wrinkled in concentration. Eventually, one of us, more nimble at mathematics than the rest, found his tongue.

"Listen, Hymie," he expostulated. "Those drinks are a dollar and a quarter apiece, which works out at twenty-five bucks for a bottle. This stuff retails for seven-fifty at a package store."

Bellwether surveyed him with Olympian scorn. "That shows what you know about the rich, wise guy," he scoffed. "Straighten yourself out. People with gelt drink exclusively from the bottle—that's their hallmark. Besides," he added reasonably, "those stiffs are going to pay for it in the end, aren't they?"

And pay they did—through the nose—even though the show irretrievably closed like an oyster a week later. Bellwether, nonetheless, was right, and I was reminded of the truism when I read a piece by Maurice Zolotow in *TV Guide* about the tribulations writers are currently experiencing on the Coast. For a variety of reasons—the frequency of reruns, the decline of the sixty-minute show, the increase of movies made for tele-vision, and the F.C.C.'s allotment of prime time to local sta-tions—a grievous dearth of jobs has stricken the industry's scribes. With dust settling over their typewriters, many an exquisite once shod by Lobb is forced to shuffle around in shoes fashioned out of old inner tubes, to redouble his visits to the phrenologist, and to practice the most stringent economies. Witness, for example, the case of one hitherto solvent writer who, says Zolotow, "has made certain compromises during the present crunch. He used to throw fabulous dinner parties with a hired-for-the-occasion chef, bartender, and waiter. No longer. The sleep-in housekeeper has been given the gate. 'I dusted off my dear and sainted mother, God bless her, and she comes here and cleans the place and cooks for me three times a week,' he says." Touching as I find this renewal of the filial bond, I detect a lurking tone of bitterness, a hint of the nagging and recrimination that undoubtedly will ensue. "So where was I all those years when you were making a fortune?" I can hear the old lady ululating. "My chicken soup wasn't good enough for His Highness. He had to have bartenders, waiters, sleep-in housekeepers yet—tramps, bloodsuckers, no-goodniks!" Perhaps the Hollywood Homicide Squad ought to plant a man outside the house just in case.

The particular passage of Zolotow's that evoked my Philadelphia memory, though, was the following: "Many [writers] don't care what they eat and drink—but worry about impressing their friends and business contacts. Olga Valence, a documentary and film writer, told me about a friend of hers who is destitute but believes he must keep up appearances when he entertains television producers, which he does now and then. 'He thinks that producers are suspicious of hungry writers and won't give them assignments,' she explains, 'so he still serves Chivas Regal, Canadian Club, Old Fitzgerald, these expensive French Bordeaux reds, and all that stuff. I wondered how he did it until he recently asked me over to help him. What he does is fill empty bottles of brand-name Scotch and wine with cheap supermarket stuff. He says that so far nobody has been able to tell the difference.' "

While Mr. Zolotow's report left me downcast, I couldn't help speculating about how the average TV viewer reacts to crises like this. Does he really sympathize with the plight of the gilded folk whose names he sees nightly on his tiny screen, those demigods supposedly immune from the anxieties besetting ordinary mortals? Perhaps, I thought, if he were brought face to face with their predicament—if the problems they now confront were dramatized, made vivid—they might excite his compassion. The *tableau vivant* that follows is no attempt to reduce anyone to tears, but it may cause him to be more resigned to his own lot.

SCENE: *The Coldwater Canyon residence of Lester Zircon, a formerly prosperous TV writer. The living-room décor is rather Spartan—the shelves bare of pre-Columbian pottery, and the concert grand repossessed by the finance company. The walls betray noticeable grayish patches, souvenirs of a onetime collection of Jasper Johns and Willem de Kooning. At rise, Zircon, his haggard forty-two-year-old face athrob with more tics than a Swiss watch, is pleading with an elderly Filipino houseman in a white coat.*

LESTER: Look, Papa, do I have to go over the whole thing again? Grimalka and I are tapped out, flat broke, behind the eight ball—do you understand? We haven't got from what to eat—we've been living on macaroni and graham crackers for seven months now! Everything's gone—the cars, the beach house, the orgone box, even my electric typewriter.

ZIRCON SENIOR: Then why are you giving this party, if you're so busted?

LESTER: Because I finally induced Lucas Membrane, the producer of the "Laugh Out Loud Show," to come to dinner. He might just throw me a half-hour segment, a few lines of dialogue to brush up, if I handle him with kid gloves.

ZIRCON SENIOR: Well, helping out I don't mind, but this coffee-colored makeup, Lester—it isn't nice, your own father schmeered up like a wetback. Suppose he says something to me in Spanish.

LESTER: Spanish? This creep can hardly talk English—he's a moron. Feed him all the booze he can hold, and whatever he says to you, don't answer—just grunt.

ZIRCON SENIOR: Like I'm a greenhorn.

LESTER: That's the idea. The main thing is not to let him know we're strapped. He's prejudiced against anyone that needs money. Where's Mother?

ZIRCON SENIOR: Grimalka's fixing up some kind of a Brazilian costume for her, with a bandanna. You couldn't tell her apart from a gypsy.

LESTER: Well, make sure she keeps her trap shut at all costs.

(*Grimalka Zircon enters unsteadily, her face pallid. She seems about to faint.*) Grimalka! What's wrong?

GRIMALKA: I—I don't know, it must be the smell of the meat. I'm so unaccustomed—

ZIRCON SENIOR (*hastily pouring a shot glass of liquor*): Here, drink this.

GRIMALKA: I can't. I spilled some on the rug this afternoon and it smoked. Never mind—I'll be all right in a minute. (*There is the sound of a car offscene. She peers out of the window.*) It's them. But why are they going around the back?

LESTER: Search me. (*Agitatedly*) Honey, turn on the hi-fi, dance the Charleston or something. Try to act carefree.

GRIMALKA: How can I? They took away the set weeks ago.

LESTER: Wait a minute. (*He rummages in a closet, extracts a tambourine.*) I'll beat on this and you snap your fingers. Vo-do-de-o-do! (*The Membranes enter through French doors rear. He is a fattish froglike twenty-nine, his countenance etched with a permanent sneer; his wife is a cadaverous blonde with an acid smile.*)

MEMBRANE: Hey, what gives here—a flamenco recital? Better watch out, Zircon—coronaries are a dime a dozen these days.

LESTER (*exuberantly*): Not in this household, fella. Grimalka and I have too much energy, if anything. We ski up at Sun Valley every weekend.

MRS. MEMBRANE: Oh, that's why you filled in your pool, is it? We thought maybe you couldn't afford it.

LESTER: Are you kidding? Confidentially, I needed the space for a vault. I've got so many blue-chip securities the bank didn't have room for them. Still, that's neither here nor there. Aguinaldo, see what our guests'll have to drink.

MEMBRANE: Dom Perignon for me, and my wife wants—do you have any genuine Rumanian slivovitz? (*With a grunt, Zircon senior pours out two shots of supermarket vodka, which the Membranes sip with relish.*) Excellent vintage, this. Bottled at the château, I suppose?

LESTER: Where else?

MEMBRANE: Brother, I need this. What a grisly sight we saw on the way over.

GRIMALKA: An accident?

MRS. MEMBRANE: No, a bunch of hungry writers waiting for their unemployment compensation. It looked like the breadlines you read about in the Depression.

MEMBRANE: Well, I can't sympathize with those vags. There's plenty of jobs available, but they're too lazy to work. By the way, Zircon, what's that cluster of "For Sale" signs doing on your lawn?

LESTER (*quickly*): The damn real-estate brokers—I *told* 'em it wasn't settled. I've been dickering for Pickfair on account of we need a larger house, so right away they start offering this place. (*His mother, garbed like Carmen Miranda, enters with a trayful of food.*)

GRIMALKA: I hope you don't mind eating in the lap. Our Chippendale table is being wormed at the moment.

MEMBRANE (*humorously*): It must be on its last legs.

LESTER: Say, that's a good one! We could build a whole routine out of it for your "Laugh Out Loud Show." A guy comes into a cabinetmaker's—

MEMBRANE (*icily*): Please—I never talk business on a social evening. What is this we're eating—pot roast?

MRS. ZIRCON (*angrily*): What did you think it was—reindeer meat?

GRIMALKA: Mama—I mean, Mazeppa—you forgot the potato pancakes!

MRS. ZIRCON: I work and I slave for your company, and that hippie there has the gall—

GRIMALKA (*hustling her out*): Here, I'll get them myself.

LESTER: Don't ever hire a sleep-out housekeeper, folks. We brought that woman all the way from Cuernavaca, and you can see the thanks we get.

MEMBRANE: You're telling me. Do you know T. S. Eleazer?

LESTER: The writer that won the Emmy Award last year?

MEMBRANE: Yep. Well, he's been on his uppers ever since, and out of pity I took him on as a handyman. He stole so many steaks from our freezer I had to prefer charges. He's doing six months in the workhouse.

LESTER: Speaking of TV, Mr. Membrane, would you settle a bet I made with a friend of mine? To what do you attribute your success in this medium?

MEMBRANE: I never surround myself with losers.

LESTER: That's exactly what I told him! You always hire topnotch writers—by that I mean ones that aren't starving. Correct?

MEMBRANE: Let me tell you something, Buster (*biting off a cigar*). I don't hire 'em *whoever* they are. I've got a new policy that's going to revolutionize this business. Writers are a thing of the past. Nobody needs 'em.

LESTER: Uh—I know, but who's going to make up the plots?

MEMBRANE: Anybody—the actors, that Filipino there, even this dummy I'm married to. You think it takes talent? Why, busy as I am, I could spin you a dozen situations which they'd be loaded with yocks. Take this very household, for instance.

LESTER: I don't get you.

MEMBRANE: Well, suppose there's an elderly guy like yourself, a poor crumb that he's practically on relief. He figures if he can get the boss in for a meal and juice him up that maybe he'll con him into a job. So he puts up a big front, gets his parents to impersonate a butler and a cook.

LESTER (*rocking to and fro*): Boy, that's a natural! I could milk that situation for thirty-nine weeks. It's got everything—humor, pathos—

MEMBRANE: Sure, and I'd be a sap to make a present of it to you. I'm going to package that idea, sell it to a network, and cut myself in for a big chunk of coin as the creative consultant.

MRS. MEMBRANE: I have to say it, even if he is my own husband. Everything Lucas touches turns to gold.

MEMBRANE: Yeah, show biz has been pretty good to me. Little did I dream when I was a pitchman for silver polish in Cleveland what the gods had in store for me.

GRIMALKA (*re-enters, eyes red from weeping*): I'm sorry, folks, but something went wrong with the potato pancakes. The cook threw them on the floor.

MRS. MEMBRANE: Well, it don't really matter. We have to be going anyway. There's an auction sale at Parke-Bernet of the effects of several bankrupt writers.

MEMBRANE: Keep in touch with me, Zircon. On second thoughts, I may have something for you—a polish job.

LESTER (*eagerly*): A rewrite? Gee, Mr. Membrane, that's right up my street.

MEMBRANE: So's the Fleetwood I need it on. Come around in the morning—two coats of wax and a good, brisk rubdown with a chamois. Think you can handle it?

LESTER: You just wait and see. I worked in a lubritorium before I came out here.

MEMBRANE: Yeah, anyone can tell from reading your scripts. Good night, all.

GRIMALKA (*as they exit*): Lester, you better go in and talk to your mother. She's threatening to put her head in the oven.

LESTER: I don't blame her, after the way she humiliated Mr. Membrane. Anyway, she's just bluffing. The old man can deal with her.

GRIMALKA: I'm not so sure. He's already got his head in there.

LESTER (*philosophically*): Oh, well, two less mouths not to feed.

GRIMALKA: Hmm, that's true. . . . You know, I think I'll have some of this pot roast—it's a shame to let it go to waste.

LESTER: That's the spirit. And let's have a little music with the meal. (*He picks up the tambourine and starts humming "I've Got a Pocketful of Dreams."*)

CURTAIN

Shubert, Shubert,
I've Been Thinkin'

Anybody who was passing through the living room of a certain apartment in the East Eighties about seven o'clock one night 32 years ago could not have helped but notice a charming domestic scene. The deponent was stretched out on a horsehair lounge, his toupee slightly askew and a tortured grimace on his face as, in a fleecy cloud directly above it, Veronica Lake pursued him about her hunting lodge, trying to smother him with kisses. A few feet away, and apparently oblivious to his plight, his wife was calmly knitting away at an Afghan, a devil of a fellow with liquid brown eyes and a magnificent fan-shaped beard. It was a picture which cried out for Currier & Ives, and it got them, for a scant ten minutes later two friends of ours named Harry Currier and Bertha Ives burst in excitedly. Pressing a hidden spring in his leg, the former produced tickets to the closing performance of *The Land Is Bright,* a play by Edna Ferber and George S. Kaufman (whose real names, it may be interesting to note in passing, were Edna Currier and George S. Ives), and before I could offer to pay my share, we were seated in the Music Box Theatre, rustling our programs and coughing for all the world like hardened playgoers.

The Land Is Bright was, as you undoubtedly know, a study of a family of American robber barons who, in spite of occa-

124

sional peccadilloes like the theft of a railroad or a Western state, eventually prove to be good kids *au fond*. It was a rich tapestry and the playwrights spared no pains to embroider it with a host of colorful characters and incidents. Lacey Kincaid and his wife, the founders of the dynasty, lacked none of the robust humor of their progenitors, Jiggs and Maggie, and the scene in which they auctioned off their daughter to an impoverished Hungarian nobleman was as memorable as anything in the *American Weekly*. In fact, the illusion was so perfect that I kept expecting H. Ashton-Wolfe of the Sûreté to enter disguised as an *apache,* arm in arm with that scientific wizard Mr. Gobind Behari Lal.

By far the most unusual feature of the production, however, was its servants. Whereas the average play limps along with a single frowzy part-time girl, *The Land Is Bright* contained at least three separate relays of butlers and maids tirelessly dishing out exposition. There was hardly a moment when the stage was free of flunkeys straightening the cushions and the plot, and when the cast took a bow at the final curtain, you would have sworn you were in a domestic-employment agency on Madison Avenue.

This kind of prodigality, of course, is the purest self-indulgence on the authors' part. Not only would one butler and maid have been sufficient but, with a slight technical readjustment, the Kincaid clan itself could have been dispensed with. The following charade, woven around a plot I found in an old rain barrel, may serve as a diagram of what I mean. Any producer who is sufficiently stirred to sponsor it is welcome to the rights; all I ask for myself is the lemonade concession.

SCENE: *The sitting room of the Fifth Avenue mansion of Burleigh Shostac, head of the vast Shostac industrial empire. The room exudes an air of quiet elegance; the floor is paved with silver dollars and the furniture upholstered in varying denominations of greenbacks. As the curtain rises, Bridget, an angular maid, enters and rekindles the dying fire with an armful of negotiable bonds.*

BRIDGET (*flicking a feather duster over the furniture*): Divil an' all, 'tis the beast of burden Oi've become, runnin' upsthairs and down constantly tindin' to the requirements of me employers, the Burleigh Shostacs, as shure as me name is Bridgid, their devoted maid of all wurrk. A hundred and sivinty rooms to take care of; begorra, it kapes a body busy from dawn till dark. Oi'd have give me notice long ago if th' masther wasn't such a swate soul, for despite his rough extherior and brusque ways, 'tis the grand ould gintleman he is, and the same applies to Mrs. Burleigh Shostac, though in lesser degree. As for their two childer, Whitney an' Brenda, Oi don't know phwhat's goin' to become of thim, indade Oi don't. Th' young felly's been a-roistherin' around till all hours with fly chorus gurrls, refusin' to take his rightful place at the helm of th' vast Shostac industrial empire, and they do say Brenda's head over heels with Grimes, th' new coachman, wurra wurra. (*She exits, shaking her head; a moment later, Uncle Cudgo, the butler, enters, bearing a feather duster.*)

CUDGO (*ruefully scratching his grizzled poll*): Lawkamassy, heah's a purty kittle ob fish, as sho's mah name is Uncle Cudgo dat's been de devoted family retainuh nigh on fo'ty yeah. Seems lak young Miz Brenda, which Ah done dandle on mah knee as a pickaninny, jist elope wif dat no-'count coachman Grimes, an' to make mattuhs worse, Whitney he gone blind fum drinkin' bad likker. De news done affeck de ole lady's ticker an' she peg out soon aftuh, closely followed by ole Mistuh Shostac, whut succumbed fum a sudden chill he cotched while horseback ridin'. Dis suttinly been a day jam-packed wif incident. (*Bridget re-enters. Her eyes flash fire as she sees Cudgo.*)

BRIDGET: Whisht, ye ould crow, g'wan with yiz! Don't yiz know Oi'm in charge of th' exposithory dialogue?

CUDGO (*blazing*): Drat yo' impudence, young 'ooman. Ah's been raisin' de curtain an' 'stablishin' de premise ebber sence de plays ob Dion Boucicault, an' Ah ain' gwine countenance no sass fum po' white trash!

BRIDGET (*with a shrug*): Alannah, ye needn't be afther givin' me the hard wurrd; there's enough for us both. Have yiz heard th' great news?

CUDGO: Yo' mean in regahds to Whitney recoverin' his sight through de ministrations of dat beautiful young nurse, which ain' no mo' a nurse dan yo' foot but is really a debutante dat tired ob leadin' a frivolous life?

BRIDGET: Th' same. Well, th' marriage has proved th' makin' of th' young omadhaun. He soon gave up his wild cronies, shouldered th' responsibilities of th' vast Shostac domain, and it says in this paper he'll soon be inthroducin' his daughter Linda to society.

CUDGO: Hit's too bad Miz Brenda, which Ah done dandle on mah knee as a pickaninny, cain't be heah fo' dat notable event, but Ah spec's she daid or sumpin'. Ah often wonduh whut become ob dat li'l boy ob hers aftuh Grimes left her 'thout no reso'ces in Champaign, Illinois.

BRIDGET: Little boy, is it? It's th' grown man Peter Grimes is an' a murtherin' Red radical to boot, bad 'cess to him, causin' disaffection in his uncle's facthories and shipyards an' settin' capital an' labor at each other's throats.

CUDGO: Linda Shostac sho' gwine break she pappy's heart fallin' in love wid sich a man.

BRIDGET: Oi'm afraid th' fat's in th' fire already. Bedad, there's th' tillyphone. Oi was just wonderin' what was holdin' it up. (*Answering it*) Yis? Phwhat's that ye say? . . . Will you give us a moment to regain me composure as ye've knocked th' wind out of me sails intirely? . . . Ye say Peter Grimes has called off th' shtroike in th' shipyards an' Whitney Shostac has consinted to his daughter's union with Peter as well as appointin' the latter giniral manager of th' vast Shostac domain? The saints preserve us, this comes as considherably of a surprise.

CUDGO (*chuckling*): He! He! He! Whut Mistuh Whitney doan know is dat de couple been secretly married all dese yeahs.

BRIDGET (*beaming*): Shure now, he'll forgive the headsthrong pair when he sees the darlint grandchild they've prisinted him with, an' her with thim eyes bluer than Killarney's lakes an' th' flaxen hair ripplin' down her back th' loikes of an angel. Well, toime certainly flies. Here it is 1942 an' Oi still haven't fixed the flowers for th' party th' three ginirations is havin' in this very room tonight afther th' curtain falls. Will Oi be seein' yiz at th' matinée tomorrow, Cudgo?

CUDGO (*morosely*): Ah doan know ef Ah's gwine get heah. Ah took de mis'ry powerful bad jist as we wuz roundin' 1900.

BRIDGET: Faith, why don't yiz stay in bed then an' phone th' dialogue in?

CUDGO: Ah will, ef hit doan make no diff'unce to yo'.

BRIDGET (*as the creditors swarm on stage and start dismantling the set*): Macushla, Oi'm afraid it don't make no difference to *anybody*. (*They exit sadly for a season in summer stock.*)

CURTAIN

Who Stole My Golden Undies?

Thumbs hooked into my waistcoat and feet squarely planted on the hearth, a sensation of utter beatitude flooding me from crown to toe, I stood in my new sublet at 61 Brasenose Mews in Mayfair that sunny autumn morning, a man at ease in Zion. Every detail fitted my preconception of the ideal flat for a three months' sojourn in London—the snug living room, with its Adam mantelpiece and well-polished brass, the delicate mahogany oval of the dining table, the tasteful mirrors, the sparkling rows of glassware in the closet bar. What if the tangerine lampshades and silver upholstery were early Evelyn Waugh, what if floral wallpaper had run riot in the bedrooms and the telephone lurked under a hoopskirted Dresden-china shepherdess? It all evoked a certain nostalgia, as though Basil Seal and Brenda Last and Lady Metroland had circulated through these rooms and might be reincarnated at the parties I foresaw. Even Leatherby's, Ltd., the sales garage below that trafficked in opulent second-hand motors, struck the proper jaunty note, and, if further cachet were needed, my windows overlooked the rear entrance of Annabel's, the playground of the overprivileged.

Yes, one might well preen himself at finding such a jewel, I reflected, thinking back on the rookeries I had canvassed in my search for a pied-à-terre. There was the basement den off the

Fulham Road tenanted by two Picassoesque giantesses in night-gowns who kept drunkenly beseeching me, amid a reek of fish-and-chips, to applaud the shadow box they had evolved from an orange crate. There was the sixth-floor aerie in Swiss Cottage Road, where a mad Rumanian graphologist resembling Zip the Dog-Faced Boy offered me a free handwriting analysis along with the lease. And the Primrose Hill bed-sitter, whose landlady admitted in a burst of candor that her garden was frequently invaded by coypus, large South American aquatic rats from the Regent's Park Zoo nearby.

Serene as my occupancy of Brasenose Mews had been thus far, though, the truth was that one irritating domestic compli-cation had arisen—the refusal of every laundry I dealt with to collect and return my linen at a definite, fixed time. Inexplic-ably, almost as if they feared prosecution under the Official Secrets Act, they all persisted in a tight-lipped silence about their schedules. Time and again, I wasted entire mornings waiting for vans that failed to materialize, fretting myself into a lather that seriously endangered my blood pressure. Even when I managed to reach someone in authority—usually a female of awesome refinement—and to protest this enslavement to a driver's whim, I was met with the same silken answer. "But surely you've staff there to cope with such details?" she would rejoin. "How curious! All the previous tenants at Sixty-one employed staff—Brigadier-General Pouncefoot, Viscountess Bulstrode, Ian Murrain of That Ilk, the Graf Frobenius zu Strabismus. Well, in that case, I'm afraid we can't accept you as a client any further. So sorry."

At last, through the intercession of friends to whom my grievance was assuming the proportions of paranoia, I was put in touch with an establishment that promised heartsease. Not only was Hackamore's in Kentish Town prompt and civil in handling my application but the leaflet enclosed in their initial delivery bespoke a desire to cooperate to the fullest. "For the convenience of certain customers," declared the text, "laundry is sometimes collected from and delivered to a prearranged place outside the security of the customer's home." The words lifted a weight from my spirit. Here was the perfect solution to my dilemma—a bunk or hideout known only to the two of us, where I could deposit or withdraw *sans peur et sans reproche*. I fumbled the phone out of the Dresden-china shepherdess, asked for the manager, and found him completely sympathetic.

"I see from your sponsor's letter that you enjoy guest privileges at the Garrick Club," he said. "Would you consider entrusting your bundle to the hall porter there?" A presentiment of myself for all the world like a Chagall peddler airborne over the portals of the Garrick with a sackful of wash arose before me, and I demurred strongly. "Quite, quite," he acknowledged. "Then how about some tradesman's in your vicinity? This bookshop in Curzon Street, where you've had an account for years?"

"No, no, entirely out of the question," I said. "Mr. Buchanan's a dear man, but I couldn't ask a bibliophile to keep track of my shirts. I mean, it would be like asking a shirtmaker to—to look after my bibelots," I finished lamely.

"Yes, that would be hard cheese," he agreed. "I say, what's wrong with using the car dealers underneath your flat—Leatherby's?"

Frankly, it was an inspiration, and the garage's response when I asked their typist if I might impose on them was unhesitating: they'd be delighted to accommodate me. The system worked flawlessly, beyond my wildest expectations. Every Monday, ulcer-free and cool as a cucumber, I sauntered unhurriedly downstairs with my laundry box, and every Friday there it lay awaiting me—collars wrinkled, buttons ground to powder, and shirtsleeves in ribbons. But such trifles were as thistledown—the vital, the paramount thing was that I was liberated, out of bondage, free to come and go as I chose.

Or so I fatuously thought until the October afternoon I was packing my bag for a weekend in Northamptonshire. In the rush of several earlier appointments, I had neglected to pick up Hackamore's box from the garage, and since I acutely needed a couple of dress shirts, I hastened down to retrieve it. To my dismay, the sole person visible was a spotty youth polishing a drophead Bentley coupé, who revealed that the typist had gone off to Paris with her chum that morning and that he himself had seen no box such as I described. However, he added, maybe Mr. Satchmole, their salesman, who was out demonstrating a Lamborghini at the moment, could enlighten me on his return. I began to feel the old familiar churning in the tripes, the constriction that portended trouble, and quickly rang up Hackamore's in Kentish Town. The manager, regrettably, had left for Portugal that morning, also with a chum, and inasmuch as he hadn't confided our secret arrangement to his deputy, the latter was powerless to aid me. He suggested, though, that if I could wait until the drivers got back to the plant at nightfall . . .

"Nightfall! Nightfall!" I shouted into the receiver. "Don't you realize, you dunderhead, that I'm trying to catch the four-fifteen to Birchstone? How can I if you don't find my night-shirts?"

"Nightshirts?" he repeated, mystified. "But you said before they were *white* shirts—stiff-bosomed ones. Could you give me the ticket number again?"

Fortunately, at that juncture Mr. Satchmole bounced into the garage—a pudgy, effusive citizen with an air of false cheer. My laundry box had indeed arrived, just as he was departing with his client, and he had cannily placed it in the boot of the Lamborghini for safekeeping. With an uprush of elation, I wheeled about to reclaim it, but he caught my arm. There was a slight hitch, he stammered; the fact was, Mr. Rowbottom had taken the car home to Bishop's Stortford for a weekend trial.

An anguished sob burst from my throat. "Of all the fat-headed, idiotic—"

"I know, I know," he blubbered. "I remembered the box too late, after he'd driven off. But I'll call him straightaway—we'll have it back safe and sound Monday, never fear. He's a splendid gentleman, is Mr. Rowbottom—a Hebrew, I think, but straight as a die—"

I ignored his panegyrics and thought furiously. Bishop's Stortford was on the northern line, midway to Birchstone, my destination. It was quite conceivable that one could stop there, pick up the laundry, and catch a later train onward. Hastily jotting down Rowbottom's address, I ran upstairs for my bag, sped through the maze of streets to the tube station at Green

Park, and reached Liverpool Street, streaming with perspiration, in the nick of time for the four-fifteen.

Needless to say, nothing resembling a cab was visible at Bishop's Stortford, but my fevered supplication to an official at last produced an old party, clearly afflicted with St. Vitus's dance, who undertook to ferry me to Rowbottom's, eleven miles distant. Mon Repos, his Elizabethan brick cottage, nestled in a lofty beech copse well off the main road, and, judging from the array of cars ranged outside, some sort of bash was in progress. The butler who commandeered my bag propelled me into a smoky, low-ceilinged room where two dozen guests were noisily congregated, pressed a Martini into my hand, and vanished before I could explain myself. Deafened by the tumult, I wove through the crush, vainly trying to elicit the whereabouts of the host. None of the folk I questioned—a leggy young model in fringed buckskin, a gaitered divine redolent of Courvoisier, and a willowy pouf sporting a monocle—appeared to have heard of him. Each of them, however, was insistent on replenishing my glass, and when a large, bland individual on the order of Godfrey Tearle approached and identified himself as the person I sought, I could sense that my enunciation had lost its usual clarity. For the life of me, I was unable to fit Leatherby and Lamborghini into the same sentence.

"Suppose we continue this in my study," he said, guiding me into an adjoining chamber. "Now then, sir, what the devil is the meaning of this intrusion? Exactly who are you?"

My head had cleared and I could not repress a smile at the fellow's coolness. "Let's not bandy words, Rowbottom. Are you the chap to whom Leatherby's in Brasenose Mews loaned a certain Italian sports car early this afternoon?"

"Why is that any business of yours?" he snapped.

"Because along with the car you took something else—something that concerns me intimately," I threw at him. "In fact, I suggest to you that it was my fiber box in the boot you were bent on acquiring rather than the Lamborghini."

"Have a care, laddie." The corners of his mouth twitched in a manner that boded ill. "You're quite positive I'm the cove you had in mind?"

"There's one way to prove it," I said. "The man I'm looking for lacks the third fingertip of his left hand."

His smile became catlike. "You mean like this?" he asked, and held up a finger with the tip missing.

"Precisely," I said, and paused, the better to marshal the charge I was preparing to launch. "Tell me, Rowbottom, have you ever heard of an organization called the Thirty-nine Gyps —a worldwide conspiracy aimed at the confusion and over-throw of everyone's sanity by deliberately misplacing his laundry?"

Had I dreamt that a man of his girth could move so swiftly, I daresay I might have sidestepped his onslaught, but it came too suddenly. The blow he loosed at me would have felled an ox; luckily, it struck the breast pocket in which I was carrying Hackamore's leaflet describing their types of service, so that its force was minimized. The split second Rowbottom needed to recover his balance proved my salvation. Thrusting a chair into his path, I sprang past him, wrenched open the French win-dows, and dove headlong into the shrubbery. As I scrambled through the great beeches encircling the house, I heard excited voices from within, a hue and cry in the courtyard, and engines revving up to give pursuit. I doubled back, veered off at a right angle, and, after slogging through interminable fens, fetched up muddied and breathless at a secluded inn. From which, thanks to a five-pound note discreetly slipped to the publican, I was enabled to proceed in the sidecar of his son's motorcycle to Bishop's Stortford, and thence, belatedly, to Northamptonshire.

Frankly, there were those among the company that weekend who betrayed some skepticism at my account of the cabal I had unearthed. I did not altogether blame them; in a Mod dinner jacket two sizes too large for me, worn over a Chimmie Fadden gooseneck sweater, I was not a figure to inspire confidence. In fact, by the following midweek I myself had begun to succumb to doubts, when the scarehead "EXCLUSIVE LAUNDRY IN ASHES" leaped out at me from my morning paper. The particulars were brief, their significance unmistakable. The night before, a fire of mysterious origin had gutted Hackamore's in Kentish Town, holder of royal patents innumerable, destroying quantities of aristocratic linen along with all the firm's records. I permitted myself a grim chuckle. So Rowbottom and his confederates had gone to this extremity to cover their tracks, I mused. Or possibly the entire story was a fabrication—perhaps they had printed just one copy of the newspaper, hoping to lull me into a false security. Well, whatever the case, the skirmish had taught me another invaluable lesson about the forces pitted against an American and his laundry. I emptied the contents of my hamper into the bathtub, drenched them with Albion, the foamier, more perfidious detergent, and rolled up my sleeves.

Slow Down—Dangerous Footlights

Apart from flensing whales aboard a factory ship in the Arctic, or pedaling a pyramid of fellow acrobats on a unicycle across the high wire, few professions seem to me more grueling than that of the actor. To spend one's waking life haunting producers' offices in search of a part; to subsist on endless containers of coffee in darkened theaters awaiting some director's pleasure; to rehearse with no assurance that the play will last beyond opening night—what other calling requires so much stamina and dedication? Only a person with Joblike patience, the most sanguine outlook, and the constitution of an ox could withstand the erosion of a stage career. And, as if the actor's existence weren't already rigorous enough, indications have been forthcoming lately that his very life may be in hazard. Yes, alarming though it sounds, under certain conditions the poor soul runs the risk of mayhem, if not total annihilation.

The first of these portents appeared in, of all places, the *Irish Times,* and read as follows: "The French actress Madeleine Robinson's allegedly too earnest rendering of the angry wife in Edward Albee's *Who's Afraid of Virginia Woolf?* will cost her 75,000 francs (£6,250) if a Paris court grants her partner's demands. Raymond Gerome, who played opposite her at the Paris Théâtre de la Rénaissance from 1964 to 1966, has sued her for damages, claiming that he suffered a nervous break-down and finally had to give up his part. Mlle. Robinson, his lawyer told the court, added her own insults to the script and threw a shoe at him harder than was necessary." Exactly how hard the script specified that the shoe be thrown, and whether Mlle. Robinson auditioned her insults in court to prove they were up to Albee's standard the dispatch neglected to say. It was abundantly clear, though, that everyone who saw that Paris production got his money's worth and more.

Quite as significant, and illustrative of the perils that lie in wait for the mummer, was an item from the other side of the world, in the *New York Times,* which ran thus: "JULIUS CAESAR ROLE PROVES 'TOO BLOODY' FOR AN ACTOR. Melbourne, Australia (AP)—The stabbing scene in *Julius Caesar* was just a bit too lifelike, or deathlike, for Brian Muir, an actor. Playing the Roman emperor, Mr. Muir slumped to the stage floor after being stabbed. 'Blood' from bags hidden in his clothing flowed freely—and so did his own. His assailants had wielded their knives too enthusiastically, wounding Mr. Muir in the arm. A tourniquet stemmed the flow sufficiently for him to continue through the next scene." Here again the report is woefully incomplete. One wonders what engendered so much zest in Muir's colleagues. Was it merely high spirits or was there a substratum of professional jealousy? I suppose we shall never know. Those Australians are a close-mouthed lot.

Between ourselves, such contretemps are no great revelation to me; I learned years ago, at first hand, how dangerous a path the actor treads. The circumstance that brought it about was a revue I was involved in produced by a social butterfly named Thurston Murk. Both in appearance and in disposition, Murk was the embodiment of George Randolph Chester's Get-Rich-Quick Wallingford. A natty, bibulous individual whose facile charm concealed a wide streak of larceny, Murk specialized in promoting funds from Park Avenue friends to back his Broad-way ventures. In *Pousse-Café,* as the revue was called, he scored what he regarded as a dazzling coup—he persuaded two wealthy families who had feuded through an entire century to invest in the show. For its components, he similarly bamboozled a composer, a lyricist, a scene designer, a choreographer, and myself, the author of the sketches, with visions of a run longer than *Chu Chin Chow* and fabulous royalties.

Like most theatrical enterprises, this one began on a note of optimism so shrill as to be nearly deafening. Everybody agreed that the songs and skits were inspired and that the stars chosen to headline the show, Robby Spark and Lily Beecham, would draw capacity audiences even if they were to read portions of the telephone book. (At Murk's insistence, I tried writing a skit on that theme, but it failed to jell.) Spark was a dynamic bantam of a man, a graduate of burlesque and vaudeville, whose stage makeup consisted of painted spectacles, a canary-colored box coat, and a cane with which he thwacked the scenery and bystanders indiscriminately. Miss Beecham, in contrast, was the epitome of elegance—a pert and saucy creature of unshakable aplomb, who could utter a low-comedy line with bombshell effect. Both of them expressed unrestrained delight at their material; not since the days of Gilbert and Sullivan, they assured the composer and the lyricist, had performers been entrusted with songs as melodious or words as scintillating. As for my contribution, our principals professed themselves unable to read their dialogue without doubling up with merriment. Each took me aside to express wonder at my artistry, which I gathered was awesome. Altogether, it looked as if *Pousse-Café* was off to an auspicious start.

By the second week of rehearsals, the picture had altered considerably. Michael Molesworth, a drama professor Murk had imported from Idaho State University to direct the piece, was visibly overwhelmed by the assignment. Though he had won numerous plaudits in academic circles for his revivals of Hauptmann, Wedekind, and Strindberg, the complexities of assembling a Broadway revue unnerved him. Endeavoring to exert his authority, he rejected half the score, infuriating its creators, and provoked fits of hysteria in the choreographer, a stormy Russian lady, with the charge that her ballets were plagiarized from *Chauve-Souris*. Of my sketches only one remained, Molesworth having pronounced the rest coarse and humdrum and substituted in their stead five poetic playlets by

Percy MacKaye and Lady Gregory. His panic naturally communicated itself to the company, with disastrous results to its discipline. Members of the cast stood about like Talmudic scholars, debating the validity of lines, musical passages, and dance steps. Spark and Miss Beecham, frightened that a debacle was impending, sent out appeals for the management to intervene. Murk, however, could not be reached. The two families backing the show had revived their feud, each threatening to withdraw its investment as long as the other participated, and Murk was feverishly trying to mollify them. Eventually, he was able to arrange some kind of shaky accommodation, Molesworth was replaced by a breezy character named Dink Feigenspan, and the revue lumbered into its third week of rehearsals.

One of the skits that Feigenspan brought with him—though practically illiterate, he prided himself on being a writer—and that, in the event, almost proved our stars' undoing, dealt with an Alpine encounter between Miss Beecham, a mountain climber lost in the snows, and a St. Bernard, portrayed by Robby Spark. So rich were its comic opportunities, Feigenspan convinced Murk, that the producer ordered a dog suit, complete with a little cask of brandy, costing nine hundred and fifty dollars. Normally, the costume would not have been available until the dress parade out of town, but Feigenspan insisted on Spark's rehearsing in it, and, thanks to a huge bonus, it was finished in forty-eight hours. Two seamstresses arrived with the suit, prepared to make any necessary alterations.

"Hey, wait a minute," said Spark after a critical inspection. "Don't the mouth open? How am I supposed to smoke my cigar?"

"Robby," Feigenspan besought him patiently. "It's not believable, a dog smoking a cigar."

"But a dog that talks is believable?" Spark countered. "Now, get this, Feigenspan. I've always been identified with a cigar. The public expects it, just like my glasses. As a matter of fact," he went on, "better have some painted on that before we open, else nobody'll ever know I'm in there."

"Sweetheart, the more legit you play it, the bigger the yocks," Feigenspan pleaded, struggling to control his temper. "I guarantee by the time the curtain goes up the civilians'll be laughing so hard that it won't matter who's in there."

As the import of Feigenspan's words sank in, Spark turned pale with outrage. "Oh, it won't?" he exclaimed. "You mean that any thirty-five-dollar-a-week actor inside could get the same reactions?"

The director, realizing his *gaffe,* hurried to extricate himself. He poured honey and balsam over Spark's ego and implored him to don the costume so it could be properly fitted. After endless fussing with the network of zippers, the seamstresses finally encased him in the suit, made a few minor adjustments, and departed. The problem of simulating an Alp was solved by Miss Beecham's posing on a stepladder, and Spark began to frisk about, rolling in the hypothetical drifts and trailing the climber to her perch. Because of his posture and his limited vision, unfortunately, he gamboled too close to the ladder and overturned it. With a shriek, she hurtled down onto the stage apron, hung there for a perilous moment, and dropped into the orchestra pit. Hearing her outcry but unable to see the cause, Spark stood up and groped his way forward.

"What's the matter? What happened, Feigy?" he called out, teetering on the edge of the apron.

"Don't move!" the director shouted, overcome with anguish. "Stay where you are, Robby, for God's sake!"

The warning came a shade too late, however; Spark was already airborne, and a second later crashed into the pit beside the comedienne. Inexplicably, neither sustained more than lacerations, but that was the end of the sketch.

Though a bit downcast by the misadventure, Feigenspan soon rallied. "To tell you the truth, I never had much faith in that shtick," he confessed to Spark when the session resumed. "It was too broad. You need something subtle—something that pokes fun at our current fads and foibles."

"That's what I've been saying all along," declared Spark. "Remember that Civil War idea I had a few days ago?"

"I remember," I put in, since I happened to be standing there. "Your notion was to show Ulysses S. Grant at Appomattox just as he's recovering from a hangover. Lee and his staff arrive to surrender and Grant offers to wrestle him to see who wins the war. Then they peel off their greatcoats, revealing themselves in blue and gray trunks."

"Say, that's a hell of an idea—" Feigenspan began enthusiastically.

"You bet," I said, "but someone else thought of it first, and wrote it all down. His name was Thurber."

"So what?" Feigenspan retorted. "Did he invent the Civil War? Does he have a patent on Grant and Lee? Don't listen to this Calamity Jane, Robby—we'll put it on the way you said, and, mark my words, it'll be a sensation!"

"Right," said Spark, rubbing his hands. "Now, like you said, Feigy, this has to be really legit. The first thing to do is find a professional wrestler to coach me. Get me somebody like Wladek Zbyszko or Joe Stecher."

A professional was found, and Spark became so proficient that on opening night, in Boston, he and his adversary wrestled nine minutes while the theatergoers slept peacefully in their chairs. The contest might have lasted longer except that he dislocated an elbow and his collarbone. Miss Beecham didn't fare much better. On our second, and final night, she had finished a recitative, daintily hoisted her evening gown, and was roller-skating across the stage when she caromed into a floodlight and lost several teeth. *Pousse-Café* never got to New York, but Thurston Murk got as far as Costa Rica before his backers extradited him. The rest of the cast, and those of us on the so-called creative side, wound up insolvent, but at least with a whole skin. Which, everything considered, is a darn sight more than your average thespian can expect nowadays.

The Pen Is Mightier—
and Also Pricier

Look, I'm a bluff and hearty straightforward sort, and I shan't beat about the bush. The whole affair would never have happened except for this damnable kink in my nature. Generosity is kind of a fetish with me. I'd give you the shirt off my back, anything I owned, if you took a fancy to it. You know those Arab chieftains which they're constantly pressing their white stallions on people who admire them? (The stallions, that is. The chieftains are odious.) Well, that's me, only I carry it to extremes—I mean, I really do. I daresay I'd have cabbage galore in the bank if I were a bit more mean-fisted, but one can't alter his nature, can one? I mean to say, I'm that way and I've got to live with it. It's my besetting sin. I mean, I'm besotted with it.

Well, anyhow, the thing actually began over a year ago in London, just before Christmas. An unbearably chintzy advertisement I came upon in the *Times* portrayed a hand holding a gold fountain pen, its clasp surmounted by a diamond the size of your pinkie. Underneath was the endearing caption "The one-thousand-guinea Sheaffer. Golden elegance from Sheaffer —perfected with a diamond. For the discriminating and very wealthy at 1,000 guineas ($2,520). This is one of a wide range of the finest pens, pencils, and ballpoints. . . . All are specially packed and ready for giving. See them at your nearest Sheaffer stockist."

Now, at that juncture two factors militated against my visiting my Sheaffer stockist—first, the few friends in Britain who rated so sumptuous a gift already had fountain pens, and, second, if I'd added up all the lolly I could muster it would have come to just under $140. So, thought I to myself, I'll just throw 'em a sop—an egg timer or a pair of panty hose; a stopgap, as it were—and next Christmas, by George, I'll knock their eye out with a thousand-guinea Sheaffer. Well, sir, a few months later, while awaiting my turn in the laundromat at the Connaught Hotel, I fell into conversation with an amiable chap who proved to be a Sheaffer executive, and when I chatted him up about his product he gave me the scam on the pen. Apparently, some oil-rich sheikh in Trucial Oman had conceived the idea of a solid gold stylus garnished with a seven-carat rock and had ordered a dozen as gifts. Shortly afterward, a Parisian belly dancer revealed in a press interview that she had received such a pen for unspecified services. (Is it all clear thus far, or am I going too fast for you? Well, *nil desperandum,* because now comes the riveting part. Take a firm grip on the sides of the roller coaster.)

It seems that Harrods, London's well-known department store, chose to put one of the thousand-guinea pens on display in an elaborate Perspex case, brilliantly floodlit and securely locked. It was marveled at, yearned for, and salivated over, and one day shortly a rather grotty individual, manifestly a hippie, accosted the clerk in charge. Was it at all possible, he inquired, to supply the pen with a platinum barrel instead of a gold one? Coming from a manifest schlep, the query was a trifle suspicious, but inquiries were put forward and the putative client was informed that the price would be approximately four times that of the sample. A knot of other folk had meanwhile clustered around the exhibit. The young man reflected for a bit and, announcing that he would mull over the matter, departed. An hour or so thence, an elderly lady with a string bag—the role usually played by Margaret Rutherford—approached the case. She peered into it, and then squeaked tremulously to the clerk, "But it's gone!"

"What's gone, Madam?" he said, giving her the amused-eyebrow routine warranted to pulverize the customer.

"Why, the p-pen," she said. "It was there when I first looked, but it's gone now."

The clerk majestically unfurled his arms and strolled over to the display. An instant later, and white with anguish, he was frantically summoning the store's security police. Their interrogation of the old party disclosed that some time earlier she had observed an ill-favored type fussing about the rear of the case. Too terrified to inform on him for fear that if he overheard he might wreak vengeance on her, she had retired for a cup of tea before revisiting the display.

"Great Scott!" the clerk burst out to the chief shamus. "That hippie—I knew in my bones the man was dishonest!"

A description was immediately broadcast, and within hours the suspect had been picked up and the darbies clapped on him. There was, however, one hitch: he was a reigning pop star in Glasgow, and his interest in the pen had been altogether legitimate. The air instantly grew sulphurous with allegations of false arrest, humiliation, and damaged charisma, but groveling apologies from the management restored his *amour-propre,* and all became serene. The actual thief, though, was never apprehended, and after a long-drawn-out insurance wrangle Harrods and Sheaffer were forced to absorb the loss in equal shares.

I steadied myself with an Armagnac. "And how many of these—ah—doodads have actually been sold?" I asked my informant.

"In all, fourteen around the world," he replied, drying his wetwash with a goblet of V.S.O.P. "It's an O.K. pen, but if you intend to get one I'd reserve it for dress wear. The diamond rather diminishes the sobriety of your morning coat and bowler."

Well, to get on with it, the stars in their courses revolved, deep summer gave way to the harvest, and ere long the present holiday loomed up before me. How was I going to repay certain people who had been extraordinarily gracious—in particular, one lady who had wined and dined me to repletion, entertained me repeatedly at her country house over the years? Foraging up and down Bond Street, the Burlington Arcade, the hushed precincts of Mount Street, where cat-footed salesmen, obsequiously washing their hands, strove to palm off rare netsuke and fertility symbols from Luristan, I became gloomier by the moment. She *owned* all this jazz. Her dwelling was filled with objets d'art: Gainsboroughs elbowed each other off the walls—she was *boiserie*-poor. And then, like a thunderclap, came the memory of that pen of pens—the thousand-guinea Sheaffer. But, of *course*—here was the gift supreme, the ultimate *bonne bouche*. I pictured Lady Francesca's long, tapering fingers, so soft and yet powerful as a strangler's, curled around the golden barrel, the diamond flashing like the Hens-and-Chickens lightship off Boston Harbor as she dashed off letters to me more graceful than the Marquise du Deffand's, instinct with wit and scholarship and ever the promise of dalliance in her cabinet. Yep, this was it, Charlie. No time for halfhearted gestures, for measly little flacons of Joy or scarves by Yves Saint-Laurent. "Back to the days of the Regency, when a man could ruin himself for a woman!" I cried, leaping into a cab and bidding the driver make haste for Lozenge's, the haughtiest stationer's on Bond Street.

Midafternoon of the ensuing Friday, I was seated in the 4:09 express to Wolverton, bound for the Christmas jollities at Hopscotch, Lady Francesca's seat in Northamptonshire. Chained to my wrist was a pouch like a diplomatic courier's, within it my offering nestled in a blue velvet jewel case. By now, the rigors attending its purchase had dimmed—the skepticism about my solvency, the microscopic examination of passport and work permit, the endless phone calls to bank managers, embassy, and tailors, the notes of hand whereby I undertook to pay the balance of nine hundred guineas over the next three years. What mattered aught, save that I was speeding toward Francesca with a present I was confident would dazzle her? A strange and dizzying sense that I was Edward VII on his way to the Countess of Warwick overcame me. Suddenly regal, I lay back in my carriage and stroked a nonexistent beard. And yet, before the train had whizzed past Watford Junction, I was assailed by doubts. Was the gift perhaps too pretentious? Francesca, of course, would never possibly intimate it, patrician that she was. But might not some of her other guests, betraying their scorn by no more than the flicker of an eyebrow like the clerk's, decide that I was a coarse-grained parvenu seeking to ape his betters and put me in Coventry? My hands grew clammy at the prospect, and I stared unseeingly at Hemel Hempstead, Leighton Buzzard, and Bletchley as the express roared past them.

Fortunately, nobody showed up to meet me at Wolverton, so that I forgot my agitation in lugging the suitcase and pouch half a dozen blocks to the nearest taxi. During the thirteen-mile ride to Hopscotch, I evolved a shrewd plan for avoiding any charge of ostentation. I would subtly lead the table talk at dinner around to the subject of writing—the first faltering efforts of cavemen, the evolution of alphabets, the growth of Chinese calligraphy, and the like—and later mingle the thousand-guinea pen with the pile of ballpoints, pencils, and crayons on Lady Francesca's buhl desk in her study. The instant she sat down next morning to indite one of her matchless notes, her eye, keen as a Brahmany kite's, would pick out the golden maverick, and then I, the donor and in future ever-welcome guest, would step forward with a polished little speech beginning, "Francesca, my dear, what gift could anyone bestow one half so precious as that beauty the gods have lavished on you, darling?"

Ah, well, it didn't turn out quite that way, curse it. During the night, some thieving s.o.b. walked off with the pen, or maybe I had a glass of port too many and mislaid it. Anyhow, the wretched thing disappeared without a trace, and of course I lost my head and started a big shauri about everybody being searched, and then a fat little person in tweeds named Miss Marple came in (played by Margaret Rutherford—my God, how that woman gets around), and she found it in the gun room, where the clumber spaniel had chewed it to bits. So of course, wouldn't you know, Lady Francesca's taken against me for creating such a row, and if I ever get invited back to Hopscotch, that'll be the day. And I have to go on paying for that bloody pen for the next three years. I wish I'd never seen that advert in the *Times*.

Don't Blench!
This Way to the Fantods

F. H. Tate, Esq.
High Housen, Hook Heath,
Woking, England.

DEAR MR. TATE:

I daresay this communication from a total stranger will mystify you. Indeed, I clearly picture you thundernook in your breakfast-struck—I'm sorry, "thunderstruck in your breakfast-nook" is what I meant—with your egg untasted, toast stiffening in the rack, and a bee from the laburnums buzzing around your jam pot. "Great Scott, Violet," I hear you exclaim, tossing my letter over to your better half. "What in perdition is this American boffin driving at? He must be bonkers." Well, I can hardly blame you; no reason why you should remember the circumstances, but they were exceptional, and since you inspired them, you're certainly entitled to an explanation.

Something like a year or so ago, you wrote the editor of the London *Times* as follows:

> Sir, Your article on "Dracula and the Vampires," December 4, recalled to me that my maternal grandfather, Louis Jelf-Petit, who knew Bram Stoker when they were both young men, used to tell me a facet of the writing of *Dracula* which I have never heard elsewhere.

The story was that Bram Stoker and a friend entered into a wager as to which could write a more horrible and frightening story. When the time limit for the wager had expired and the tales were submitted to the adjudicator it was decided that Bram Stoker had lost his bet. The other story has never been published!

I wonder if anyone more closely associated with Bram Stoker has any confirmation of this legend?

Now, let me confess straight off, Mr. Tate, that apart from horripilating as a stripling at the book and Bela Lugosi's screen version, my only association with Bram Stoker's classic was fortuitous. In 1964, at the instigation of an editor who thought there might be a story in Count Dracula's castle, I spent three weeks in Rumania searching for it. My sole clue, that it was located in a place called Bistrica, entailed two thousand miles of driving, during which I subsisted on leathery Wiener schnitzels and slept in roach-ridden beds that would have intimidated even a vampire. In the end, I unearthed three Bistricas without, however, any verification of the myth. The real Count Dracula was apparently nothing like the legend. He was a jolly, happy-go-lucky sort, liked to take a little blood now and then, sure, but definitely was no problem drinker. I wish I could say the same for the editor.

Nonetheless, central to your mention of unpublished horror stories, I *can* be of some service to you, having recently heard one that should give you a *frisson*—as gruesome a tale in its way as F. Marion Crawford's *The Upper Berth* or Montague Rhodes James's *The Mezzotint*. The protagonist was a diffident, middle-aged chap named Felix Gosling whom I vaguely recall meeting at sessions of the P.E.N. Club and the Authors' League. He had watery blue eyes, a pronounced overbite, and hair roached down to cover his incipient baldness, and he wrote picaresque novels that drew plaudits from the reviewers like "Sparkling, well-researched. A must for anyone interested in the Wars of the Roses," and "A rousing yarn of the Spanish Main. Satisfies the reader's thirst for derring-do." None of his half-dozen books had ever reached the best-seller list, but they were the kind of bilge that does well in rental libraries, and occasionally he had a windfall, as when *Laughing Cavalier,* a work in which he had drawn rather heavily on Rafael Sabatini's *Scaramouche,* was plagiarized by a Hollywood film company and Gosling collected substantial damages. He was, in short, an inoffensive, diligent hack—a salesman, as it were, in the literary department store who never aspired to be floorwalker—and his existence was as colorless as the glassfish in his aquarium in Greenwich Village.

One spring afternoon, just as Gosling had completed the seventh chapter of *Laughing Bombardier,* a romance strikingly parallel to Baroness Orczy's *The Scarlet Pimpernel,* a strange lassitude overtook him. The pages before him, the first editions and etchings by Anders Zorn lining the walls, his entire life, suddenly felt stale and devoid of purpose. He was not given to melancholia, but he knew the potential in himself and he dreaded it. Sheathing his typewriter, he made his way down Bleecker Street and turned into Mulligatawny's, a bar he sometimes patronized. The place was deserted at that hour, and Gosling, sunk in contemplation of his second Manhattan, was recovering a shred of self-esteem when he became aware of an insistent nasal voice. It was proceeding from a florid, white-haired party in a dizzying tweed jacket who had materialized on the adjacent stool.

"Down in the mouth, eh?" the stranger inquired. "How would you like to hear about the trip my wife and I made last month from St. Petersburg to Pompton Lakes, New Jersey?" Before Gosling could moisten his lips to refuse, the other plunged ahead. "Well, brother, if I'd known what we were getting into, we could have saved ourselves plenty of grief. We started out in our Pontiac bright and early on a Tuesday—no, a Thursday—yes, it must have been Thursday because we figured to spend the weekend in Charleston."

"Look, Mister," Gosling broke in. "I was just sitting here—"

Pitiless as a juggernaut, his neighbor rolled over him. "Anyway, we took Route 17-A north to Gainesville," he swept on. "About three miles south of there, the wife thought we ought to branch off onto U.S. 1, but I decided on 122 to Ocala to avoid these big rigs barreling through. I mean, it winds around hell-and-gone, all those jerkwater towns, but at least it's easier on the nerves—am I right? So we're tootling along, happy as a clam, when just past Palmdale, we meet the intersection of 47-W and the Grapefruit Trail—that's the one leading east—and end up at Cornelius. Now, at Cornelius you have a choice of Highway 8-B or Florida 177, depending on which way you're traveling. I mean they both go there, only the shorter one is really longer, if you add it up mileage-wise."

Gosling felt a cold drop of perspiration trickle down his back. "Excuse me, but your sleeve is in my drink," he said feebly. "Would you mind—"

"That was the first day," the narrator pursued relentlessly. "The next morning we headed for Duckworth on 225-J, thinking to connect with Georgia 112 and go straight through to Pflaumsburg. Well, halfway to Falcon City, it starts raining cats and dogs, so we switch to Interstate 77 . . ."

The horrid sensation that his supply of oxygen had been cut off assailed Gosling. There was a loud buzzing in his ears, the world turned dark, and he slid off the stool onto the floor, where he lay sprawled like a starfish of the genus *Echinodermata*. Aroused by the other's call for help, the bartender surfaced, cast one look at Gosling, and sped to the adjoining building for a doctor. The physician, who happened to be shaving, responded on the double, chops flecked with foam and suspenders flapping. He loosened the patient's collar and rolled back his eyelids. Then, after a cursory test of his pulse, he straightened up.

"Nothing to worry about," he said crisply. "The man's just fainted from boredom. Rub his face with an ice cube—he'll be O.K. in a minute."

The prognosis was accurate, if only in part. Within half an hour, Gosling was back in his domicile, glumly pondering the import of his seizure. To collapse in such ignominious fashion plainly meant that his resistance was low, which called for a medical checkup. Yet why borrow trouble? A day or two in the country, a change of scene might help restore his zest. He began ticking off friends to whose houses he could invite himself. The

Waxwings had young children, Nelson Broom was still convalescent from an attack of the mumps, Diana and Marvin Sweetmilk were divorcing . . . Then, miraculously, he had an inspiration—Fatima Ann Drumright.

Fatima Ann Drumright, the relict of a millionaire Buffalo insurance broker, was a patroness of the arts, the author of three sheaves of poetry visible in any remainder bin, and an indomitable huntress of literary personages. Whenever she met one, no matter how minor, she showered him with invitations to dine at her town house, to weekend at her estate in Manhasset. Thus far Gosling had always sidestepped entanglements of the sort, but the prospect of having his ego caressed while relaxing in luxury was the very tonic he sought. He began quickly thumbing through his address book.

At 11:15 that evening, Gosling sat in a high-backed Jacobean chair in Mrs. Drumright's cavernous drawingroom on Long Island, struggling to keep his eyes open as his hostess read the final canto of *Eheu Sigismonda,* a narrative poem of the Risorgimento she had composed. Clad in a shimmering purple-and-gold Fortuny gown, her massive neck encircled by rubies the size of Catawba grapes, she flung forth a braceleted arm and declaimed her clotted periods with all the magniloquence of William Jennings Bryan, the Boy Orator of the Platte. Out of the corner of his eye, Gosling saw her pet chihuahua twitch convulsively on the cushion where it lay, but his mistress was too intoxicated by the divine afflatus to notice. A sudden compulsion to yawn afflicted him, so painful that he gritted his teeth to stifle it. Mrs. Drumright paused in midsentence.

"You liked that passage, didn't you?" she boomed. "I saw you smile—it's one of my favorites, too. I'll read it again."

As she made good her threat, each syllable chewed like nougat, his hands grew clammy. The woman was an ogress, an incubus into whose power he had deliberately committed himself, and this was to be the pattern of the weekend—an endless poetry recital punctuated by haphazard meals. Desperate, he cut her short, pleading exhaustion from overwork and the need for a night's rest to properly appreciate her verse.

"Well, don't stay in bed all day," she enjoined him, visibly displeased. "There's another version of the first two cantos I want to try out on you." She reached over and pressed the boneless little canine to her bosom. "You'll take care of Mummy, won't you, José? We don't need that old sleepyhead."

An hour later, Gosling lay rigid in his room, waiting for the nepenthe tablet he had swallowed to function. His head ached and his throat was constricted in anguish at his predicament. Finally, irrigated by repeated sips of water from a carafe, the Luminal took hold and his drowsiness merged into slumber. Sometime well before dawn, he awoke feeling parched, and reluctant to switch on the lamp, crawled out of bed and groped around in the darkness for the carafe. Its cold metal surface eluded him, but his fingers dipped into some indefinable fluid and he blundered on, encountering curtains, a lampshade, several walls. Unable to quench his thirst and leaden with fatigue, he abandoned the search and lurched back into bed and oblivion.

The scene he beheld on waking the next morning extruded his eyeballs in dismay. Overturned on the flowered carpet amid a large blue-black stain was a double inkwell he remembered seeing beside the carafe. A series of inky footprints radiated away from it toward the yellow silk draperies, curtains, and wallpaper, all of which bore chilling testimony to his nocturnal jaunt. As his stricken gaze traveled around the room, noting the flecks of ink on the upholstery and bed linen, Gosling's bones turned to water. Fatima Ann Drumright would never credit this as accidental; beyond any doubt, she would interpret it as a spiteful critique of her poetry, as cold-blooded vandalism wrought by a jealous colleague. In the next instant he was on his feet, scrambling into his clothes, feverishly lacing his shoes. No time now to pen apologies or retrieve his possessions—all that mattered was flight before the misdeed was discovered. As delicately as if he were treading on spider web, he tiptoed around the trail of ink, opened the door, and with a swift glance left and right, stole down the corridor.

In the three days following his ordeal, Gosling remained indoors cut off from the world, his telephone and doorbell unanswered, his mind a maelstrom of anxiety, guilt, and fear.

Unendingly, he summoned up visions of the retaliation Mrs. Drumright was preparing—arrest for malicious mischief, damage suits that would impoverish him, denunciation *coram populo* at the Authors' League's next meeting. In the fullness of time, though, a measure of calm supervened and he began to regret his cowardice. Rather than hide like a poltroon, would it not be more manly to face the music, to seek out the woman and ask forgiveness? After all, terrible as her wrath might be, she was bound to have some compassion for human frailty, and in any event, the outcome could be no worse than the remorse consuming him.

It was in much the same mood of lofty resignation with which Sidney Carton had mounted the guillotine, therefore, that he ascended the steps of Mrs. Drumright's town house in the East Seventies that afternoon. The equine-faced butler who admitted him was frankly dubious that Madame was receiving callers, but he conducted Gosling into the library and left to ascertain. As the door closed behind him, an almost intolerable sense of panic invaded Gosling's breast. His hands trembled, his forehead mantled over with perspiration, and he felt his legs giving way under him. Tottering across the room, he dropped heavily into a leather chair. Simultaneously, a muffled squeal rent the air and he felt a small form squirm and convulsively subside under the impact of his body. Springing up, he spun around to discover Mrs. Drumright's pet chihuahua outspread on the seat, flattened as neatly as a flounder.

Well, Mr. Tate, that's pretty much the story, and if I've kept you and your good lady from your breakfast, I apologize. On the other hand, I always think that a soupçon of horror lends tang to one's mundane existence, and you certainly must, else you wouldn't have written such a beguiling letter to the London *Times.* So *bon appétit,* may your shadow never grow less, and toodle-oo from

Yours cordially,
S. J. PERELMAN

The Art Is Long,
the Crisis Fleeting

The moment Fritz Larkspur slithered into my studio that morning, his eyes crinkled up in his characteristic smirk and his voice dripping Mazola, I knew it was destined to be one of those days. Everything had been going far too smoothly; the mural for the Woonsocket Hilton was two-thirds complete, my dealer'd had a nibble from some chatelaine in Bala-Cynwyd for a portrait, and for once it looked as if I might get up Fidèle's alimony payment on time. Not that Fidèle needles me, mind you—sometimes she waits a whole hour before unchaining the process servers, and, under pressure, will accept certified checks in lieu of cash. Anyhow, I was cleaning my brushes after breakfast, scanning the mural before the model arrived, and I couldn't help but pat myself on the back. Nine out of ten painters, had Conrad Hilton commissioned them to decorate the lobby of a skyscraper motel in Woonsocket, Rhode Island, would have chosen some banal motif, like Indian sachems and Pilgrim fathers smoking the pipe of peace, a steatopygous nude pouring knitwear out of a cornucopia, or whatever. My design, contrariwise, was inspirational—in essence, the Boniface spirit subjugating the unknown. It depicted Hilton, astride a white charger on a hilltop, surveying a panorama of jewelry mills and pointing at a huge bird perched on a nearby knoll. Emblazoned across the pennon that fluttered from his standard was the device, "On this roc will I found mine caravansary." Along the base of the composition, for symmetry, I portrayed a frieze of domestic fowl and shellfish—quahaugs, soft-shell clams, etc.— and a band of colonists, under the leadership of Roger Williams, initiating the red man into the secrets of tobacco. If I say so myself, it was an adroit compromise between the brooding realism of Orozco and the luminosity of Maxfield Parrish.

At any rate, I could tell right off from Larkspur's mealy-mouthed expression that trouble was brewing. "A great conception, old boy," he said, patting my shoulder. "The organization's crazy about your mural—can't wait for Mr. Hilton to see it." Then the anxious cough I was expecting. "A couple of minor details, though. The—er—the chickens, for one thing."

"You told me they loved them."

"Oh, they do, they do!" he bleated. "But you know how conservative the brass can be. Some of the older executives felt that—well, in these troubled times, Rhode Island Reds or anything smacking of Communism—I mean, couldn't they be Leghorns or Wyandottes just as easily?"

"Relax," I said. "If they want real security-type poultry, I'll make them Plymouth Rocks. What else?"

"Nothing drastic." He hesitated. "There were one or two murmurs about Hilton's jowls. They pointed out that physique-wise as well as hostwise, he's in the pink—he plays handball, football, eyeball, noseball—"

"I'll tighten up the sag throughout," I assured him, and tapped the curve of Hilton's buttock. "As a matter of fact, I'll minimize this area as well. It's accentuated by the horse's crupper."

His gratitude was so copious that I had a devil of a time shooing him out, and by the time the model arrived and mounted his sawhorse, the morning was half shot. I'd barely striped in the brick factory walls à la Ben Shahn when Predatore, my dealer, rang up. The Bala-Cynwyd portrait was off; the prospect wanted something she could fondle instead, preferably an emerald choker. And a split second later, of course, came the cherry on the parfait: a hysterical call from Fidèle about her basset hound. The son-of-a-bitch had swallowed a rubber ball or a shoehorn or something and needed an oxygen tent. When we finally finished screaming at each other, my knees were rattling like castanets. It was all I could do to dismiss the model and dig the cork out of the slivovitz.

So just as the pressure in my temples was subsiding, there came this timid knock at the door, and a young fellow named Lewando, one of the half-dozen artists in the rear of the building, sidled in with a canvas under his arm. We'd met now and then on the stairs and he seemed mannerly enough, but I knew nothing about him or his work. After profuse excuses for his temerity, he accepted a drink, made some very flattering (and, I thought, perceptive) comments on the mural, and finally dropped his domino.

"Maybe I ought to sketch in my background," he began. "I'm from Toledo originally, but I grew up in Chicago and got my training there—at the Institute."

"I know it well. They've turned out some very distinguished artists."

"Oh, I don't mean that one," he said, blushing. "The Institute of Applied Cuisine, over on South Randolph. I took their short-order course, and a postgraduate in baking."

"But I thought you were a graphics man," I said, perplexed.

"I am. I only studied cookery so I could specialize in painting food. You know, like Teniers and some of the Dutch school, or Courbet and Cézanne. Those men, I figured, had gone back to the kitchen for inspiration, so why couldn't I do likewise—translate a juicy dish of sauerbraten, say, or a Brown Betty with hard sauce into an important visual experience?"

"Because nobody's interested, that's why," I rejoined. "All they care about nowadays is this bloody abstract stuff. Mescaline visions and slavish little copies of Mondrian and Klee."

"You said it," he concurred somberly. "Things were pretty rough after I got to New York. When the dealers saw my meatloaves and rolypoly puddings, my kebabs and Danish coffee rings, they were outraged—they called it rotisserie art. I did all kinds of hackwork to survive—frankfurter signs, display ads for cupcakes thirty feet high—always hoping for some courageous patron who'd recognize my potential. My first break was a spaghetti place in the Village that needed a mural of the Bay of Naples. I wove in a festoon of pizzas, using olive oil in the pigment so the splashes from the minestrone and salads wouldn't show. Then the Shad Shack, a seafood restaurant over on Third Avenue, gave me a wall for a finny theme, the Seven Ages of Chowder. That brought a commission from the Shanghai Zesture—an ornamental scroll of crispy noodles, egg rolls, and subgum wonton. Forgive me," he broke off apologetically. "I've abused your patience, and I didn't mean to. I just wanted your honest professional opinion of this canvas."

"Certainly. Put it up on that easel."

He extended a newspaper clipping. "Maybe you'd better read this first. That's what motivated the painting. It's from my hometown paper."

The item, abstracted from an editorial in the Toledo *Blade,* began on an abject note of self-criticism. "Something is missing from the Toledo Museum of Art," it declared. "There is no reproduction of a great, beautifully frosted layer cake—the like of which delights a grateful public in the full-page color advertisements of the makers of cake mix, cake flour, and shortening. There is a time for Rembrandt's subtle blendings of lights and shadows, or Rubens' sweeping lines and sensuous portrayals of flesh and fabrics, of Renoir's soft tones midst rich, dark contrasts, of Van Gogh's brilliant colors. But there is another time, too—a time for the overpowering beauty of line, and color, and contrast in the glorious frosted swirls and rich textures of chocolate layer cake."

"Well and bravely spoken," I applauded. "An artistic Declaration of Independence. A challenge to every American limner to fulfill his birthright, and one that I'm sure you've risen to."

Sanguine though I was, I was unprepared for what followed. The impact of Lewando's still life was so immediate, so irrefutable, that I was struck dumb. It was indescribably lovely—the cascades of luscious butter icing, poignant as music, that trembled on the perimeter of the cake, the yellow, steeply layered interior of the excised wedge, the succulent beads of frosting that adhered to the doily and inflamed one's senses to white heat. Combining a knowledge of skillet and spectrum vouchsafed to few mortals, Lewando had produced a masterpiece. I was overwhelmed.

"Great Scott, man," I exclaimed. "Do you realize what you've done here? You may have altered the whole current of modern art! This picture could be as decisive as Monet's *Dejeuner sur l'Herbe!*"

"Do you really like it?" he asked tremulously.

"Like it?" I repeated. "Does one *like* the Alhambra, or 'The Eve of St. Agnes,' or the Kamikura Buddha?" I offered him my hand. "Lewando," I said emotionally, "may I be the first to say it? You're a very great talent."

His gratitude was pathetic. "Thank you," he said, his eyes bright. "I just hope the Toledo Museum agrees with you."

"Are they considering it?"

"Their curator, Keith Dulcimer, is coming by this morning. Would you mind if he looked at it here? My own studio's so cramped—"

"I'd be honored," I said, and returned to my scrutiny of his work. "What are you calling it?"

"Just 'Carbohydrates.' Do you favor something more poetic, like—well, 'Beat Till Fluffy'?"

"I certainly do. I'd go for 'Rhapsody in Flour,' or even 'The Culinary Diamond.' "

Lewando pondered. "M-m-m, that sounds a little boastful . . ."

He broke off as the door opened and a plump hyperthyroid in a dove-gray Chesterfield entered. He carried matching gloves, a homburg, and a snakewood stick, and his pate was bald enough to have inspired that classic of social obloquy, "Too Late for Herpicide." His birdlike glance flickered around the studio, missing nothing. Then he skipped forward and flashed a brief, triangular smile. "Mr. Lewando? I'm Keith Dulcimer. Could I see the painting, please? I have a cab downstairs."

"The Medici kept theirs waiting," I was tempted to say, but Lewando found his voice first. As he began expounding his theory of food in art, Dulcimer betrayed marked impatience. Yes, yes, he said fussily, he quite agreed that a renaissance of food painting was overdue; he had, in fact, prevailed on the Toledo *Blade* to write the editorial Lewando spoke of, but he would be obliged if he might inspect the painting without further ado. Somewhat abashed, Lewando wheeled the easel about. Dulcimer stepped back a pace, cocked his Crenshaw melon of a head, and submitted the canvas to a long critical scrutiny. There was no clue to his feelings when he spoke. "Humph," he said. "Evocative. What is it?"

"Why, a cake," Lewando stammered. "A chocolate layer."

"Poppycock," the other snapped. "A chocolate layer is all dark inside—a devil's food cake. This one's white with dark frosting. Surely you don't think a museum of standing like the Toledo would put its imprimatur on such—such a hybrid concept?"

"Just a minute, you two-penny Duveen," I burst out. "Where do you get off, haranguing a friend of mine that way? He's forgotten more about baking than you'll ever learn!"

"And who are you, pray?" he said, inflating himself like a blowfish.

"I'll tell you who," I retorted. "I'm the guy who owns this studio, and I've had a snootful of expertise from pipsqueaks like you."

He jerked his head toward my mural. "Well, it's obvious you don't follow it," he said with a sneer.

"That tears it," I said wrathfully. "Get out of here before you're carried out!" Wresting a Zulu knobkerry from the wall, I made for him, but he ducked past Lewando and went squealing downstairs, his cane clicking against the balustrade. I pitched his hat and gloves after him and returned to Lewando, who sat collapsed on the divan, Veronese green around the gills.

"It's my own fault," he said lugubriously. "I should have known better than to tackle a controversial subject. I may as well go back to painting wienies."

"What kind of a pantywaist are you, man?" I demanded. "Don't let an obscure measle like that dishearten you. Fight back—make him eat his words!"

"O.K. for you to talk—you're a success," he said. "But what'll *I* eat in the meantime?"

"The dry crust of fortitude," I told him. "The same fare that has sustained every artistic visionary from Caravaggio to George Petty. Don't you realize that the Pharisees always react this way to the innovator? Your day will come, Lewando—perhaps after you're dead, but I promise you—"

"Someone's knocking at the door," he interrupted.

"Let 'em knock," I said, swept away by my fervor. "Recognition will be yours, never fear. Think of Salvator Rosa—Alma-Tadema—Nell Brinkley!"

"Excuse me, sir," said a voice from the doorway. "I was told I might find Mr. Lewando here."

One glance at the elderly party on the threshold, peering benignly through pince-nez secured by a black ribbon, sufficed to tell me that he was a connoisseur. His long sensitive fingers, caressing an aquiline nose like a bit of medieval ivory, the deliberate Bohemianism of his dress—all bespoke the fastidious collector accustomed to indulge his whim. "Pardon the intrusion, gentlemen. Are either of you the painter Lewando?"

"This is he of whom you speak," I averred.

"Then my long search is ended," he said joyfully, advancing on Lewando with outstretched hand. "Permit me to introduce myself. I am Jared Mallomar, president of Loose-Wiles, the Bakery of a Thousand Windows. At the risk of seeming headlong, I shall be succinct. My company has recently completed a fifty-eight-story building on Park Avenue at a cost of four million simoleons. Our executive offices, paneled in rich Circassian walnut and carpeted in fabulous Einstein-Moomjy rugs, lack but one thing to achieve perfection. Can you divine its nature?"

"Let me hazard a guess," I put in. "Do you perchance covet a still life of some edible object—preferably a cake—painted with such exquisite realism that it typifies your firm's cherished tradition?"

"So much so that we are prepared to pay through the nose for it," he declared, pointing to his nose and extracting a sheaf of the long green. "And unless I am very much mistaken, there is one on this here easel that for sheer impasto and brilliance of execution, not to mention downright yumminess, surpasses anything in the Uffizi. Mr. Lewando," he went on, "I bid you welcome to the company of Snyders, Herman Fogelson, and other Dutch genre painters too numerous to mention. I have prepared a little reception at the Metropolitan—the Museum, that is, not the insurance people—where some of the most illustrious figures in the bakery world and the arts eagerly wait to bleat your praises. Will you and your friend accompany me there?"

Little else remains to be told. Today the most trifling pastiche by Duncan Lewando—an éclair or a dish of blintzes—commands astronomical prices. He is married to Jared Mallomar's niece, a pretentious fat girl with presbyopia and two children by a former husband, and occupies a triplex studio on Sutton Place. As for me, the mural for the Woonsocket Hilton is coming along nicely, though Fritz Larkspur is still bothered about the hens. I think I'll recommend Rock Cornish and get Lewando to paint them—broiled, of course. It's the least he could do for me, after what I've done for *him*.

Sleep Tight, Your Honor

Pardon my buttonholing a stranger in this abrupt fashion, stranger, but would you happen to have an inkling you could spare? Not much of an inkling—just enough to straighten me out on something that's been bedeviling me lately. For instance—under what circumstances is it permissible for an English magistrate to play with a piece of string? Or when is a litigant in Britain justified in pitching a book at him? Or, alternatively, can furniture in the United Kingdom ever be sold as carrots? . . . Yes, I quite realize how bizarre these speculations must seem to you, but then it's unlikely you've been reading the law reports in the London *Times,* and even if you have you're more confused than I am. The fact is that anyone who drowses through those reports—and it takes a heap of pinching to keep oneself awake—is likely to wind up enmeshed in fantasy. The further you get the more they resemble *Alice in Wonderland* crossed with a D'Oyly Carte operetta. Could it be that, despite all evidence to the contrary, Lewis Carroll and W. S. Gilbert are alive and well?

My earliest intimation that English jurisprudence was a tangled skein was an account, in the *Times,* of a symposium of lawgivers that read thus:

> A High Court judge advised magistrates to be careful what they ate in the luncheon adjournment to avoid looking sleepy in the afternoon. Mr. Justice Lawton told 300 magistrates at the start of their training conference at

Nottingham University: "Nothing can tarnish the image of justice quicker than the appearance of somnolence. Those of us who find, or think, they can concentrate better with their eyes shut, should seek other ways of bringing their minds to bear on the case. Playing with a piece of string or sucking the mint with the hole is better than slumping in a chair with eyes closed. . . . It may be the gin and tonic, or the meat and two veg or the prunes and custard. Whatever it is, cut it out if it leaves the public in court to think you are sleepy."

Maybe it was this kind of judicial torpor, engendered by a surfeit of bangers and mash and prune whip, that aroused a lady to violent behavior in an ensuing legal action:

Miss Vera Beth Stone, aged 37, heard the Court— Lord Denning and Lords Justices Harman and Diplock —dismiss her *ex-parte* application for leave to appeal against a decision on a review of taxation. Then she picked up two books and threw them towards Lord Denning, saying that it was not a personal matter but that she hoped by this means to bring her complaint before the Court. The books—copies of Butterworth's Workmen's Compensation Cases—taken by her from the Court library, passed between Lord Denning and Lord Justice Diplock, Miss Stone saying that it did not have to be tomatoes. She was restrained as she picked up a third book, remarking that she was running out of ammunition. . . . As Miss Stone left the Court with the tipstaff, she said to Lord Denning: "May I congratulate your Lordship on your coolness under fire?"

Lord Denning's aplomb, to be sure, could have had a simpler explanation; perhaps he was so rapt in playing with a piece of string or sucking the mint with the hole that he was unaware of the books flying past. It was in a third *Times* story, however, that I became convinced I had been projected bodily into Andrew Lang's books of fairy tales. The case, headlined "Furniture Cannot Be Sold as Carrots," was rather intricate, but the salient point was that some furniture dealers had circumvented a statute forbidding their goods to be sold on Sundays. Inasmuch as British law allows the sale of vegetables on the Sabbath, the defendants opened a shop where they sold carrots, it being tacitly understood that the customer was receiving an equivalent amount of furniture. "On one occasion," the charge against them stated, "they sold a carrot for £520 and on other occasions for £20 with free gifts of furniture. . . . When a Sunday customer went to the office, he was asked if he agreed to enter into a contract to buy only a carrot to the value of the free gift selected, and he was handed a carrot."

By a dizzying coincidence, I myself was embroiled in an affair so similar to the foregoing that the ice in my veins turned to blood when I read it. Casting about for a furnished flat in London not long ago, I was shown one ideally suited to my needs. It was cozy, quiet, and altogether tip-top but for one slight detail; it was devoid of furniture other than an armchair, a Georgian shaving stand, and a bed. Miss Crackthorpe, the rental agent who accompanied me, pooh-poohed my expostulations.

"Not to worry," she said airily. "You can chink in whatever you lack—bureaus, couches, tables—at Thimblerigg & Bilk in Gudgeon Lane this very weekend. It's a wildly popular place, only open on Sundays, so be sure to get there early. Here's the address."

At eight-thirty on Sunday morning, accordingly, I raced to the shop with a list of my requirements, and straightaway ran into a predicament. Instead of the showroom I expected, the premises were a mere hole in the wall—a greengrocer's establishment displaying a rather dispirited stock of vegetables and fruit. As I hesitated on the threshold, a sharp-featured character in sleeve garters, with a bowler smartly cocked over one ear, approached from the rear. "Greetings, mate. I'm Thimblerigg," he saluted me. "Up bright and early for the bargains, eh? Well, we've got 'em. How about a nice overstuffed suite in genuine rat hide, with a bar to match? Or a Chinese sideboard of crushed mahogany that converts into a vanity? I can see from your clothes you're a trendy type."

"Well, I *was* looking for a few unusual pieces," I admitted, "but I must have strayed into the wrong—"

"Ah, yes," he said smoothly. "You didn't expect a green-grocer's shop—right? Think nothing of it. We've got exactly what you're after, but we merchandise it in a totally novel way. Take this cauliflower, for example," he said, selecting one from a bin. "That'll come to sixty-eight pounds and thirty pence. What you're really buying, though, is a kneehole desk, four kitchen chairs, a floor lamp, a hat rack, and an ironing board you can use as a stepladder. You get the idea?"

Plausible as the fellow seemed, I fortunately had my wits about me, and, sensing that he was trying to pull the wool over my eyes, retorted that I had never heard anything so preposterous. To my surprise, he agreed wholeheartedly. The principle of Sunday substitute shopping was such an innovation, he acknowledged, that it had swept Britain like wildfire, yet it was backed by an ironclad warranty, and thousands of satisfied customers bore witness to his claim.

"Here's the way it works," he went on, producing a handsomely illustrated catalogue. "You simply pick out whatever strikes your fancy, scratch your name on this agreement, and we deliver the furniture to your door in forty-eight hours. Now, which type of veg would you prefer—cucumbers, artichokes, one of these big luscious eggplants?"

Well, it was all I could do to repress a giggle. Anyone chuckleheaded enough to fall for such a yarn must be naïve indeed—and yet maybe it wasn't so fanciful at that. Miss Crackthorpe had recommended the place, the items in the catalogue seemed trustworthy—possibly I was suffering from an excess of caution. I stood irresolute for a moment, and then, gambling on my instinct, decided that I had misjudged Thimblerigg, mistaken his Cockney shrewdness for charlatanism. Selecting a divan, some end tables, a couple of mirrors, and a club chair from the catalogue, I signed a contract, handed over my check for three hundred pounds, and, in turn, was handed two cabbages, a bunch of carrots, and a bagful of peanuts and spring onions. As he escorted me to the door, Thimblerigg besought me to pester him if the furniture did not arrive as guaranteed. The watchword of the firm, he declared, was integrity, uncompromising and foursquare; without those components, any business was a mockery and a sham. And when he reached into the cab to shake hands with me the candor that shone in the man's eyes dissipated any lingering doubts. If ever I saw bluff English honesty, it was in that chap's visage.

Nine days elapsed before it finally percolated through to me that I had been yentzed and flensed to a fare-thee-well, and it was confirmed by an expert—Mr. Thaddeus Shadbolt, the bulky, white-haired solicitor to whose chambers I fled in panic when the realization jelled. Shadbolt reacted with the typical cynicism of his profession as I poured out my recital of the facile excuses given me by Thimblerigg & Bilk for their failure to deliver my purchases.

"Quite, quite," he said, drumming impatiently on his desk top. "They told you they were installing a new computer system, that their warehouse had burned down, and that they were bankrupt. The procedure is altogether ritual, classic—and so is ours. We'll lay an action for fraud against the bleeders. I needn't tell you, of course, that the courts are clogged with matters like these, and normally it'd be months before the case is heard. However, I may be able to winkle it through with a bit of influence. Just leave it with me."

Whose ear he whispered into I never learned, but on an unseasonably warm April afternoon three weeks later, the two of us sat at a table in court before a lay magistrate named Mr. Cyril Trouncer, listening to Thimblerigg's evidence in the witness box. Never, he affirmed to his counsel, had there been any undertaking on his part to supply me with furniture; his firm was a long-established greengrocer's licensed to sell produce on Sundays, and to assert that it dealt in any other merchandise was nonsensical.

Shadbolt sprang to his feet. "This is a monstrous perversion of the truth, Your Honor!" he protested. "Does the witness seriously ask us to believe that my client paid three hundred pounds for a few paltry vegetables? What kind of a simpleton do you think he is?"

The magistrate, who had been leaning back with his eyes

closed, came to with a start. "What did you say?" he demanded. "I didn't catch that. I had a fairly heavy lunch—two pints of bitter, silverside and Brussels sprouts, and gooseberry fool, and I'm a trifle sleepy." He swung around to his clerk. "Where's that length of string I usually play with? . . . Good. Now, Shadbolt, let's have that objection again."

"Oh, never mind," Shadbolt fumed. "I withdraw what I said." He resumed his seat, snatched up a pencil, and scribbled distractedly on a pad. "Damned old fogy," he muttered. "This is what comes of rushing a case through the docket. If I can't get his attention, we'll be in a hell of a fix."

We certainly would be, I surmised as Thimblerigg again began droning his bland denials. I looked around desperately for some way of vivifying the magistrate, and suddenly, in a flash of inspiration, it came to me—the thick law volume I saw peeping out of Shadbolt's briefcase. I plucked it out, stood up, and, summoning all my strength, flung it at Mr. Trouncer's head. It missed him by a good seven inches but struck a picture immediately behind, shattering the glass into a thousand fragments. There was a momentary hush, and then all was confusion. The clerk leaped forward to assist Trouncer to his feet, a constable pinioned my arms, and the half-dozen spectators in the court burst into excited babble. Shadbolt was aghast.

"Great Scott, man, have you gone bonkers?" he snarled at me. "Assaulting a Crown magistrate—you'll get three years in quod for this! Please, Your Honor, give me leave to explain. My client's an American; he's unfamiliar with our judicial process—"

Mr. Trouncer readjusted his tie, cleared his throat, and held up his hand for silence. "The Court is not interested in your explanations, my dear Mr. Shadbolt," he said with icy calm. "I'm quite capable of drawing my own conclusions, and I wish to say that in my seventeen years on the bench no litigant has ever shown such initiative, has behaved with such total disregard for legal flummery and red tape, or given so convincing a demonstration of his faith in English justice. Bring forward the plaintiff, constable, so that I may commend him."

In the electric moment that followed his words, I managed to retrieve my voice. "I—I apologize for hurling that book at you, sir," I stammered. "My motives were of the best—"

"Of course they were," said Trouncer with a kindly smile. "You saw before you an old foof, sodden with alcohol and overindulgence at table, and with characteristic Yankee ingenuity you chose the only means at your command to restore his concentration. Startling it undeniably was, but it achieved its purpose; and now that you have cleared my head, I can proceed to render a verdict proper to the evidence. I direct Thimblerigg & Bilk to repay your three hundred pounds at once and to sustain all costs in this action without benefit of appeal. And," he concluded with a twinkle, "if you and your counsel care to join me in my chambers, I can promise you a glass of the crustiest port either of you has tasted in many a moon."

Well, there it is, one man's experience with English law stripped down to its essentials, and that, parenthetically, still holds true of my furniture—a bed, an armchair, and a Georgian shaving stand. One of these days, if I can catch up with her, I must present Miss Crackthorpe with some sort of *bonne bouche,* like a nice beefsteak and a bagful of fresh vegetables, for involving me with those muzzlers in Gudgeon Lane. She can always throw away the veg, but the beefsteak should be an absolute godsend for her black eye.

Whenas in Gilt
My Julio Goes

GOLD THREAD SUIT—£250.—A cloth with a genuine
gold thread has been produced by a Yorkshire mill and a
suit made from it would cost at least £250, it was stated
today.

The cloth, trade named Golden Cashanova, is a blend
of worsted and cashmere in navy blue or dark grey with a
pin stripe of fine gold thread made by a leading London
firm of gold and silver wire drawers. . . . Mr. Walter
Otten . . . of Wain Shiell & Sons, Ltd., London woollen
merchants . . . said today: "Frankly, we have made a
cloth with snob appeal. It is the man's answer to the
women's mink coat. . . . Our customers will probably
be very wealthy people, businessmen and film stars, but
even they will have to wait. The Americans are already
after the cloth, but I have had to tell them that they can
have enough for only four suits at the moment. That is
what I call really exclusive."—*London Times.*

Of a wild and windy night this winter, any noctambule
pausing to light his cheroot (or extinguish it; it comes to the
same thing) outside a public house off Shaftesbury Avenue
called the Haunch of Pastrami might have observed two individuals of no special distinction descending from an equipage
before the premises. The elder and portlier, under whose lux-

uriant crêpe whiskers were concealed the features of Prince Florizel of Bohemia, preferred to be known as Theophilus Godall, proprietor of a cigar divan in Rupert Street. The younger, his confidant and Master of the Horse, Colonel Geraldine, passed under the sobriquet of Major Alfred Hammersmith, a currently unemployed member of the Fourth Estate. In the manner of a certain fabled Caliph of Baghdad, it was the Prince's whim, whenever threatened by *tedium vitae,* to thus disguise himself and his *fidus Achates* and to court such adventures as might befall them. The locale chosen by the pair tonight, however, seemed less than promising. None in the crowd peopling the bar was in the least eccentric or provocative in his conduct; and casting a keen glance about him as he finished his negus, Prince Florizel was constrained to remark how commonplace their existence in London had become of late.

"True, Sire," his aide concurred. "Still, it was in circumstances very like these that we encountered the young man with the cream tarts who led us into that extraordinary affair of the Suicide Club."

"Far from heartening me, your optimism only aggravates my ennui," the other returned. "There is nothing in the world so tiresome as those who persist in looking on the bright side."

"Forgive me, Highness," Geraldine apologized. "I was merely contributing some exposition to help the reader identify us—the sort of thing a housemaid is usually discovered prattling over a flower arrangement when the curtain rises."

"In that case, I withdraw the rebuke," said the Prince graciously. "But what is this? A young person, his cheek mantled by a hectic flush, has just entered, bearing a tray laden with a dozen or so hard doughnutlike discs, heavily varnished and garnished with a fishy pink-and-white substance."

"Yes, and he is importuning everybody to take one free gratis," Geraldine chimed in. "Here he comes now. What can be his purpose?"

Pausing before their table, the object of their speculation bade the duo a civil good evening in an American accent and urged them to sample his provender. "Should you be toxiphobic, I can dispel your fears at once," he told them. "I have already eaten fourteen and, apart from a slight nausea, have experienced no noxious effects."

"They are tiptop," the Prince declared, chewing one meditatively. "What are they, if I may inquire?"

"As to that, I can best respond with a brief anecdote," said the young man. "Are either of you gentlemen familiar with Rivington Street in New York?" They shook their heads. "Ah, well, no matter. It is an area rather like your Golders Green, thickly populated by a particular ethnic group whose notables range from Gyp the Blood to Spinoza. At any rate, it appears that a UFO, a flying saucer, was forced down there, owing to failure of its landing gear. The pilot, a small emerald-hued Venusian with ears like catalpa leaves, roved about until he came upon a delicatessen, the window of which contained a panful of these biscuits. Entering the shop, he indicated them and said, 'I need a couple of those wheels.' The counterman regarded him pityingly. 'Listen, greenhorn,' he said, extending one. 'These aren't wheels—they're bagels. They're meant to be eaten.' The Venusian took a bite or two and stood plunged in thought. 'You know what would be real tasty with these?' he said. 'Lox and cream cheese.' And that, in a word, gentlemen, is what you are munching at the moment."

The Prince chuckled almost as though he grasped the point of the story. "I shall not conceal from you, sir, that you intrigue me vastly," he said. "Would it be presumptuous to ask why a seemingly rational American (unless that is a contradiction in terms) is engaged in distributing bagels in so alien a milieu?"

"Not at all," replied the young man. "There is, indeed, a cogent enough explanation, but, to be candid, it involves a somewhat lengthy preface, and the hour is late."

"You have our complete attention, to say nothing of our appetite," the Prince assured him, reaching for another of the delicacies. "Not having supped yet, my companion and I will gladly liquidate the rest of these. Pray enlighten us."

"Very well," the young man acceded. "Let me begin with a query. Do you believe in the power of suggestion—specifically, in mesmerism?"

"I most emphatically do not. I consider it so much tommy-rot."

"Really? Then I fear I must differ with you, since it is my livelihood. My name is Julio Hoblitzelle."

"What!" exclaimed Geraldine in startled tones. "Not Hoblitzelle the Great, Hoblitzelle the world-renowned, Hoblitzelle the master hypnotist, who has been packing them in nightly at the Palladium to boffo grosses—"

"Enough already," the young man broke in. "Yes, I am he."

"Then I owe you a profound apology for my skepticism," the Prince averred. "I myself saw you hypnotize a chicken in Antwerp which subsequently passed through the audience and clucked out the serial number in people's watches. Is that fowl still part of your repertoire?"

"No, I ate him right after the performance," said Hoblitzelle. "But to resume my explanation. Did either of you, perchance, happen to see a jotting in the *Times* here relative to a gold-thread suit?" His auditors signified that they had. "Well, that item had a profound consequence. It set me to reflecting whether the apparel might not prove tremendously valuable to me in my profession. Up till then, in order to hypnotize a person I had asked him to concentrate on a shiny spoon, coin, candle flame, or the like. Here, though, was an absolutely infallible means of inducing the hypnoidal state. Under ordinary stage lighting, the suit would appear to be merely a garment with tiny metallic accents. The instant I stepped into a spotlight, however, the material would sparkle and shimmer like a Burmese pagoda, automatically throwing my subjects into a trance. It was so simple I was astonished that I had never thought of it before. Conceive, then, of my frustration when, on hying myself to such prestigious tailors in Savile Row as Huntsman and Hawes & Curtis and Anderson & Sheppard, I found not an inch of this Cashanova fabric available—not even a swatch. To add to my chagrin, I was reminded with a taunting smile that the supply for America had been restricted to enough for only four suits, and that Dean Martin, Liberace, and similar peacocks were offering as much as one hundred pounds a yard for the goods. So daunting was the taunting that I was ready to abandon my quest, but destiny willed otherwise. The very next evening, I happened to be dining by myself in a Turkish restaurant in Old Compton Street."

"I know it well," said Florizel. "It is called the Paunch of Hastrami. The owner is an Anatolian with a big fat belly."

"Correct," said Hoblitzelle. "Halfway through my dinner, a brash and patently offensive personage strode in, accompanied by a very pretty girl. They were shown into the booth adjoining mine, separated from me by a café curtain, and as they sat down I stiffened in surprise. The man was wearing a *gold-thread suit*. Need I tell you that from that second my meal went untasted? At first, their conversation dealt with the usual banalities—the choice of apéritifs, some heavy gallantry she evidently welcomed, judging from smothered giggles. Suddenly I was riveted; she was admiring the texture of his jacket, and he, fatuous booby, began to preen himself on his cleverness. The material was well-nigh unobtainable, he reported smugly, but he knew of a source . . . And at that exact juncture fortune smiled on me. The headwaiter's voice interrupted him, announcing that he was wanted on the phone. It was a heaven-sent opportunity, and I seized it. Allowing just enough time for him to lumber off, I extracted my silver cigarette case, thrust aside the curtain, and held it mirrorwise before the understandably astounded beauty.

" 'Do not be alarmed, lady,' I told her in a low, urgent voice. 'Just concentrate on this surface, this shining silver object. . . . No, no, not at me. Look right at the case—yes, straight at it . . . Good—perfect. You are getting drowsy . . . sleepy . . . drowsier, sleepier. . . . Oh, so relaxed . . . Fine! Now, listen to me. When your swain reappears, you will ask him where—*where*, do you comprehend?—he got that cloth. Repeat after me, "Where did that cloth come from?" . . . Right. . . . Yes, now wake up,' I commanded, snapping my fingers, and drew the curtain back into place."

"Your stratagem worked?" the Prince asked, his eyes sparkling.

"Like a charm," said Hoblitzelle. "Within five minutes after her escort returned, I had the requisite information and was speeding homeward. At eleven the following morning, in his dingy burrow in the Portobello Road, a dwarfish Pakistani tailor, richer by the sheaf of banknotes I had tendered him in advance, finished taking my measurements. That a sartorial triumph would emerge from such frowsty surroundings may seem incredible, but in fact the result was most gratifying. Indeed, when I confronted my image in the cheval glass, using a powerful lamp to study the effect of its rays on the gold thread, I was so dazzled I nearly sank into a trance myself. Hence you may imagine with what buoyancy—nay, with what glee—I awaited the première of my new costume. As luck would have it, it was a command performance at the Albert Hall. The whole Royal Family, numerous European heads of state, members of the peerage, ambassadors, and dignitaries of the court were arrayed in the boxes and stalls, and all the performers, if I may risk sounding vainglorious, were ornaments of our profession. One after the other, my colleagues went through their turns to tumultuous cheers. Never had we known an audience so appreciative, so unsparing of its applause; and when the time came for my specialty the assemblage was wax in my hands, to mold as I willed. Resplendent in my Cashanova, I sallied from the wings to a storm of handclapping, took a bow, and signaled for a spot to be thrown on me. The house blacked out, there was a flourish from the orchestra, and there I stood, the only figure visible, bathed in a cone of light."

The mesmerist paused, drew forth a handkerchief, and sponged his forehead. Openmouthed, their ears strained to catch every syllable, the Prince and his aide sat waiting for Hoblitzelle to continue. When he spoke again, it was in a tight, curiously flat voice, devoid of timbre.

"Do you know what it is like to be confronted by six thousand spellbound people? I don't mean fascinated or deeply absorbed—I mean people asleep with their eyes open."

"Are you trying to tell us—" Prince Florizel began.

"Precisely," said Hoblitzelle. "In my rapture at achieving the suit, I had underestimated its candlepower. Such was its effulgence, its sheer and blinding radiance, that the entire audience—even those already asleep—was hypnotized. The realization of what had occurred only dawned on me when, receiving no answer to my appeal for volunteers, I shaded my eyes and peered into the orchestra pit. Twenty-seven union musicians and their conductor, frozen like Madame Tussaud's waxworks, stared up at me; beyond them were row on row of mummified faces. In the same breath, the significance of the terrible power I possessed overcame me: with a few words, I could implant a command in these monarchs and ministers that would affect the lives of millions for good or evil. It was a responsibility no mortal should be vested with. I bent over the footlights, wrested the timp stick from the inanimate hand of the percussionist, and struck the kettledrum a resounding blow that freed the spectators from my thrall. Then, with the house lights on and all shimmer spent, I proceeded with my act—which, I may say without vanity, brought me the longest ovation in the history of the Albert Hall."

"Amazing! Unparalleled in my experience!" Florizel pronounced, exhaling slowly. "To think that for one instant you were as close to being divine as man has ever come! Do you agree, Hammersmith?"

"Er—yes, I certainly do," said the latter. "The only trouble is—the thing that confuses me—"

"What are you brumbling about?" the Prince demanded sharply. "Speak up, man. Get the marbles out of your mouth!"

"Well—uh—don't you remember?" Geraldine reminded him. "He still hasn't told us. I mean, why is he giving away free bagels?"

Hoblitzelle nodded patiently, gestured to the pair to lean closer, and gave them a sly wink. "I know," he said. "I was coming to that. You see, friends, it's like this. Between you and me and the lamppost, and don't breathe it to a soul, hypnotism is for the birds. It's kaput—finished—napoo. The real dough is in standup comedy—you dig? So now that you've enjoyed our little feed, I'd like to try out a couple of shticks on you. Purely for reactions." He arose, rubbed his hands, and in a plangent voice that embodied the less endearing facets of Jerry Lewis,

Alan King, and Joey Bishop, saluted the occupants of the bar: "Good evening, folks. Say, I shot a little pool yesterday afternoon and a funny thing happened on the way to the taxidermist's. Yuk, yuk. I ran into a guy named Booth, who has a booth in the diamond center, and what d'ye think? He's got a wife named Ruth, forsooth. . . ."

Watch the Birdie,
but Hire a Mouthpiece

> Another animal doctor told of the Park Avenue ma-
> tron whose parrot has its own room in her handsome
> duplex, complete with television and hi-fi set. When the
> parrot took sick, the woman canceled a trip to Paris;
> only when assured the worst was over did she make new
> plans to travel. She hired round-the-clock help to care for
> the bird during her absence, insisting she be called home
> if the bird took a turn for the worse.
> —*Claire Berman, New York Times Magazine*

It was the last night of my fleeting revisit to London, and
given a choice, the last place in the world I wanted to spend it
was a dinner party at the Wormwoods in Chester Square. I
hardly knew my hosts; we had met for an instant at a publisher's
bash the week before where, just as I was making headway with
a dazzling Titian-haired beauty aptly named Rosy Cleavage,
they had pounced on me with their invitation. So deafening was
the noise and so spectacular the lady, whom I hoped to scale
like the Matterhorn, that I nodded distractedly and shook them
off. And now, on this evening when I might have been persuad-
ing the lovely Rosy to stoop to folly, here I was, trapped between two unidentified females, both long in the tooth and
strikingly devoid of charm. Furious at the Wormwoods, but

even more at myself for being such a spineless, pliant nincompoop, I sat grinding my dentures in rage.

"The *salt*," said an icy British voice in my ear. "Might one intrude oneself on your reverie so far as to ask you to pass the salt?"

"Oh, yes—yes, of course," I exclaimed. My hand shot out, neatly overturning the shaker so that it caromed into my other neighbor's lap. "Forgive me, Miss—er—"

"Quite all right," she assured me. "I don't think we've met, incidentally. My name's Millicent Proudfoot. I'm from New York."

"So am I." As I introduced myself, I realized that my first impression had been unjust. She was a rather imposing woman in her mid-fifties, with the kind of classic features popularized earlier in the century by Charles Dana Gibson, and it was apparent to even a heterosexual eye that her gown was the last work in chic. Like myself, our chitchat disclosed, Mrs. Proudfoot was a bird of passage, en route to the States after a fortnight in Paris.

"As a matter of fact," she said, glancing at her watch, "I should be getting an overseas call from New York any moment. Someone in my household's quite ill."

"Nothing serious, I trust."

"Nobody seems to know. It's a mysterious ailment they haven't been able to diagnose as yet."

I mumbled some sympathetic bromide, and as predicted, Mrs. Proudfoot was summoned to the phone shortly. She looked so stricken on her return that I asked what the report was.

"Very bad, I'm afraid. Raimondo's nurses—he's got three around the clock—say he's unable to talk and refusing nourishment. It's silly of me, I suppose, but I'm terribly worried."

By a coincidence, I happen to be fairly skilled in these matters, having spent a year or two as a premedical student back in 1922. "That's undoubtedly the fever. What's his temperature?"

"They've tried to take it, but he won't let them."

"Yes, that's often the case in high fevers," I said judiciously.

"Still, there's no need to be alarmed if he's receiving adequate medical care."

"I'm not sure he is." The woman was plainly upset. "I may have to leave sooner than I thought—tomorrow, if I can. Do you think there might be any room on the plane you're taking?"

Well, now that I look back on it, the whole thing must have been foreordained. Half an hour later, and with profuse apologies to the Wormwoods, I was escorting Mrs. Proudfoot back to her hotel in a cab. Instead of subsiding, though, her anxiety seemed to redouble; a stream of conjecture, ever more apprehensive, poured from her lips. What if Raimondo was allergic to the medication he was receiving? What if his heart weakened through lack of nourishment? Raimondo—Raimondo—at the reiteration of his name, I finally grew suspicious. Clearly he wasn't a husband or son, since she'd referred to him as a member of her household. Could he possibly be her gigolo, one of those sleek lounge lizards rumored to cluster around wealthy women? Yes, I decided, that must be it; Raimondo was her South American cicisbeo, otherwise she never would have displayed such concern for his health.

The next morning at Heathrow, there was no sign of my dinner partner among the passengers awaiting our flight, but no sooner had we reached cruising altitude than she materialized from first class. "I was lucky, I just managed to squeeze on," she said breathlessly. "I thought you'd like to know, though— Raimondo's holding his own. The nurses say his appetite's improved since yesterday, thank God. I'll see you at Kennedy when we get in." It began to dawn on me that willy-nilly, my destiny was becoming entwined with Mrs. Proudfoot's, and the realization irked me. What kind of imbecility was this, involving myself with a society woman and her plaything—a hot-blooded Latin, moreover, who might stick a knife into me at the drop of a hat? Better steer clear of this lady, chum, I told myself, or you'll be spread out all over some dissecting room in Bellevue like a chicken in parts.

Alas for my noble resolutions—cornering me at the baggage claim in New York, Mrs. Proudfoot, in a voice husky with emotion, requested a favor. I had been so sympathetic about her trouble, so understanding of her fears; would I now lend my moral support and accompany her home? Surely I couldn't refuse this small boon in her hour of need? I listened impassively, and folding my arms, crumpled like a wet paper bag. Within the hour, the two of us were ascending in an elevator to her Park Avenue duplex.

The nurse who answered the door was as close to hysteria as anyone in my entire medical experience; only when I shook her repeatedly was she able to frame a rational response. "Raimondo!" she choked out. "He's disappeared—vanished! I looked everywhere when I came on duty—"

Mrs. Proudfoot emitted a strangled cry. "What are you saying?"

"I called the super, the janitor, but they don't know anything," the nurse blubbered. "The registry doesn't have the other girl's number. Oh, Mrs. Proudfoot, I'm so ashamed—I've never lost a patient before!"

The task of coping with two overwrought women, frankly, is not one at which I excel. Eventually, I managed to convince both, however, that sobs were unavailing and recrimination useless. Then, banishing the nurse to the kitchen, I talked to Mrs. Proudfoot like a Dutch uncle. The sooner she notified the police, the better, I counseled her; the Bureau of Missing Persons was adept at handling such cases.

"No, no—that's out of the question," she said vehemently. "If this ever got into the press, the publicity would be disastrous. Nobody—well, nobody would understand about me and Raimondo."

I certainly agreed; a socially prominent matron offering a reward for her *cavalier servente* would make a juicy newspaper feature. All of a sudden, another and more sinister aspect of the affair struck me. "Look here," I said. "Maybe Raimondo didn't leave of his own free will. Is there anyone who might profit by his disappearance?"

She stiffened as though I had proposed a dip in the nude together. "I don't think I quite understand."

"I'm sorry, Mrs. Proudfoot, but this could be essential. Is Raimondo by any remote chance a legatee in your will?"

"The only one." Her answer was instant and unhesitating. "Upon my death everything in the world I own becomes his."

"You don't say." The poor creature was really infatuated. "One more question. Was there ever at any time another beneficiary?"

Her mouth tightened. "Yes. A nephew of mine, an utterly worthless ne'er-do-well named Sprague Fishlock. I disinherited the blackguard after he was caught cheating at cards."

I don't pretend to be Sam Spade or Philip Marlowe, but I know a homicide motive when I see one, and I followed up on it fast. "O.K., Mrs. Proudfoot, I'll do what I can if you just cooperate. You have a picture of Raimondo?"

"No." Her eyes avoided mine. "The truth is, we never went out in public together."

"Not even to places like 21 or El Morocco?"

"No, I couldn't risk taking him to restaurants or discotheques."

And neither could he, I echoed silently—a person of his caliber probably had a record as long as your arm. "That isn't vital, actually, but I will need a photo of Sprague Fishlock."

"Oh, that's simple enough." She crossed to the bookshelves and rummaged in an album. The snapshot she handed me showed a youth with a weak, handsome face astride a motorcycle, a cigarette dangling from his lips. The eyes under the linen cap were shifty.

"Good." I pocketed the photo, stood up. "I've got to go and make a few calls now. You'd better get some rest."

Her lip quivered. "Do—do you think Raimondo's in any danger?"

"No, I don't," I said to reassure her, and added a proviso I was destined to remember. "Just so long as he doesn't lose his head."

At 11:45 the following morning, I stood huddled in a mackintosh across the street from Sprague Fishlock's apartment midway between Park and Lexington Avenues. It was a good two hours since I had begun my vigil in the rain, and reviewing the story told me by Nora Lynch, the other day nurse, I wondered whether it could have led me on a totally false scent. According to her, Fishlock had arrived at the sickroom the previous afternoon carrying a hatbox, and had demanded to be left alone with Raimondo. Subsequently, she had overheard angry voices inside and something resembling a scuffle, but inasmuch as the visitor was Mrs. Proudfoot's relative, she had suspected nothing and gone off duty without checking her patient's condition. I stepped back to avoid being splashed by a furniture van and cursed myself for yielding to Mrs. Proudfoot's blandishments. But for her I might be snug at home in my bed, or better yet, in somebody else's in Britain . . .

Suddenly I froze; a figure bearing a hatbox, indubitably that of Fishlock, had emerged from the house opposite and was hailing a cab. I dashed into the street, flagged another one, and set off in hot pursuit. Within three or four blocks, his vehicle swerved into the transverse bisecting Central Park, but my driver hung on grimly. Speeding toward the West Side, I racked my brain over the puzzle confounding me. What was in that hatbox—the weapon with which he had dispatched Raimondo? The latter's valuables? Then, in a blinding flash, the solution burst on me. Like Robert Montgomery in the film of Emlyn Williams' famous play, *Night Must Fall,* Fishlock was carrying his victim's head in a hatbox to some unknown destination.

"Driver!" I shouted through the barrier separating us. "The next traffic cop you spot—slow down! But don't let that taxi get away!"

He called back some inaudible reply in which I caught the word "loonies," but thankfully did not slacken his speed. Pellmell we went across Central Park West and Columbus Avenue, and at Amsterdam, my heart leaped exultantly—a policeman, bulky in rainwear, stood waving at the intersection. I tore open the door and grabbed his arm ere he could protest.

"Come on—no time to explain," I yelled, pulling him into the car. "That cab up ahead—there's a killer inside!"

"Who perpetrated the crime? Is the perpetrator armed?" he stuttered, fumbling for his holster.

"Search me," I said frantically. "All I know is, he has someone's head in there—a gigolo! We've got to nab him before he hides it!"

Unhappily, at that moment the lights turned red, and by the time our command to jump them animated the driver, the other taxi was blocks ahead. When at last we caught up, it had stopped beside a row of small shops and Fishlock was nowhere in evidence. The driver, absorbed in writing up his tally sheet, reacted at the sight of the law.

"My fare?" he asked, startled. "Why, he went in that store there."

In a bound, I was across the sidewalk, the policeman on my heels. The interior of the place was as brilliantly lit as a delicatessen and clamorous with sound—puppies barking, canaries trilling, and over all, the bray of rock-and-roll. Up at the further end, the young bearded proprietor was just handing Fishlock several bills. At his feet lay the sinister hatbox.

"There he is, officer!" I cried in a ringing voice. "Sprague Fishlock! I order you to arrest him for the murder of Raimondo Gonzaga y Freluche de la Pintada. Do your duty!"

As all three stared at me fascinated, I advanced on the pair, snatched up the box, and unzipped the lid. With an angry, ratchetlike croak, a rainbow-hued Amazon parrot flapped out and, beating its wings furiously, perched on the cash register.

So there you are, and that's the thanks one gets for being a Good Samaritan. I'm facing a damage suit in six figures for false arrest, three Broadway columnists have already run veiled references to the matter, and as you might expect, Mrs. Millicent Proudfoot has behaved like a perfect swine, dissociating herself from the affair and claiming she never met me in her life. At any rate, the experience has taught me one thing at least. From now on, any woman I sit next to at a dinner party, here or in London, is lucky to get a peep out of me. Unless, of course, her name happens to be Rosy Cleavage.

The Machismo Mystique

It was 3 P.M., that climactic midafternoon moment toward which every gallant worthy of the name bends his energies, and I'd done all the preparatory work time and an unencumbered credit card could accomplish. I had stoked my Chilean vis-à-vis with three vodka martinis, half a gallon of Sancerre, and two balloons of Armagnac until her eyes were veritable liquid pools. Under my bold, not to say outrageous, compliments her damask skin and the alabaster column of her throat glowed like a lovely pink pearl; her hair, black as the raven's wing, shimmered in the reflection of the boudoir lamp shading our discreet banquette; and every now and again as my knee nudged hers under the table, my affinity's magnificent bosom heaved uncontrollably. I had glissed through all those earnest confidences that begin, "You know, I've never said this to anyone before," to, "Look, I'm not very articulate, but I feel that in these parlous times, it behooves us all to reach out, to cling to another lonely person—do you know what I mean?" Suddenly I had the feeling that she knew what I meant, all right. In a swift glance, I encompassed the small chic restaurant whence all but we had fled—its idle barman and the maître d'hôtel stifling a yawn—and I struck.

"Listen," I said as if inspired. "This friend of mine, the Marquis de Cad, who has a wonderful collection of African sculpture, was called away to Cleveland, and I promised to stop by his flat and dust it. Why don't we pick up a bottle of lemon oil . . ."

Inamorata threw back her sleek head and shouted with laughter. "Stop, *querido,*" she implored. "You're ruining my mascara. Such *machismo*—who would have expected it from a shrimp like you?"

Quicker than any hidalgo of Old Spain to erase an insult, I sprang up prepared to plunge my poniard into her bosom (a striking demonstration of the maxim that man kills that which he most loves). Unfortunately, I had left my poniard at home on the bureau and was wearing only a tie-tack that could never penetrate anyone so thick-skinned. Nonetheless, I made the hussy smart for her insolence. "Let me tell you something, Chubby," I rasped. "Never underestimate the American male. I may not dance the mambo or reek of garlic, but I'm just as feisty as those caballeros of yours below the Rio Grande. Remember that our first colonial flag in Kentucky, the Dark and Bloody Ground, portrayed a coiled rattlesnake over the legend, 'Don't Tread on Me.' "

"Big deal," she scoffed. "Do you want an example of real *machismo*—the kind of masculinity Latin-American men are capable of? Tell them to bring me another Armagnac."

Downcast at the realization that our matinee had blown out the back, I sullenly acceded. The story as she related it dealt with a bar in Guatemala City called *Mi apuesta* (The Wager) after a bet once made there. Two young bloods or *machos,* it appeared, had swaggered in one evening, stiff with conceit and supremely self-confident, arrogant as a pair of fighting cocks. Lounging at the bar over a glass of manzanilla, one of them remarked to the other, *"Te apuesto que no eres bastante macho para matar al primero que entre"* (I wager you're not man enough to kill the first hombre who comes in).

The other sneered thinly. "No?" he said. "I bet you fifty *centavos* I will."

The bet was covered, whereupon the challenged party extracted a Beretta from his waistband, and a moment later, as a totally inoffensive stranger stepped through the saloon door, a bullet drilled him through the heart.

"Madre de Dios," I exclaimed, shocked. "What happened to the assassin?"

"Niente," said Inamorata calmly. "The judge gave him a three months' suspended sentence on the ground that the crime was in no way premeditated."

Needless to say, whenever Inamorata rang up after our abortive meeting and besought me to lunch her again, I showed her a clean pair of heels. (They were two fellows who dispensed towels at the Luxor Baths; they pursued her madly, and I hope with more success than I had.) At any rate, in pondering the whole business of *machismo,* of male bravado and excessive manliness, it occurred to me that I had met quite a few *machos* in my time, both in the entertainment world and belles-lettres. The one I remember most vividly in the former was a Hollywood screenwriter—a big redheaded blowhard I'll call Rick Ferret. A Montanan who claimed to have grown up on the range, Ferret was forever beating his gums about his amatory exploits; by his own blushing admission, he was Casanova reborn, the swordsman supreme, the reincarnation of Don Juan. According to him, women in every walk of life—society leaders and shopgirls, leading ladies and vendeuses—fell in windrows in his path, and though it was obvious to his auditors at the Brown Derby that he dealt in quantity rather than quality, the references he dropped to his nuclear power and durability left us pale with jealousy.

One evening, I attended a party at his house in Laurel Canyon. Living with him at the time was a lady named Susie, quite well-endowed and with a rather sharp tongue. So late was the hour when the bash ended that the two insisted I stay over, and the next morning, while I was adjusting my false lashes, Ferret entered the bathroom and proceeded to take a shower. Just as he was snorting and puffing like a grampus, I chanced to observe a quite formidable scar on his *Sitzfleisch.* With an apology for the personal nature of the question, I asked if it was a war wound of some kind.

"Yes, in a way," he said carelessly, turning off the taps. "There's quite a story attached to it." He opened the door of the bathroom to disperse the steam, and I glimpsed his Susie breakfasting in bed a few feet distant. "The fact is," he went on, "it happened some years ago down on the south fork of the

Brazos while I was rounding up some mavericks. This gang of rustlers from Durango way cut into the herd, and I took after them hell for leather. Well, the greasers were spoiling for action, and they got it." He chuckled. "Before I could yank out my six-guns, they creased me here, but I managed to rub out the whole dad-blamed lot."

"Oh, for *God's* sake, Ferret," I heard Susie's voice croak from the bedroom. "You know perfectly well you had a boil lanced on your tail only last Tuesday."

The two most celebrated *machos* I ever knew, I suppose, were Ernest Hemingway—unquestionably the holder of the black belt in the Anglo-Saxon world—and Mike Todd, who, to pilfer a phrase from Marcel Proust, might aptly be termed the Sweet Cheat Gone. My go-around with Hemingway took place in the winter of 1954, directly after his two widely publicized plane crashes in East Africa. He was borne into the New Stanley Hotel in Nairobi in a somewhat disoriented state, suffering a double concussion, a smashed kidney, and alarming symptoms of *folie de grandeur*. I turned up there two days later from Uganda with fourteen women comprising the first American all-girl safari (quite another story), and since my room was adjacent to his, saw a good bit of him thereafter. What with his tribulations and frequent infusions of hooch, Papa was inclined to ramble somewhat, and it was not always easy to follow the thread of his discourse. Once in a while, though, the clouds dissipated, and we were able to chat about mutual friends in the Montparnasse of the 'twenties. It was on such an occasion, one night, that he told me an anecdote that stunningly dramatized his *machismo*.

It concerned a period when he used to box at Stillman's Gymnasium in New York, a favorite haunt of enthusiasts of what is termed the manly art. His adversaries, Hemingway blushingly admitted, never matched his own speed and strength, but one of them improved so under his tutelage that occasionally the pair had a tolerable scrimmage. Thinking to intensify it, Hemingway suggested they discard their gloves and fight bareknuckle. This, too, while diverting, soon palled, but at last he had an inspiration.

"The room we boxed in," Hemingway explained, "had these rows of pipes running along the walls—you know, like backstage in a theater? Well, we flooded the place with steam, so thickly that it looked like a pea-soup fog in London. Then we started charging each other like a couple of rhinos. Butting our heads together and roaring like crazy. God, it was terrific—you could hear the impact of bone on bone, and we bled like stuck pigs. Of course, that made the footwork a bit more difficult, slipping and sliding all over, but it sure heightened the fun. Man, those were the days. You had to have real *cojones* to stand up to it."

The same hormonal doodads were imperative in order to cope with Mike Todd and his vagaries. Todd's *machismo* was that common form that afflicts all undersized men—megalomania. He freely identified himself with Napoleon, P. T. Barnum, and Carl Laemmle, Junior, not to mention the Roman emperors of the decline. Whereas the latter, however, believed in giving the populace bread and circuses, Todd gave them circuses and kept the bread. Rarely if ever has there been anyone more unwilling to fork over what he owed to those actors, writers, and technicians who aided him in his grandiloquent projects of stage and screen. The little corpuscle, in short, believed in flaunting money where it made the most impression—at Deauville, Monaco, and the gaming tables of Las Vegas. In this respect, he was a true *macho*. My sole souvenir of our frenetic association is a replica of the carpetbag Phileas Fogg carried on his celebrated journey, a thousand of which Todd distributed in lordly fashion to Broadway companions, investors, accountants, dentists, and other sycophants. But surely, his admirers have since queried me, I must have been awed by his tremendous vitality? Only in part, I respond: *Moi-même,* I prefer the anthropoid apes. The gibbon swings farther, the chimpanzee's reflexes are quicker, the orangutan can scratch faster, and the gorilla—my particular love object—has been known to crunch a Stillson wrench in his teeth.

Of such literary *machos* was the late Robert Ruark, who of course patterned himself slavishly on Hemingway. Their careers afford ample demonstration of my two favorite maxims: a) that the gaudier the patter, the cheaper the scribe, and b) that easy writing makes hard reading. The legend of Ruark's fatal charisma with women still gives one a pain in the posterior when recounted, and his press interviews, studded with reference to the millions of words he merchandised, act as a tourniquet on bleeders like myself who labor over a postcard. Even John O'Hara, somewhat more talented, was not above buttonholing acquaintances and boasting that he had written this or that deathless vignette in three quarters of an hour. It is interesting, by the way, that Scott Fitzgerald, with whom O'Hara was given to comparing himself, never made any claims to his own facility when I knew him in Hollywood. On the contrary, both he and Nathanael West were continually obsessed by delusions of their inadequacy with sex and their small literary output.

Looking back over a long and mottled career, I think the best illustration of real *machismo* I ever beheld took place on the terrace of the Café du Dôme in Paris in 1927. I was seated there at dusk one day with a fellow journalist when an enormous yellow Hispano-Suiza landaulet driven by a chauffeur drew up at the curb. From it emerged a tall and beautiful, exquisitely clad lady, followed by another even more photogenic—both clearly high-fashion mannequins. Reaching into the tonneau, they brought forth a wizened homunculus with a yellow face resembling Earl Sande, the celebrated jockey. Hooking their arms through his, they assisted him to a table farther down the terrace. I turned to my *copain* with my eyebrows raised, searching for some explanation of the phenomenon. A slow smile overspread his countenance, and he held his hands apart as does one when asked to steady a skein of wool.

That's *machismo,* sweetheart.

Nostasia in Asia

I—A Nutmeg for the Master

One January evening in San Francisco back in 1949, I was given a rather curious assignment. Poised to embark momentarily for the Far East with my wife and children, I attended a small celebration honoring the seventy-fifth birthday of W. Somerset Maugham. The old party, as Mr. Maugham persisted in characterizing himself after the age of forty, got moderately juiced on Dom Perignon and began quizzing me on our itinerary. I said that among other areas, we intended to visit the Netherlands Indies, specifically the portion of the Malay archipelago east of Java encompassing Celebes, the Lesser Sunda Islands and the Moluccas. It was quite a mouthful, considering that the wine had turned my tongue to flannel, but I managed to choke it out.

"Capital," he approved, "then you can do something for me as well as yourself. A hundred and thirty-odd miles southeast of Amboina, the port of Ceram, there's an extraordinary place in the Banda Sea that I used as background in a novel, *The Narrow Corner*. It's a tiny cluster of islands where the Dutch found cloves and nutmeg and mace when they wrested it from the Portuguese in the seventeenth century." He went on to extol the beauty of Banda Neira and Lontor, the principal islands, the plantations the patroons had cultivated there, and the sumptuous houses they built on the profits of the spice trade.

"Now, make no mistake," he continued. "The journey there may be a trifle hazardous—I'd park the family somewhere and go it alone." (Maugham's attitude toward family ties was a matter of record.) "In any case, I promise you it'll be a memorable experience. Cable me at Villa Mauresque if you get there and bring back a nutmeg or two for my cook."

Well, the old party was right. The Dutch mailboat I sailed on was a mere cockleshell in those mountainous seas, its skipper was awash in Bols, and I aged ten years in the process, but I made it. Naturally, in the twenty-five years since Maugham's visit, the place had gone down appreciably, what with Japanese wartime occupation and the Indonesian struggle for independence. The once stately mansions were mildewed and roofless, the nutmeg gardens choked with vegetation; nevertheless, one got an inkling of the splendor in which the perkeniers had dwelt from the marble Corinthian porticoes and handsome tulip-tiled floors, the bits of ornate woodwork that had resisted the inroads of time. Like all such remnants of colonial glory, of course, Banda was tinged with melancholy, but somehow it exerted a fascination that haunted me long after I had left.

A short while ago, in a gypsy tearoom cater-cornered from the New York Public Library, an aged crone of twenty-three in a see-through blouse read my fortune as part of the 85-cent lunch.

"Mm-m," she muttered, massaging my pinkie in a most interesting fashion. "I see a long journey by water . . . coconut palms . . . a dusky-skinned maiden with bewitching dimples."

"That's your reflection in my glasses, honey," I explained. "Look, what time do you finish here? There's a snug little drop—"

"Islands," she interrupted, unheeding, "a name like Fonda—Honda—I can't tell exactly. You're going back there very soon—you can't help it. It's like a nostasia thing, you're fated to return."

Well, the old crone was right. Some nineteen days thence in Amboina, now called Ambon, I teetered up the gangplank of the S.S. *Kakatua* on a hot and cloudless Sunday morning, outward bound on a voyage scheduled to include not only Banda but the Kai and Aru Islands and the Tanimbar group in the Arafura Sea. The 600-ton vessel, so named because its captain never sailed with less than five sulphur-crested cockatoos on the bridge, was busy loading cargo and deck passengers, and the tumult was deafening. My cabin, a lazaret on the port side, seemed to guarantee privacy until I detected five faces peering through the window at my underthings and realized the passage was going to be one long striptease. It also came as a surprise, on rinsing my hands, to find my shoes full of water; someone had removed all the piping under the bowl, doubtless to cool his feet. With a fatalistic shrug, I mounted to the boat deck to watch our leave-taking. A huge truck was drawn up on the jetty, pumping diesel fuel into the ship, but closer inspection revealed a branch pipe diverting the fluid into another truck concealed behind a godown. I pointed it out to a swarthy individual beside me on the rail, observing that our skipper ought to be apprised of the flimflam. My knowledge of Malay, admittedly, is sketchy, but I read his answer loud and clear.

"I happen to own those trucks, Charlie," he said, baring his teeth in an evil smile reminiscent of Lon Chaney's. "So take my advice and shut your yap. The captain's getting a good hosing."

The hullabaloo of departure reached a crescendo as friends and relatives swarmed aboard with last-minute gifts for passengers—seaweed knishes, crates of live chickens, and a tray of fat little puppies for broiling on skewers. Finally, amid farewells operatic enough for a four-year whaling cruise, the *Kakatua* edged into the stream and began the eighteen-hour run to Banda. By now every inch of deck space had been pre-empted; families huddled over rice bowls, consuming dried fish pungent with *trassi*, infants bent on self-destruction crawled headlong into the anchor chains, and sleek teenyboppers armed with tape decks chatted up any girl who looked available. The sunset, over a sea rippling like a mill pond, was breathtaking, especially as viewed through a highball in my cabin; and I was just composing a poem that would have surpassed Shelley's "To a Skylark" when there came an insistent knocking on my door. The second officer, whose empurpled nose and rheumy eye clearly bespoke a wet brain, had discovered by some telepathy that I harbored a quart of Black Label. Explaining that although a devout Muslim he had no prejudice against grain alcohol, he proceeded to knock back a good third of it. As the voyage progressed, his nightly visits soon exhausted the bottle, and on applying to our purser for something to wet my whistle, I was given a mason jar of Indonesian whiskey containing two embryonic baby deer. It is an elixir much esteemed in that part of the world as promoting agility and fleetness of foot, but one with small appeal to the squeamish. My incubus, though, drained it in two sessions, smacking his lips and pronouncing it far superior to any Western tipple.

Shortly after daylight next morning, we steamed into the harbor of Banda Neira in the shadow of its great volcano, the Gunung Api or Mountain of Fire. To the casual eye, the past quarter of a century had wrought few changes; the old mansions, now roofed over with rusting corrugated iron, sheltered five or six Indonesian families apiece, many of the soaring kanari trees I remembered had been cut down for firewood, and the bust of William of Orange facing the Dutch administrative buildings, not unsurprisingly, was gone. However, I did succeed in verifying a weird story related by a Dutch priest in Makassar a few days earlier. According to his informants, some unhappy person had incised a suicide note with a diamond ring on a window of the governor's residence at Banda before dispatching himself. The island's controller, a most amiable chap, readily confirmed the tale and showed me the graffito. It was a fairly orotund quatrain in French, dated 1 September 1932 above an indecipherable signature, that read in rough translation:

> When will the time come to free my spirit?
> When will the clock strike to sound the hour,
> The moment I again glimpse the shores of my country,
> The faces of the family I love and whom I bless?

Disappointingly enough, the official could impart no further information, but he was vehement in declaring that the room was haunted and that everyone who had tried to spend a night there swore to having seen a bloody hand tracing words on the windowpane. There was indeed a quality of horror about those spidery lines etched on the glass in a dusty sunlit room that recalled the ghost stories of M. R. James and Algernon Blackwood. I took a short-cut back to the ship, frequently whirling about to make sure I was unaccompanied, and felt no intolerable anguish when the cone of Gunung Api faded over the horizon.

Tual and Elat, our ports of call in the Kai group twenty-six hours onward, were singularly devoid of glamour—the usual ramshackle godowns for storing copra, the string of *tokos* operated by Chinese and Hindu merchants retailing sleazy printed cottons, kerosene and sandals of old carpeting, and a pullulation of shanties housing several thousand underfed and apathetic inhabitants. Visiting the islands in 1857, Alfred Russel Wallace, the great naturalist and coauthor with Darwin of the theory of natural selection, was overwhelmed by the lepidoptera he saw, the magnificent butterflies, and beetles; I personally was thunderstruck by the diseases. Never, except possibly in Calcutta, had I beheld so spectacular a display of trachoma, such a profusion of rickets, jaundice, beriberi and distempers arising from malnutrition. Whether it was their cumulative impact or the oppressive heat, I experienced a sudden vertigo and stumbled into a grocer's shop for some Orange Crush. The proprietor was a benign old Cantonese, with a marked resemblance to Chairman Matzo Tongue, who reacted excitedly to the discovery that I was an American. What was my candid opinion of Mr. Nixon? he queried eagerly. I told him, and apropos of regurgitation, he produced a block of ambergris spewed up by a whale in the vicinity, which he presented with his compliments. It is symbolic little courtesies like this, I contend, plus a frank exchange of views, that lead in time to a better understanding between peoples.

In the course of numerous trips to the Orient, I had long yearned to ascertain the truth of an oft-repeated legend, that at Dobo in the Aru Islands, our next stop, one could obtain genuine pearls the size of Muscat grapes, to say nothing of

Ming Dynasty ceramics, for a handful of chickpeas or goobers. No sooner had the *Kakatua* anchored in the roads there, accordingly, than I raced ashore to investigate. (In actuality, I was carried ashore piggyback by a crippled urchin whom I paid off in chickpeas, but that is not central to the narrative.) Anyhow, after hours of bargaining with a heavily enameled Eurasian lady who could have doubled for Florence Reed as Mother Goddam in *The Shanghai Gesture,* I came away richer by a necklace unobtainable this side of Attleboro, Massachusetts, for love or money, as well as two Ming snuff bottles with their original contents intact. I took the latter, on my return to London, into Fribourg & Treyer's in the Haymarket, a firm that has made snuff for donkey's years, and they confessed they had never seen anything like it.

At Saumlakki in the Tanimbars, our circumnavigation of the islands reached its southernmost periphery; Australia was a scant overnight sail across the Arafura Sea, and our cargo, hitherto copra and the trepang or sea slug relished by the Chinese, became more varied—baby kangaroos earmarked for European zoos, cages of brilliant-hued lories and flycatchers, and roots of the Larat flower, an orchid highly prized by fanciers. I was now on such terms of intimacy with the captain that we had worked out a *modus vivendi;* I kept my nose out of the chartroom, and in return he thrashed his small daughters whenever they played scales on my typewriter. Stimulating though the voyage had been thus far, I was beginning to feel a mite peckish from our unvarying diet of roast fish, parboiled rice, and hot water masquerading as tea, and I longed to get on with the next stage, a revisit to Bali. Unhappily, since no air service however primitive exists in the remoter Moluccas, I was compelled to backtrack to Ambon, Makassar, and all the way to Surabaja in order to reach Bali, and as it turned out I should have stood in bed.

The Golden Gamelan, a few miles distant from Denpasar along the coast, was a glittering nineteen-story hotel run on the principle of "Why send out the tourist to be dry-cleaned when it can be done on the premises?" To this end, the proprietors had built a better mousetrap, an enclave that guaranteed instant

Bali amid hygienic surroundings. No facet of its culture—
music, dance, sculpture, painting, gastronomy—had been overlooked. Three nights a week, *rijsttafel* was served up under the
stars, along with a terpsichorean *bouillabaisse* of native dancing
and clangorous gamelan rhythms. Inside the hotel, the guest's
credit card was relentlessly wooed by shops chockful of batik,
wayang dolls, blackwood carvings, devil masks, nielloware, fly
whisks, Benares brass, lacquered betel boxes, and all the machine-made schlock that covers the Far East like a mulch. If
one so desired, he could loll drink in hand by a beach where
minions ceaselessly raked away seaweed threatening to entrap
his feet, or puff his Corona while skimming the bluest of
lagoons in an outrigger. The lengths the management had gone
to in its effort to cushion the visitor against reality were awesome. Anything that might conceivably offend foreign sensibil-
ities had been expunged—malodorous drains, pie dogs, tropical
insects, beggars; and after three days there, I became so surfeited that I took action. The clerks at the reception desk must
have sensed my outrage, because I was shown into the manager's office straightaway. The portly individual engaged in
counting several foot-high stacks of currency on his desk looked
up questioningly.

"Look here," I said without any preamble. "Have you
stopped to analyze how you came by that scratch?"

"No, that's the auditor's job," he said. "I just like to run my
hands through it. Boy, isn't it great? We ought to clear a million
on the week."

"Yes, but what good is it?" I flung at him. "This place isn't
Bali—it's a movie version, a fake. People save up their hard-
earned pennies, travel thousands of miles to see the last para-
dise, and what do they find? Walt Disney!"

"Gee, I never thought of it that way," he said, tugging at his
earlobe. "It *is* sort of a betrayal, in a sense. Golly," he sighed,
"we've been like immersed in our little store here, orientated
pelfwise and not caring a snap for ethics, and suddenly along
comes a person which he shakes us topsy-turvy. Maybe we
ought to give back the money."

"I don't care what you do with it," I rejoined. "You can burn it for all I care. I'm flying to Australia first thing in the morning."

"But you can't do that, fellow!" he pleaded, his face ashen. "You can't walk in here and question our values, bring down our world around our ears. . . . Who—who are you?" he asked superstitiously.

"Just say—" I turned, my hand on the doorknob, "just call me a carpenter. A carpenter of words, Mister—Mister—?"

"Sauerwein—Abraham Lincoln Sauerwein," he said, and smiled sadly. "They used to call me 'Honest Abe,' back there in the Garment Center."

"And will again, Abe," I said. "Don't despair. Out of our meeting, strangers in a strange clime, may yet come understanding and—who knows?—retribution. Goodbye."

And that was how I left Bali, lovely enchanted isle in a turquoise sea. I like to think it was a little better for my coming, and a lot better for my going. One day, perhaps, I shall return, but only if tied between the tails of wild Caucasian horses. *Selah.*

II—The Egg and Ainu

The whole affair began under somewhat bizarre circumstances, with a crisp and sizzling fried egg that a crisp and sizzling press agent I knew in Tokyo carried around in his pocket. The day after my arrival in Japan last fall, I was having a late breakfast with the chap, a free spirit named Windy Maelstrom, in a crowded restaurant off the Ginza and, overcome by euphoria and three Bloody Marys, I launched into a dithyramb about Japanese taste and craftsmanship. Maelstrom concurred wholeheartedly, and in support brought forth the egg—an amazing replica, its golden yolk shimmering in a snow-white plasm pocked with tiny globules of fat.

"Well, fan my brow," I said, dazzled, "that's real pop art. What gallery did you buy it from?"

"Ach, there's a wholesale district full of this stuff," he said.

"They duplicate all kinds of food in plastic for display—steaks, chops, poultry, fish, salads, desserts—you name it. Of course, I use it for a particular purpose."

"To wit?"

"Goosing headwaiters." He cast a quick look about, placed the egg on the table, and sprinkled it with bread crumbs. "Just watch."

For a moment there was no visible reaction; then the steely-eyed maître d'hôtel patrolling our section froze in his tracks. Plainly classifying us as a couple of dirty feeders, he hissed at our waitress nearby to clean up the debris. The girl seized a rag and complied, but the egg evaded her and coyly slid away. Mystified, she made another attempt, this time pursuing it like a hockey puck around our table and onto the one adjoining. Suddenly the truth dawned on her and she fled, a hand clapped over her mouth to suppress her giggles. Stiff with outraged dignity, the headwaiter, who had been looking on transfixed, bathed us in a murderous glare and stalked off.

As Malestrom was about to stash the egg, I intervened and examined it. "You know," I said thoughtfully, "it's a shame a lovely object like this shouldn't be utilitarian as well. What if you scooped out the reverse side of the yolk, for instance, and installed a mirror and a powder puff?"

"A compact!" he exclaimed. "Hey, that's a sensational idea! I can just see one of the Glorias—Vanderbilt or Steinem—taking it out to repair her makeup as she's finishing lunch at La Grenouille. Every columnist in New York would flip!"

"Right!" I said, feverish with creativity, "and maybe for a lipstick, she could use a little plastic pickle—a gherkin."

Maelstrom gazed at me in awe. "Helena Rubenstein, move over," he murmured. "In my humble opinion, friend, this is the greatest. . . . Wait! Wait! I've got it!" A look of positive ecstasy overspread his face. "You know what she'd sign the check with when it comes? A chicken leg that's really a ballpoint pen!"

"Maelstrom," I said emotionally, "you and I have just become the two richest men in the Klondike." We arose and shook hands formally. "Now, all we need is a good catchy name for our company. What about 'Big Ball of Wax, Limited'?"

"Masterly. It's powerful, arresting, yet greasy—everything our product stands for," he exulted. "I'll mail our incorporation papers to Delaware this afternoon. How long are you staying in Tokyo?"

"Well, I'm undecided. Everybody says I ought to see Kyoto and Nara, and Mount Fuji—"

"For Pete's sake, man, are you out of your mind?" His nose wrinkled in disgust. "Those are all tourist traps. I wouldn't be caught dead there. Why don't you do something worthwhile—like flying up to Hokkaido to visit the Hairy Ainus?"

I protested that I knew nothing about them, and he shook his head commiseratingly. Here was a golden chance to see one of the strangest, most mysterious folk on earth in their native habitat, to study their origin, folklore and customs. Was I so blasé, so bereft of curiosity that I begrudged them a ninety-minute flight? If it was merely a question of *money,* he went on loftily, I could put up my shares in Big Ball of Wax, Limited, as collateral, and he'd advance my expenses.

"But how do you communicate with an Ainu? I don't speak Japanese."

"No problem at all. I'll get you an interpreter, a beautiful girl who's a trained researcher, and brother, what a shape." He whistled. "O.K., here's what you do. Go back to your room, send out your laundry—"

"I haven't any."

"I'll get you some. Anyway, relax and leave everything to Katie Shlimazu. She'll be in touch with you inside an hour."

Now, needless to say, I had no intention whatever of embarking on any such harebrained expedition, but by sheer chance I happened to be in my room at the Okura when a caller arrived. She was a Japanese person—a big, bouncy sort of girl—and being as she was bigger than your average Japanese person, some people would have deemed her sweater too skimpy for her frame, but not me. I don't know why, but tears welled up in my eyes.

"I'm Shlimazu-san, your interpreter," she said. "What's the matter? Why are you crying?"

"Uh—er—it's nothing," I said, gulping. "I—I'm allergic to cashmere, and your sweater—it *is* cashmere, was it? I mean, is it?"

"Oh, I'm sorry," she apologized, and lowered her eyes demurely. "I can't very well take it off, there's nothing underneath—"

"Atchoo! Harooch!" I sneezed. "Never mind. Listen, how soon can we leave for Hokkaido or wherever those Ainus are? If we're going, no sense dragging our feet. You follow? You see what I'm driving at?"

That was her instinct too, and she went into action at once. Well, talk about dynamos—Katie Shlimazu was a regular whirlwind. By noontime the next day, all travel arrangements complete, the two of us were aboard a jet speeding toward Hakodate, the southern gateway to Hokkaido. My fair companion was spoon-feeding me such background as I might need on the Ainus, and I was doing my best to concentrate.

"Science is still puzzled about their history," she explained. "They're not ancestors of the Japanese, as many think, nor are they Eskimos. In the old days, they roamed all over our northernmost island, hunting and fishing, but now there are less than 17,000, most of them in the general area of two villages to the north of Hakodate across Volcano Bay."

"What kind of perfume is that you're wearing?" I asked curiously. "It smells a little like Mitsouko, only more flowery."

"At one time the Ainus used to have long beards and the women wore a design tattooed around their mouths," she went on. "Nowadays this is no longer the custom."

"I'm glad of that," I admitted. "I don't approve of permanent lipstick. Your shade, by the way, is very becoming—did you know that? It's halfway between coral and peach, I'd say. That's so attractive on someone with a creamy type skin."

An abrupt warning of turbulence ahead set us to buckling our seat belts—I had some trouble adjusting Katie's but it was worth it—and we descended at Hakodate in the teeth of a raging snowstorm. After jolting for an eternity through suburbs devoid of life, we arrived at a museum renowned for its collection of Ainu artifacts. Unhappily, the curator's two-hour lecture in Japanese was so interminable that I blacked out and pitched forward into the tea ceremony, demolishing a fair amount of porcelain. As a result, I had only a fleeting impression of the artifacts—bows and arrows, beaded headbands, harpoons, and mortars and pestles—but sufficient to recapture the anguish of being dragged through similar dusty memorabilia as a schoolboy.

Deliverance, however, was at hand. Later that night, a complex parlay of trains, buses and taxis ferried us to Noboribetsu, a spa where mixed bathing, my guide blushingly revealed, was a feature of our hotel. Visions of sugarplums danced in my head as I conducted Katie to her door, and with a frolicsome injunction not to keep me waiting at the halter, or rather the lack of it, I raced to my room.

The moment I entered it, all rhyme and reason vanished. Two frozen-faced maids straight out of *The Mikado* seized me in a hammerlock, and burdening me with kimono, slippers and towel, thrust me into a cell with a sunken bathtub five feet deep. Apart from a scalp wound, none of the contusions I sustained in my dip was grievous, but even had I concussed myself, the maids were too busy to notice. They had meanwhile redecorated the room with *tatamis* and a low table, at which they forcibly knelt me and began plying me with a variety of dishes compounded of raw fish, squid and eels. In vain I kept struggling to make them understand that I had an assignation at the communal baths. Finally, overwrought at the thought that Katie might contract pneumonia in her birthday suit, I wrenched myself free and plummeted down three flights of stairs into what turned out to be the lobby. The manager and the cashier, both impeccable in morning coats and pencil-striped pants, surveyed my kimono and tousled hair with cold disapproval.

"The baths!" I gasped. "The mixed noodles—I mean, the nude poolroom—"

"Terribly sorry," the manager returned in a Cambridge accent, "we have dispensed with mixed bathing. It attracted the wrong clientele."

There being no other place to recline, I spent the remainder of the night on the floor of my room, composing a heated letter to Emperor Hirohito about luring tourists to his country with false promises.

The next phase of our journey, Katie apprised me the following morning, was an interview with an authentic Ainu chieftain at Nibutani, one of the tribal enclaves she had spoken of. Hours later, spent from zigzagging along Hokkaido's bleak coastline and floundering through Arctic drifts, we reached Mr. Nuki's abode. The chieftain, a burly individual whose beetling eyebrows somehow reminded me of Mack Swain, Charlie Chaplin's scourge in his early movies, was engaged in excising the centerfolds from a pile of tattered girlie magazines, with which, I gathered, he intended to paper the walls of his living room. Disposing ourselves on the floor around his smoking oil stove, we toasted each other in thimblefuls of Manischewitz laced with neat's-foot oil while Shlimazu-san questioned our host. Were there any Ainu myths or folktales, memories of a racial past, to indicate where his forebears had come from?

"Look, it's impossible to sort out the wheat from the chaff, the warp from the woof," she translated his reply. "Last night at the firehouse, some character says to me, 'You know what I think? I think maybe we all came from Woonsocket.' How do you like that—Woonsocket, way over in Rhode Island! So I say to this dummy, 'That's brilliant. I suppose we all flew over here by Northwest Orient?' That shut him up, all right."

"Still, if you could prove it, it'd be a wonderful ad for Northwest Orient," I pointed out. "Ask him what other theories there are."

"Well, let me see," Nuki pondered. "They'll also tell you we're Norsemen—Vikings. If that's so, why don't we have smorgasbord? In my opinion—and mind you, it's just an educated guess—the Ainus are Romanians. And why do I say that, you ask? Because only a Romanian would have the gall—the *chutzpah*—to migrate to a place like this."

So scalding yet logical was the man's conclusion that my eyes widened in surprise, and in widening detected that his arm had encircled my companion in an amorous squeeze. Yes, he was right, for who but a Romanian would be capable of such *chutzpah*? I gently disengaged his grasp, assisted Katie to her feet, and as Nuki, with a philosophic shrug, resumed scissoring his centerfolds, we pressed on to Shiraoi, our final objective. There as nowhere else, if one could believe the reports, was the hub of Ainu activities; there they could be seen in a faithful reconstruction of a native village—a sort of Ainu Williamsburg—living and working as they had from the dawn of time.

Through grimy industrial wastelands and over tundras measureless to man we went, in a journey beside which those of Shackleton and Peary paled to small potatoes, and came at last to a windswept suburban plot exhibiting a cluster of empty straw huts. Nearby and drearier than a small-time carnival on closing day stood a double row of souvenir booths that displayed row on row of wooden bears with fish in their mouths, Irish shillelaghs, footstools, pennants and post cards. Not a single patron, let alone a Hairy Ainu, was in sight, and the few shopkeepers huddled in the booths lacked even the energy to accost us. Ultimately, it emerged by dint of close questioning that some Ainus, bankrupt after an unsuccessful attempt to sell fried chicken in the huts, had departed but had left behind a number of rare artifacts that our informant might dispose of cheaply.

"What kind?" I asked, my memory still smarting from the accumulation in the museum at Hakodate.

"He says very old, very choice," reported Katie. "Beaded headbands, harpoons, bows and arrows—"

"O.K., honey, that tears it," I snapped. "Back to Tokyo, and believe you me, a certain press agent is going to get an earful, as sure as God made little green suckers."

Which, of course, never came to pass, because when we got there, as you will have guessed, Mr. Windy Maelstrom was gone, and with him all the assets, stock, and goodwill of Big Ball of Wax, Limited. That's right—the whole blasted trip to Hokkaido was just a ruse to get me out of town and loot our enterprise, and here I was, a stranger in a strange land with nobody to lean on. And if it hadn't been for a Japanese party, a wonderful person who'd give you the shirt off her back—ah, but that, as they say, is a whole other ballgame.

III—Paradise—Once Over Lightly

Sometime during the winter of 1915, an 11-year-old youth in Providence, Rhode Island, whose razor-keen mentality, Napoleonic ego and steel-rimmed spectacles strikingly corresponded with my own, received a letter from the editors of the *National Geographic* in Washington. It read as follows:

"Dear Sir: Your recent communication in hand and contents dully noted. (Also smear on envelope manifestly arising from contact with jelly sandwich.) The proposal you advance—that we outfit an expedition led by yourself to explore the Seychelles Islands in the Indian Ocean for buried treasure—unfortunately duplicates one already in progress. Tom Swift, with whose exploits we feel sure you are familiar, left here last Tuesday in his Giant Electric Submarine for those waters. Tom, as you know, is a resourceful, quick-witted lad, and we have every expectation that his project will shortly bear fruit. Should no fruit be forthcoming, we shall of course signal you posthaste at your moorings, c/o the Candace Street Grammar School. With every good wish, etc., etc."

While downcast at the revelation that Swift had stolen a march on me, I never forsook hope that one day I would set foot in the Seychelles, whose name possessed an undefinable quality of magic for me. Perhaps it was their remoteness, a thousand miles off the coast of East Africa, as well as the scarcity of information about them, that made them a challenge. Over the ensuing years, I picked up odd bits of hearsay and conjecture—that Yankee whale ships, for instance, cruising what their captains termed the Eastern Grounds, used to call in there for fresh water, mangoes and dalliance with exceptionally lovely females; that Chinese Gordon, the hero of Khartoum, had located the Seychelles as the indubitable site of the Garden of Eden; and that there one could behold the last stronghold of British colonialism, full of retired officers imbibing pink gins and pettishly snapping their copies of *The Times* of London in the imperial afterglow. To these was added an even more tempting rumor that ships' telegraphers, seeking to enliven the midnight watch, were wont to tap out racy stories to each other, all relayed through the central office of Cable & Wireless at Seychelles. What a mine of nuggets, a veritable Golconda, awaited anyone who could persuade the staff to disclose their favorite yarns! My head swam at the prospect.

In 1952, miraculously, the opportunity presented itself. I was holidaying in Kenya, cushioned by royalties from a Broadway play that wiseacres predicted would outrun *Chu Chin Chow,* when a deck passage aboard a vessel from Mombasa to the Seychelles was offered me. Despite the obvious rigors of three nights in a sleeping bag and preparing my own food, I jumped at the chance. In a lightning circuit of the bazaars, I laid in enough canned goods and thermos flasks, halazone tablets and sunburn lotion to equip a two-months' safari, wrote several hysterical farewell notes to family and friends, and stayed up all night swallowing Mothersill's Seasick Remedy in preparation for the voyage.

Fate, however, willed otherwise. Two hours before entraining for Mombasa, my agent in New York hurled a thunderbolt— the only collect thunderbolt in the annals of the weather department. My play, overtaken by anemia resulting from a newspaper strike, had breathed its last. One ray of sunshine alleviated the debacle, however. If I returned to New York within thirty-six hours, said the agent, he might be able to land me a job as a busboy at Schrafft's.

Confident that one day the proper conjunction of stars in my astrological sign would favor my design, I lay doggo for a decade, and then the penny dropped. The United States built a satellite tracking station in the islands for its astronauts, the British installed a runway for jet aircraft, and suddenly a buzz arose in the press of feverish real estate speculation, new hotels and tourist activity. Last December in Tokyo, I learned that scheduled flights to Seychelles via Ceylon now existed, and though it would knock all my plans into a cocked hat, I luckily possessed the requisite headgear. The dream I had so long cherished was on the verge of fulfillment. Distending my nostrils (at best a hazard in Tokyo's pollution), I could already smell the perfumed trade winds of the Seychelles, laden with cinnamon and cloves, and hear the rhythmic clash of the surf on its snow-white beaches.

The clash I heard, however, was the difference between the dream and the reality. Disembarking late one evening at the airport of Mahé, the principal island, I was assailed by a downpour so torrential as to rival the Victoria Falls, whipped up by a Force 6 gale, and I was drenched to the skin before I managed to find the sole taxi in sight, a heap with an equally decrepit driver.

"A hundred rupees to the Esmeralda Hotel?" I stared at the Jehu in disbelief. "That's twenty dollars, Buster! It's only thirteen from Kennedy to the Astor Hotel."

"Then if I were you I'd take that instead," he recommended, sucking on his pipe. "The only thing is, you might get a surprise. They tore down the Astor six years ago."

"A smart apple," I said savagely. "That's what a man needs after a nine-hour plane trip—a smart apple. You ought to be ashamed, asking twenty dol—" A prolonged screech, ending in an apocalyptic crash, cut me short. "What was that?"

"Oh, just the roof of the airport peeling off," he said, craning his neck. "No, sir, I'm not a whit ashamed. In fact, sitting here in this nice dry vehicle, I don't see a particle of guilt. All I see is a man with water pouring out of his hat. I guess that's what they call a cocked hat, isn't it?"

"Take me to the Esmeralda and minimize the chin music," I snapped and yanked open the cab door. The hotel, or such portions as I could distinguish in the tempest, consisted of a dozen cottages grouped around a reception facility; but my room, on the upper floor of a two-story annex overlooking the ocean, thankfully afforded much more privacy. I awoke the next morning to a paradisiacal view lifted from a travel poster:

glossy foliage fringing a mile-long beach, a serene cloudless sky and an illimitable sea unbroken by a single sail.

"Care for a little eye-opener before breakfast, friend?" a hospitable voice inquired. I turned and beheld the occupant of the room adjoining mine, a toothy, fattish gentleman in a Hawaiian shirt, extending a pint bottle of applejack. His face and forearms were a glowing pink, whether from overexposure to the sun or the sauce was uncertain. "Go ahead—plenty more where this came from. I always carry a few quarts when I travel."

I excused myself with the plea that I drank only cologne or an occasional witch hazel and water, and my neighbor identified himself. A dry-cleaning tycoon from Southern California, the owner of thirteen stores in the San Diego area, Mr. Norman Bromwich was on a six-week tour of the world and hungry for companionship. Over breakfast he gave me a painstaking review of the countries he had visited, interspersed with footnotes on the state of dry cleaning abroad, which he deemed deplorable. Fascinated as I was by his discourse, though, I began to detect the sensation of acupuncture, of pins and needles in the extremities, that attacks one when told more than he wants to know. I proposed, therefore, that the two of us drive into the island's principal town in the car he had rented, and we set forth over the steeply winding roads dotted with hairpin turns that led to Victoria.

It promptly became evident that Bromwich was one of those drivers with unbounded faith that their reflexes can extricate them from any plight, however hazardous. Time and again our wheels hung suspended over dizzying chasms of rocketed headlong around blind corners, kicking up showers of gravel as we sideswiped oncoming traffic. Frightened faces peered out of the shacks we sped past, chickens flew squawking into the banana palms, and the squeal of pigs in their death agony surpassed even the most lurid descriptions in Upton Sinclair's slaughterhouse classic, *The Jungle*. Of no avail were my entreaties to slow down; Bromwich, his muscles taut with adrenalin, only laughed maniacally and ground the accelerator to the floor.

There was little in Victoria to warrant our breakneck journey

—the usual seedy depots of mixed merchandise run by Indians, a bank and a post office, and a museum containing a plethora of tortoise shells and cannon, even for those who had never seen a tortoise or a cannon. Remembering, however, that the Cable & Wireless office here was reputed to be an incomparable archive of naughty stories, I left Bromwich to his own devices and sought it out. The manager of the branch, a sallow dyspeptic evocative of Mr. Coffee-Nerves, compressed his lips as I bumbled through a halting explanation of my errand.

"Look here, my good man," he demanded, his voice rising, "are you suggesting or in any way implying that our facilities were used to transmit the type of risqué anecdotes that men chuckle over when ladies leave the table?"

I reddened to the roots of my hair. "No, no, I didn't mean quite that—"

"Well, then, you're a dolt," he retorted, "because it's one of the most intriguing notions I've ever heard—our directors'll turn handsprings when I pass it along. You've just talked yourself out of a fat fee, brother. There's big money in porn these days. Anyhow, thanks loads and stay away from chipmunks."

Somewhat crestfallen at having missed the brass ring, but consoled in part that I had brought good fortune to a fellow man, I rejoined Bromwich, and we made our way back to the Esmeralda for lunch, wreaking havoc on any livestock we had missed earlier. A surprise, and a disquieting one, greeted me in my bedchamber. My flight bag, containing passport, valuables, and a cache of chocolate peanut clusters that I kept for emergencies, gave clear evidence of pilferage. The fabric was torn in places as if someone, failing to force the lock, had tried to slash open the cover. Quivering with agitation, I hastened to report the offense to the desk clerk, who could not have been more sympathetic.

"I don't blame you for being upset, sir, but we often get similar complaints from our guests. It's only the rats seeking to nibble on your sweets. That annex you're in is alive with them."

"Oh, is that all?" I said. "Pretty sizable, are they?"

"Yes, quite hefty. Those Indian shops down in Victoria tan

their skins for floor coverings. People like to take them home as souvenirs."

"I don't suppose it would be possible to buy a live one, would it?"

"No, sir, I hardly think so. You see, the government forbids their export on the ground that it might weaken the strain."

"To be sure," I said. "That's basic ecology, and I say bravo. Well, I must pick up a skin or two before I leave."

"When will that be, sir?"

"Fairly soon, fairly soon. By the way—I've been meaning to ask. Does the name of Tom Swift ring a bell with you? He was over here a while ago in an electric submarine, looking for buried treasure."

"No-o, I don't seem to recall him. But if you're interested in treasure, the person to talk to is Reginald Wilkins, a remarkable chap up the coast. He's been tracing a pirate hoard there for more than twenty years."

And talk to him we did, Bromwich and I, the very next day, though it was mainly a monologue from Wilkins, four hours long, describing an incredible quest. The treasure, by his estimate worth a hundred million pounds, had been hidden by Levasseur, an eighteenth-century buccaneer, and Wilkins had doggedly uncovered acres of terrain in the search, unraveling a series of clues only comprehensible to a classical scholar—which Wilkins obviously was. In his account to us, he related how he had discovered the formula used to conceal the wealth, the Twelve Labors of Hercules, and how he had painstakingly re-created them one by one. Unhappily, midway through the twelfth, the syndicate funds backing him had dried up, and now he was trying to promote the grubstake—little enough, he assured us—that would unearth the treasure, eighteen feet below a site on the beach which he pointed out to us.

So impressed were we by the man's tenacity, the hypnotic effect of his narrative, that we were homeward bound in the car before either of us spoke, and when Bromwich did, I sensed the excitement underlying his words. "Listen," he began. "I'm not a gambling man—"

"Neither am I," I burst forth, "but if I could possibly raise the cash—"

"It wouldn't take much," he interrupted. "The cost of shipment and the advertising to build up consumer confidence—that's all. Once you got the ball rolling, the rest would be gravy!"

"What ball?" I asked, confused. "What are you talking about? I meant the money to finish the dig."

"Oh, *that*," he said contemptuously. "I stopped listening to him the minute the idea hit me. The Treasure Island Dry Cleaners—I guarantee you it'll rock the industry!" His words tumbled over each other. "First, I'll have to patent the name, else competitors might steal it. Then we approach the airlines for the lowest bid. Next, how much to tack onto the price of the average garment? Three dollars? Four dollars?"

Fearful lest he run us into the ditch, I finally prevailed on Bromwich to explain. His notion, baldly stated, was that dry cleaning lacked romance, that hitherto nobody has ever stressed its joyous, adventurous aspects. Now, for a slight premium, his new Treasure Island service could undertake to transport clothes, neckwear, drapes, upholstery—anything the customer desired—to be processed in the world's most exotic milieu, the Seychelles.

"Think of the snob appeal," he exulted. "Imagine a hostess saying to her dinner guests, 'Yes, I just received back these divinely fresh curtains from Mahé in the Seychelles, and Ricky was so dazzled with them that he's sending his pants there.' Why, once our female clientele discovers it's the smart thing to do, there won't be enough planes to accommodate our orders."

"But who knows anything about dry cleaning here?" I protested. "You'd have to train the labor, build a plant—"

"Right, and there's where you come in," he said triumphantly. "Being as you were with me when I hatched the concept, I'll let you in on the ground floor. You put up the cost of the plant, I do the brainwork and we'll go halvies—we'll split seventy-thirty."

Well, I did my damnedest to bring him to his senses, but it was like arguing with a stone wall. The man had an *idée fixe* and a captive audience, and the more I objected, the more insistent he became. He was still bombinating away at nightfall and doubtless would have continued at breakfast, except that by then I was en route to the airport. In my haste, I forgot to pick up one of those rodent hides from the dealers in Victoria, but I guess I can live without it. If there's any shuddering to be done, I merely open an atlas to the Indian Ocean, and I'm assured of little black specks before my eyes. They're a thousand miles due east of Africa, and they're called the Seychelles.

IV—No Starch, No Tunic, No Chicken Fat

Freshly hatched by the big silver bird that had borne me from Singapore, I stood at the baggage claim in Hong Kong's Kai Tak Airport amid the hundred-odd other passengers on the flight, waiting for the mechanism to disgorge the three bulky suitcases I had been toting around the Orient. As boxes and bales, satchels and cartons, tin trunks and bedrolls of every description lurched into view with no sign of my impedimenta, I began trembling with anxiety. Already I could hear the facile excuses of airline officials—the bags had been dispatched in error to Sumatra, Tasmania or West Africa; no effort would be spared to trace them, but I must appreciate that cable facilities were minimal in those places and it might be a week before a report was forthcoming; and in any case, the company's liability was limited, as I would know had I read the fine print on my ticket. Then, just as I was fizzing up like a Seidlitz powder, the suitcases catapulted onto the revolving belt, and I threw myself on them, smothering them with kisses. The brisk young Chinese customs inspector on whose bench I tumbled my accumulation tapped the largest bag questioningly. I told him that it contained shirts—seventeen white ones, to be exact.

"The color is immaterial," he said stonily, "open up." I complied, and he rummaged through every cranny, visibly chagrined at finding no heroin. "These shirts," he said, "are you an importer? You intend to sell them here?"

"No—to wash them," I replied. "I can't get anybody to iron a shirt without starch. They say they will, but then they turn around and spite me."

He stared at me fixedly. "You mean you brought these all the way from—where is it, America? England?—just to have them washed in Hong Kong?"

"That's right. Here," I said, "feel the collars and cuffs. You see? Full of starch. Every laundry I've sent them to—in New York, London, Paris, wherever—they come back stiff as a board. And if I write 'No Starch' in big letters on the slip, you know what they do? They put in *twice* as much. I tell them 'no starch'—"

"Yes, yes." He closed the bag, scrawled a chalk mark on it. "Temporary visit for purpose of maundering—excuse me, laundering." His expression, inscrutable till now, became more scrutable. "Then apart from this, I take it you won't conduct any business or commercial activity while you're here?"

"Well, I don't know," I hesitated. "Would—would it be okay with you people if I got a new suit?"

"Why, of course, my dear sir." Beaming, he whisked out a business card. "Here, look up my uncle, Tin Horn Moe—he'll treat you right. The address is New Era Togs, Room 267 in the Gloucester Building. Finest workmanship, a wide selection of handsome British woolens."

I thanked him effusively and, once aboard the Star Ferry to Hong Kong Island, dropped the card over the side; life was complex enough without entangling myself in a web of Chinese family relationships. Viewing the island's profile as we approached, it struck me how materially it had altered since my visit a scant eighteen months before. A couple of dozen new skyscrapers seemed to have sprung up, chief among them a vast perpendicular one with circular windows, resembling a colander or a slab of Swiss cheese, that was locally referred to as the Hong Kong Stilton. The superb panorama of the harbor from my hotel window, likewise, now embraced a row of huge neon signs on the Kowloon side advertising various brands of aspirin, beer and electronics. There was one reassuring element in the scene, however; as I unpacked, a game of cricket was in progress on the pitch of the Hong Kong Cricket Club fifteen stories below, in the very shadow of the Bank of China—striking testimony, if any was needed, to British sangfroid. The Empire might be dissolving like a wet paper bag, but such amenities as tea and scones and cricket were being observed to the last.

My seventeen shirts entrusted to the hotel valet with a passionate homily against starch, I set about the next item on my agenda—the new suit I contemplated. Twenty-five years earlier, a tailoring establishment here called the Swatow Lace Company had supplied me with a traditional Chinese suit of glazed black cotton with a stand-up collar, a tunic secured by frogs and wide flowing trousers. It had proved an ideal garment for summer wear around my home in Bucks County, even though I was eyed askance for a time by my neighbors as a Manchu, a transvestite, or both. When some unprincipled person borrowed it for a costume ball and vanished, I swore that one day I would replace it and the hour was now at hand. I struck out purposefully for the Swatow Lace Company.

Miraculous to relate, the shop was still at its original site, and the old gentleman in charge chuckled delightedly at my chronicle. Eventually, however, his chuckles subsided, and he asked whether I would mind if he spoke frankly. I urged him to, and he began by saying that he was 83 years old, that in the course of a long business career he had mingled with all sorts of men, and that of all the preposterous rubbish he had ever heard, the account I had just given him was without parallel. Not only had he never sold a suit of the kind I described, but in his judgment any Westerner who voluntarily donned Chinese dress was either a con man or a lunatic. He invited me to choose my own category.

Shrewdly putting two and two together, I concluded that I must have procured my outfit elsewhere. A canvass of four other shops in the vicinity, though, was equally unproductive. Left with no alternative, I decided to have a duplicate made to order. The only goods I could find resembling the original material was maroon in color and as thick as toweling, but by that time I had ceased being a purist. The son of the cloth merchant, a wide-awake lad of 11 who spoke English, guided me to a tailor who did not, and served as translator while I was measured.

"Are you positive he understands what I want?" I questioned the boy. "Stand-up collar, four pockets, lots of room in the seat?"

"Sure, sure—real mandarin style," the nipper responded. "He say you pay him now in advance, tomorrow deliver suit chop-chop to you hotel."

At the risk of sounding boastful, I felt I had handled the whole affair so deftly, with such a minimum of fuss, that I couldn't help but preen myself. Faced with like obstacles, your ordinary tourist would have thrown up his hands and quit, whereas I, skilled in the ways of the East, had met the challenge and triumphed. Well, perhaps "triumphed" is a shade excessive and should be qualified. In actual fact the garment that arrived next day was a botch—the most catastrophic botch imaginable. A long sheath with four pockets, it resembled nothing so much as a red nightgown with a stand-up collar that you wouldn't wear to a dogfight. It was roomy enough for a mandarin, all right, but not knowing any mandarin to foist it on, I gave it to a fat bellhop at the hotel and wrote the whole thing off.

One of Hong Kong's principal attractions, as all epicures know, is its food, its wealth of restaurants tempting the palate with exotic dishes drawn from every province of China. Just prior to my trip, some epicure alerted me to the existence of a place in Kowloon called Cindy's East, with a particularly exotic menu. It was, he said, modeled on Cindy's, the famed Broadway restaurant of yesteryear, and dispensed the same luscious victuals. Corned beef! Pastrami! Cheesecake! My eyes grew starry at the prospect and I salivated freely. I sorely needed some kind of heart balm—and heartburn—such as this to compensate for the Chinese suit debacle, so off I trotted to Cindy's East.

The insolent waiters and the noisy potpourri of songwriters, racetrack touts, and vaudeville agents that had made Cindy's in New York a watchword were nowhere evident in its celestial counterpart, tucked away upstairs in an office building. Two

Chinese businessmen, whom I judged to be slaves of the poppy-seed roll, were huddled over coffee cups and appeared to be the only patrons. I sat myself down in a far corner, ran my eye over a menu containing no mention of chopped liver, marinated herring, potato pancakes, or matzo ball soup, and realized with a sinking heart that another illusion of mine had evaporated. Presently a somnolent young waiter materialized, and I understood why chicken fat was missing from the bill of fare. He obviously had appropriated it to dress his hair.

"Bring me a lean corned beef and a bottle of Dr. Brown's Cel-Ray Tonic," I directed. He gave me an unobstructed view of his adenoids and a headshake to indicate he had never heard of the beverage. "Okay, then, do you have any egg cream or cherry soda?" Another headshake. "For pity's sake," I exclaimed, "what sort of a fraudulent joint is this? I'll bet you don't even have any sarsaparilla!"

"I bring you Orange Crush," he said. "Velly good with corned beef."

I repressed a shudder, and curious to ascertain who had conceived and brought forth the enterprise, I asked him to fetch the manager. After a bit, a languid young Englishman ebbed in and introduced himself as Angus Smedwick, the owner, and collapsed in a chair. In an accent I took to be Cantabrigian, he informed me that he had stayed up till dawn playing bridge, and ordered himself a stoup of black coffee. He was so unlike the Broadway hustler I expected that I asked what had impelled him to open a supposedly ethnic restaurant.

"I didn't," he returned. "I won it in a card game from a New York chap, name of Manny Rosemont, who started it. At the time I didn't know anything about this sort of food, but I soon mastered it. Take the dish they call cheese blintzes, for instance. You'd think it was a form of curry, wouldn't you? Well, it's just a hard doughnut garnished with smoked salmon."

"I thought that was called lox on a bagel."

He gave me a tolerant smile. "So do a lot of our customers, but I soon straighten them out."

"Where does most of your clientele come from?"

"Tourists mainly," he said, deliberating. "We get quite a few of those tribal fellows—I can never remember the word. They hail from some island off the American coast."

"You don't mean *Hebrews,* by any chance?" I asked, arching my back.

"That's it—from Manhattan. Nice blokes, but it's funny—they only come in once. I can't figure out why."

I could have told him, but I didn't bother. My sandwich had arrived meanwhile, and after a tentative bite or two, my curiosity was satisfied. "Tell me," I said, "where do you get your corned beef? I suppose you fly it in from San Francisco."

"Not at all—it's cured right in our kitchen. We take a side of beef, rub it with a corncob, and presto, it's ready to serve." He surveyed my plate. "What's the matter? Anything wrong with your meal?"

"No, it was delicious, but I must run along . . . late now . . ."

Smedwick uncoiled himself and snapped his fingers. "A check here, Wing Fu, and take this sandwich back, we can use the meat again. Well—" he stuck out his hand—*"au revoir,* and tell your friends about us, what?"

I faithfully promised to, and I not only did; I told a few strangers as well.

"And is that your final, irrevocable decision?" the Governor-General asked. "Can nothing we do or say influence you to reconsider?"

"Nothing, Your Excellency," I said, meeting his gaze squarely. "I've weighed your arguments, and valid though they are, I cannot accept them. I leave Hong Kong tonight."

"But Great Scott, man, think of the consequences," he pleaded. "Do you realize the impact on tourism—to name only one facet of our economy—when news emerges that we failed a hitherto devoted guest, that he quit us in high dudgeon vowing never to return?"

A groan issued from the throats of the assemblage hanging on our words, as impressive a company as had ever been summoned to Government House in moments of crisis. They were all there—the colony's military and social leaders, its banking heads, the *taipans* of its great business houses like Jardine Matheson and Butterfield & Swire, its Chinese industrialists of incalculable wealth, and dominating them all the Governor-General, a fine figure of a man with an eagle's profile like that of C. Aubrey Smith.

"Let me once more recapitulate my position, gentlemen," I said. "I came here with three objectives in mind: first, to get seventeen white shirts laundered without starch; second, to duplicate a Chinese suit I was attached to; and third, to check out a restaurant patterned on one I loved. This shirt," I said, holding up a specimen that glistened with starch, "strikingly demonstrates how fatuous my initial errand was. As for my two other objectives—"

"Please," interrupted the Governor-General pettishly. "You've already told us about the red nightgown and Smedwick's corned beef. There's no need to belabor the point. We fully understand your frustration, but can't you give us a few days to make amends? We'll wash your shirts again, make you another suit—only don't go away mad, I implore you."

"I'm sorry, sir," I said, crossing to the door. "It's too late. You had your chance and you blew it. Farewell, gentlemen, and God grant that all of you profit from this experience."

Such in essence was the scene I visualized as taking place when I exited from Hong Kong, but damned if those *taipans* ever sent for me. I hung about Government House the whole day rehearsing my speeches until I almost missed the plane, and did any of them give me a tumble? Don't make me laugh—I've got a split lip. Oh, well, *ish ka bibble.* When their lease on the place expires in 1997, those cats'll be around looking for sympathy, and I can tell them where to find it. In the dictionary.

V—*Barefoot in Burma*

With a smile unctuous enough to fry half a dozen hamburgers, U Glib, bureau manager of the Amalgamated Press in

Rangoon, bent toward me, clinked his glass against mine, and pinned on me a moist brown eye brimful of insincerity and subterfuge. A lean, coffee-colored dyspeptic with a luxuriant guardee mustache bisecting his face, he had been recommended to me in Hong Kong as one who could facilitate my week's sojourn in Burma, and he had responded to my phone call with such alacrity that I immediately suspected him of ulterior motives. Confronted with him now in the bar of the Strand Hotel, I was all the more convinced that he was a stool pigeon.

"And what is your reaction to our country thus far, my dear sir?" he inquired effusively. "Do you approve of us? You do? You don't? Are you elated by what you've seen? Disappointed? Please—" He checked me before I could answer. "I realize, of course, that you arrived only last night, that you haven't had a chance to look around. Still, an observant person like yourself must have picked up certain vibrations . . . even gossip, so to speak . . ."

I assumed that startled-fawn expression a maiden evinces when she detects a suitor's hand stealing up her pantyhose. "Jeepers creepers, Mr. Glib," I protested. "I'm just a tourist—a sightseer, that's all. I came here to see your temples and pagodas, to hobnob with your monks, to steep myself in Buddhism. Man, I sure look forward to that Buddhism—it's the greatest. You know something? It's just about my favorite religion."

"Yes, yes," he grunted. "Our cultural heritage and so forth—very fine. I merely wanted to make sure you weren't one of those muckrakers who go around poking their snoot into political matters. You know what I'm hinting at?"

I did indeed, and as the rivulets of goose grease began dripping from his chops, it all became abundantly clear. Under his journalistic cover, U Glib was Military Intelligence, and he was giving me a quick brainwash to offset any preconceptions I might have about the regime. In particular, he cautioned me, I must be on guard against numerous malicious stories being circulated about its leader, General Ne Win.

"Certain destructive émigré elements," he confided, "are

propagating a myth that our head of state is a brutal, unfeeling tyrant. In actual fact, he is compassionate to a fault, another St. Francis of Assisi. On several occasions I have seen him descend from his bulletproof limousine to rescue a tiny wounded bird which otherwise would have been crushed beneath the wheels. So harrowing was the effect upon the thousands of soldiers linked arm to arm along the roadway that many burst into tears and had to be given restoratives to resume their duties."

"What better proof of a beautiful nature," I agreed. "Would it be possible to meet whoever is entrusted with planting small wounded birds in the route of the motorcade?"

"No, that person is not available at the present time," U Glib returned, and stared at me suspiciously. "Why did you want to see him?"

"Oh, nothing," I said. "What other calumnies should I be on the lookout for?"

"The fiction that he's a womanizer," he said. "Hell, we all goof off with a chick now and then, the General's got a few phone numbers like everyone else, but I defy you to produce a snapshot of one single orgy he's participated in. He and his wife are like two lovebirds."

It was obvious from U Glib's ornithological allusions that he had some sort of avian hangup, but I did not pursue it. "Speaking of the General's lady," I said. "They say she was involved—"

"You mean that Interpol caught her smuggling rubies and other uncut stones into a locked account in Switzerland and that the Burmese ambassador to the UN was flown overseas to pay a £300,000 fine?" he asked. "Look, suppose it *is* true. Is any of us perfect? Remember what your own great spiritual leader said: 'If there be any among you without sin, let him cast the first uncut stone.'"

"Well, I've certainly enjoyed being keelhauled by you, Mr. Glib," I excused myself, "but I've got an errand or two—"

"To be sure. Forgive me for detaining you, but I found your conversation so arresting that I lost all track of time." The reference to detention and arrest may have been purely accidental, but when he arose, extending his hand ceremoniously, his trouser leg slid up to reveal a tape recorder strapped to his leg. "Welcome to Burma, Land of Smiles. I envy you your trip upcountry."

I assured him I expected a million chuckles, saw him to the door, and dodging a swarm of black marketeers thirsting to convert my dollars, went out for a look at the city. It was a ghostly experience, almost as if Piranesi and Giorgio di Chirico had collaborated to design the setting. The majority of the lofty porticoed buildings in the quarter around the hotel were in a state of acute disrepair, their makeshift roofs of corrugated iron rusted and their facades stained with mildew, and the few pedestrians visible under the arcades, inert and dispirited in the stifling heat, seemed totally out of scale with the architecture. The further downtown one got, the dingier and more ruinous the scene became; grandiose structures formerly occupied by European and Indian business firms were heavily shuttered or had crumbled into a patchwork of dark little shops crammed with outworn automotive parts and cheap dress goods. Even the traffic seemed to have succumbed to the same corrosive process; the few private cars visible were superannuated American models that clanked approach from a block away, interspersed with buses and lorries belching forth clouds of effluvia. By the time I tottered back to the hotel, drained of energy, instinct told me that another day in the sepulchral gloom of Rangoon would be sheerest masochism. Accordingly, I bucked my way into the crowded government tourist office adjacent to the Strand, and there, by dint of screaming above the uproar, prevailed on a teen-aged female clerk to devise an itinerary to Taunggyi, Pagan, and Mandalay—three localities, she screamed back, of transcendent beauty and historic interest to the foreign visitor.

Taunggyi, I discovered from a promotional leaflet I read on the aircraft flying me toward it the following morning, was a hill town in the Shan states near a body of water named Inle Lake, upon which the lake-dwellers propelled boats with their legs rather than arms. I took this to mean some sort of treadle mechanism pumped with the feet, like that used in swan-boats; and my heartbeat slowed down as I envisioned myself afloat in a Fitzpatrick Travel Talk sunset, with Lowell Thomas droning in my ear, "And it is with this thought that we take leave of beautiful Inle Lake, home of the coffee bean, where time stands still." As it developed, my aquatic adventure was even less stimulating. The technique of leg-rowing was, in reality, a form of sculling—the boatmen wrapped one leg around an oar held upright and laboriously kicked the water past them. Providentially, an easier form of locomotion was granted the sightseer. A motorized sampan snaked me through a labyrinth of canals carved out of the reeds to the center of the lake, where a well-tended pagoda sparkled in the sun. Nearby it was a cluster of huts built on spiles, housing a colony of weavers who sang and chirruped as they industriously plied their looms. And well they might, for in terms of workmanship, design, and color their textiles were as paltry as any to be found in the Far East.

The second objective on my journey, Pagan, lay two hours distant by plane on the east bank of the Irrawaddy. The seat of a long line of Burmese kings, it had reached its zenith between the eleventh and thirteenth centuries and bore the grandiloquent title of the City of Four Million Pagodas. Of the five thousand still visible in various stages of ruin, I climbed through half a dozen, careful to remove shoes and socks as prescribed by Buddhist ritual. It proved something of an ordeal, what with pebbles lacerating my toes and clouds of bats dive-bombing my head, but compared to what Fate had in store for me, it was a chocolate ice-cream soda. On emerging from the sixth and last pagoda, I was unable to find any trace of my footgear. Some accursed urchin—or even worse, some minion of U Glib's?—must have been shadowing me and had made off with the shoes while I was inside. Of all the dilemmas to be caught in, this surely was the cruelest: a savage noonday sun overhead, not a blessed soul in sight, and a mile of burning asphalt between me and my hotel. I gritted my teeth as firmly as malocclusion allowed and struck out, cleaving to the verge wherever I could but occasionally forced to prance on the crown the road like an Indian fire-walker. Half an hour later, as I shuffled along in unspeakable agony, deliverance came in the form of a peasant's cart drawn by a water buffalo. The miracle was compounded when, at the hotel, the driver refused the greenback I attempted to press on him. He was either an angel or he had a premonition that our currency was about to be devalued. Whichever the case, may he flourish like the green bay tree.

That night, recuperating in the bar of the hotel, I was moved to comment on the experience to the barman. "Is it not ironic," I remarked, "that a person too chicken to pass a cemetery at night in his own country should girdle the globe at staggering expense to root around in a lot of old Buddhist tombs? I refer, of course, to myself."

"Excuse me if I differ with you, sir," he replied. "Carried to its extreme, your logic would inevitably spell the end of tourism, forcing this hotel to close, depriving me of my livelihood, and reducing my loved ones to beggary, to say nothing of yourself. You would then be overwhelmed by such remorse that I quail to think of it."

I quailed also, and seeking to recover my equilibrium, threw down another drink and still another, with the result that I overslept and almost missed the flight to Mandalay. Like many Westerners, my only association with Burma's former capital was Kipling's poem, and it had a special relevance for me. Back in the palmy days of vaudeville, there was a baritone on the B. F. Keith circuit named Lieutenant Gitz-Rice, a particularly hateful personality, who used to sing the ballad version to climax his repertory, and now, after many decades, his voice came back to me with nauseating clarity, thundering out the lines: "Ship me somewhere east of Suez, where the best is like the worst/Where there aren't no Ten Commandments an' a man can raise a thirst." For one horrid instant, I was seized with the delusion that I was back in high school, that I had sneaked away to attend a matinee instead of translating those fifty lines of Vergil, and I cowered in my seat riddled with guilt. Then the liquid accents of the Burmese stewardess dissolved the nightmare, and I was buckling my seat-belt for the descent to Mandalay.

The guidebook speaks emotionally of Mandalay's artistic treasures—its monasteries, its pagodas, its seven hundred monoliths inscribed with Pali texts—but I must confess that a great deal of it struck me as so much cotton candy, as architectural marzipan. Every detail is so ornate, every curlicue so encrusted with gilt or gingerbread or fretwork that the eye shortly becomes surfeited. The outstanding example of embellishment there is the Kyauk-Tawgyi Pagoda surmounting Mandalay Hill, which is reached by a thousand steps circuitously winding up the eminence. Why I made the ascent I cannot say for certain; it probably was a mixture of what the French call *boy-scoutisme* and bravado. At each successive platform, as I puffed onward, there was a Buddhist shrine more rococo than the last, with hawkers retailing joss-sticks, flowers, and gimcrack merchandise, as well as beggars soliciting alms, and the hotter I grew with exertion, the more importunate they became. A peachy anticlimax greeted me when I ultimately achieved the summit. The spectacular view promised in the literature—"the whole sprawling city and its myriads of white pagodas"—was blanketed by a layer of smog worthy of Los Angeles. I mooched disconsolately around the battlements and came upon an Indian fortuneteller casting the horoscope of a newly wedded Burmese couple. After dismissing them with predictions of bounteous wealth and parenthood, he applied himself to scrutinizing my palm.

"You will live to the age of ninety, maybe longer," he declared. "I see you in days to come clad in a Norfolk jacket, wearing a long white beard and writing many successful plays."

I wondered how Bernard Shaw had intruded himself into my future, but I forbore to inquire. "What is your projection about romance?"

"Tumultuous," he said. "Here it says you will have forty sweethearts, while there," he peered at my other hand, "it says you will die an old maid."

"That seems to indicate a change of sex," I said anxiously. "I am reminded of the plight of James Morris, the British journalist, who had himself converted into a sweet, middle-aged spinster named Jan Morris and thus became his children's aunt, much to their stupefaction and mine."

"Anything can happen these days," he said with a shrug. "Do

you know a lean, coffee-colored dyspeptic with a guardee mustache? He wears a tape recorder on his left leg."

I stiffened. "Yes, I certainly do. What about him?"

"You should beware of this man. He means you no good."

"You may be right," I said. "As a matter of fact, I had a feeling in Pagan that someone was tailing me."

"No, that's just your natural paranoia," he said. "But watch out for this man in Rangoon. He is preparing a trap." I rose to my feet and thrust a banknote into his lap. "Wait, I'm not through—I can tell you how to deal with him."

"You don't have to," I called back over my shoulder. "I already know."

And I did. I was in Rangoon airport by midafternoon, and thanks to a lucky connection with an eastbound 707, dining with friends in a Hong Kong restaurant late that night. Halfway through the meal, who should come in but the very chap who originally sent me along to U Glib.

"What, back so soon?" he exclaimed. "You couldn't have had a very good time." I assured him that on the contrary, I had loved Burma. "I knew you would. It's different, isn't it?"

I'll say it is. You'd have to see it to believe it.